Australian
food

11/99

Australian food

In celebration *of the* new Australian cuisine

Introduction *by* Alan Saunders

Photographed *by* Rodney Weidland

Compiled *by* Barbara Beckett

Ten Speed Press
Berkeley, California

PAGE ONE: A case of freshly opened Sydney
rock oysters.

PAGE TWO: Jacques Reymond's very splendid Broth
of Oriental Flavours with Yellowfin Tuna Tagine
and Spaghetti Vegetables (page 140). A refreshing
way to serve tuna—the tuna is first coated in the
tagine paste and then seared, before being served
in an Oriental broth to keep the rich light tasting.

PAGE THREE: From left to right: Cattle grazing on
spring pasture in the Southern Highlands,
impervious to the threatening clouds; bunches of
fresh asparagus temptingly displayed at Fuel,
Sydney; a winter agricultural landscape of vines in
the Yarra Valley, Victoria; freshly cooked Coffin Bay
scallops at Wockpool, Sydney.

PAGE FIVE: Vignettes from the kitchen at Chateau
Yering, Victoria.

Published in the U.S.A. by Ten Speed Press in association with
Lansdowne Publishing Pty Ltd

Ten Speed Press
Box 7123
Berkeley, California 94707
www.tenspeed.com

Distributed in Canada by Ten Speed Press Canada, in South Africa by Real Books, and
in Southeast Asia by Berkeley Books.

Library of Congress Cataloging-in-Publication Data on file with publisher.

Printed in Singapore by Kyodo Printing Pte Ltd.
First printing, 1999

1 2 3 4 5 6 7 8 9 10 — 04 03 02 01 00 99

Contents

The Flavour *of* Australia
by *Alan Saunders* 7

Soups *and* Starters 43

Salads *and* Vegetables 71

Meat *and* Poultry 95

Fish *and* Shellfish 123

Barbecues 159

Fruit *and* Desserts 175

Brief Biographies 207

Further Reading 221

Index 222

It's not a surprise to me that people are talking about an **Australian cuisine.** *We are amongst the most open-minded and sophisticated people, so why would it be surprising if we spawn great food innovators? Very few cultures have the same variety of cultures and influences to call upon. We have all these flavour experiences, so we can do non-traditional things and be inventive. I'm a cheese maker. Just because fine cheese making hasn't happened here earlier, I can't see any reason why any type of cheese can't be made in Australia.*

RICHARD THOMAS

It's multicultural, it's happening, my food is not pure French because it is influenced by local products.

DANY CHOUET

Australian cuisine has advanced light years in a matter of twenty years. It is diverse, honest and built on fine, naturally grown raw materials. **I'm proud to be an Australian cook.**

DAMIEN PIGNOLET

Australian cuisine *is coming of age at the dawn of a new century. Chefs are cooking confidently in a variety of styles which all say modern Australian cuisine. There is enough room for everyone to produce what they want.*

PETER DOYLE

And now we're witnessing an **Australian renaissance** *in food. Arising from the ashes of an overcooked and often monotonous national food is the most vital new cuisine on the planet today—shamelessly and profitably plundering ideas and ingredients from neighbours and new arrivals alike; developing exceptional regional produce; and daily discovering natural riches that the original Australians knew about all along.*

STEFANO MANFREDI

A few of our wonderful chefs are reaching a new dimension—I like the way **my mind expanded** *when I tasted their food.*

MARGARET FULTON

*I think Australian cuisine is epitomised by the lack of tradition—it moves forward because it's not held back by tradition. It can't be judged by the past. Tradition is a great thing, but it can prevent the move forward—***we are looking positively forward***, we are not nostalgic for the past.*

RALPH POTTER

As long as we have Australian ingredients, we have an **Australian cuisine.**

PHILIPPE MOUCHEL

The Flavour of Australia

Alan Saunders

The Flavour of Australia

Eating in the World's Next Great City

There are three great cuisines in the world: French, Chinese and the other one. What the 'other one' is depends on who you're talking to and, more to the point, whence they come. Japanese is certainly a contender; contenders also are Italian, Turkish, Moroccan and anything from Mexico except the stuff we normally think of as Mexican food. Then there's Indian (or, to be more precise, there are Indian, because, although Indian cooking is sometimes described as the third best in the world, the truth is that India is a land of many regions, each with its own cuisine and the people of one region seldom eat the food of another). All in all, however, it seems to be the case that, whatever this third cuisine might be, it doesn't export itself with quite the swagger of the French and the Chinese.

Exporting, of course, is the point (or, at least, a lot of it). However much some of us might talk about the importance of climate, season, soil and local produce, when we describe French cuisine as a great cuisine, we don't mean merely that it's great in France, but also that it's great everywhere. French cuisine is thought great partly because French restaurants appear in so many restaurant guides published in so many cities of the world.

Take, for example, just one Australian city: to be more precise, take the Sydney of about ten years ago, when it became my home. There was no doubt there and then as to which were the two most significant cuisines. Fifty-nine French and fifty-nine Italian restaurants were considered good enough to make it into the 1986 edition of the *Sydney Morning Herald Good Food Guide*, which at that time was edited by Leo Schofield ('with John Amery' it said on the title page, although Leo alone signed the introduction). But for Sydney in 1986—or at least for Leo Schofield—the identity of the third most important cuisine was difficult to determine. It certainly wasn't Chinese, which scored only twenty-one entries and was beaten easily by a category labelled 'seafood,' which rated forty-one mentions. 'Seafood,' however, is a name tag for raw materials, not a cuisine (it's a long way from sashimi to bouillabaisse or bacalao), so naturally one looked to see what came next. And what came next, in fourth place, with thirty-three restaurants to its name, was 'international' cuisine.

This is a deeply disturbing and ambiguous label. Fatally, it conjures up in the mind the sort of place memorably evoked by the American food writer, Calvin Trillin. 'In American cities the size of Kansas City, a careful travelling man has to observe the rule that any restaurant the executive secretary of the Chamber of Commerce is particularly proud of is almost certainly not worth eating in,' said Trillin. 'Its name will be something like La Maison de la Casa House, Continental Cuisine; its food will sound European but taste as if the continent they had in mind was Australia.' Now, *there's* a man who really knows how to wound. To be fair, though, Trillin was writing in 1974, a time when Australia could have served

PREVIOUS PAGE: In this dish, the soft noodles are the main texture, with the oysters and the chewy squid providing the contrast. Ralph Potter's Oyster and Braised Baby Squid Noodle Salad with Soy, Rocket, Oil and Ginger (page 69).

as well as Ethiopia or Antarctica as the space on the culinary map at which cartographers give up for lack of information and hand the pen over to more decorative and imaginative artists. Moreover, Trillin, a man ahead of his time, was engaged in a righteous crusade to persuade his fellow Americans to appreciate the culinary treasures on their doorstep rather than to hanker after poor local imitations of what was happening many thousands of miles away.

There may be a lesson here for Australians, but it's not a simple one. Trillin thought that visitors to Atlanta—which in 1974 was cutely describing itself as 'the World's Next Great City'—should be taken to Mary-Mac's on Ponce de Leon for a bowl of pot likker (a frugal but delicious Southern soup made of the water in which greens have been boiled), but where, in 1974 or 1986, was the equivalent of pot likker to draw the visitor to Australia away from the dull but dependable pleasures of international cuisine? Australia, it seemed, had no such homely local specialities and, lacking them, was doomed to dine at La Maison de la Casa House or wherever else its chambers of commerce deemed desirable.

Something else, however, was happening in Australia—and some of it was happening under that unpromising banner of international cuisine. In 1986, Kinsela's in Bourke Street was one of the Sydney *Good Food Guide*'s international restaurants, but what was on offer here (and, sadly, I have to rely on repute rather than on personal experience) was a world away from the Frozen Duck à l'Orange Soda Pop that Calvin Trillin used to encounter at La Maison de la Casa House. Yes, there was a French accent to the food—international cuisine has always spoken in the tones of Inspector Clouseau—but it was the French not of somebody who has been mechanically trained in a catering college far from Paris, but of a genuine amateur, someone who had come to French food out of the love of it. Moreover, that somebody, Tony Bilson, had working with him a sous-chef of startling originality who was ultimately to combine the French technique that he had learned in Australia with the food of his native Japan in a marriage so seamlessly perfect that it was as though the two had never lived apart. His name was Tetsuya Wakuda, and, ten years later, he was in the *Good Food Guide* with a restaurant of his own.

By then, the number of French restaurants listed in the Sydney *Good Food Guide* had shrunk to twelve, Italian to twenty-five and international to just four. Real comparison is impossible, however, because the most remarkable characteristic of the 1996 edition—the first to be edited by Terry Durack and Jill Dupleix—is the baroque proliferation of categories in its index: American/ modern Australian, Australian regional, Cantonese, Cantonese seafood, Cantonese/Chinese regional, Chinese regional, French/Australian, French/Japanese (there was only one of these and it was Tetsuya Wakuda's restaurant), French/modern Australian, French seafood, Italian/modern Australian, Italian seafood, modern Australian country, modern Australian/Italian and modern Australian seafood.

Of all the categories represented, the biggest was one that hadn't appeared at all in 1986: 'modern Australian,' which weighed in with 121 entries. (In the most recent edition, which is a little less extravagant with its category chopping, the

Damien Pignolet's Bistro Moncur.

ABOVE: Tony Bilson's Grilled Fillet of Snapper with Saffron and Citrus Sauce (page 129)—a sweet and sour flavour structure perfectly suited to full-bodied Chardonnay.

modern Australian label is applied to 161 out of the 385 establishments listed.) Clearly, something significant had happened over that decade. In 1986, 'Australian' had been an uncertain label applied alike to steak houses and to places that offered you duckling with cherries. Difficult and interesting restaurants were described either, like Kinsela's, as 'international' or (and this was a real abdication of responsibility) as 'individual.' In 1986, Perry's restaurant in Paddington was 'individual;' by 1996, its eponymous chef, Neil Perry, was in confident command of the Rockpool, an establishment the *Good Food Guide* had no hesitation in calling 'modern Australian.'

But what *is* modern Australian cuisine? This is clearly not a category that is infinitely elastic—as we've seen, Tetsuya Wakuda's food, some of the most interesting I know, is still described by the *Good Food Guide* as 'French/ Japanese'—but its boundaries are by no means firm. Some of the restaurants thus described are primarily Italian in influence, others draw their inspiration from

Our food came alive with the Asian overlay. You cook Western food differently once you have learnt Eastern food—you are never the same again. The Asian migrants cooked their traditional food here and we responded. We didn't 'Australianise' it—we were ready to accept it. Australians are happy to be inventive. A lot of us are cooking in a different fashion. Our food works well with the ethnic flavours that make up part of the Australian psyche.

NEIL PERRY

RIGHT: Neil Perry's King Prawn Cake and Scallops with Spicy Prawn Sauce (page 60). The mousse has a wonderful fragrance of lemon grass, ginger and aromatics, with a very spicy sauce flavoured with lots of Thai basil, peanuts and coconut cream.

North Africa or from Asia. Does this seem to imply that eclecticism is the salient characteristic of modern Australian cuisine? Perhaps it does, but this is hardly a uniquely Australian quality: 'In reality, British food is, and always has been, a hotchpotch of culinary ideas,' writes Sybil Kapoor in the introduction to her *Modern British Food*, published in 1995. 'We have pilfered recipes from around the world and then subverted them to our own particular taste and needs.' British food, she continues, is characterised by 'elegant simplicity,' 'innovative use of ingredients,' and 'fresh flavours'—all of which is more or less what a lot of people would say about modern Australian food. To help us out of these difficulties, we need to ask ourselves what the qualities are that make for an international cuisine.

Throughout the globe, the cuisines of sedentary cultures—those, that is, that aren't nomadic—tend to be characterised by two things: a favourite, staple source of carbohydrate and a group of flavours which is used to make that carbohydrate a little more interesting. In much of Asia, the carbohydrate comes in the form of rice or noodles; in Africa, it's often a porridge made of millet. In each case, the cuisine is given its local twist by the flavours—deriving from animal proteins, vegetables and spices—that are used to lend interest to the starchy staple. International cuisines, however, operate rather differently. What makes them special is their technique.

So let us ask ourselves how the French and the Chinese came to be so firmly established in the first and second, or joint first, positions in the global league

table of great cuisines. In the case of China, size certainly helps. China is a huge country with varied climates, varied produce and a gastronomic history stretching back at least as far as the Zhou Dynasty, which began in the eleventh century before Christ. It also has boundless national self-confidence, surpassing even that of the Americans. It's true that China has often sold its food to the rest of the world in quite modest terms, but this is an expression of confidence rather than the lack of it: the ideas behind Chinese food are so clear that they will survive any number of alterations in basic ingredients.

Twenty years ago, Kwang-chih Chang, in the editorial introduction to a valuable collection of essays called *Food in Chinese Culture*, pointed out that Chinese cuisines distinguish between a staple of rice, millet or some other starch (which in both Mandarin and Cantonese is called *fan*), and vegetable or meat dishes (*t'sai* in Mandarin, *sung* in Cantonese), and that this principle of division is so fundamental that it will continue to operate even where Chinese ingredients are not available:

Chinese grocer in Sydney's Haymarket.

Send a Chinese cook into an American kitchen given Chinese or American ingredients, and he or she will (a) prepare an adequate amount of fan, *(b) cut up the ingredients and mix them in various combinations, and (c) cook the ingredients into several dishes and perhaps, a soup. Given the right ingredients, the 'Chineseness' of the meal would increase, but even with entirely native American ingredients and cooked in American utensils, it is still a Chinese meal.*

And it's a Chinese meal even if the *fan* is fried rice and the *t'sai* or *sung* consists of little balls of minced pork fried in a thick batter and then served in a sticky orange-coloured sauce filled with lumps of canned pineapple. If that or chop suey are what the rest of the world wants, the Chinese have been quite happy to provide it.

The French, though they cannot claim anything like so ancient a tradition, are nonetheless heirs to a technique which has turned out to be both highly refined and highly exportable. They, too, do not entirely lack self-confidence and, even when they're trying to be nice, know that what they have to offer the world is better than what the world has to offer them.

In the early 1990s—which some might think was rather late—a serious attempt was made to export French technique to Australia in the form of a branch in Sydney of the Cordon Bleu cooking school. But what, the sceptical observer might have asked, could a French school possibly have to say to Australia in this day and age? It's true that we are wide open to whatever influences the rest of the world has to offer us—how, without a commanding culinary identity of our own, could we not be?—but these days an Australian chef is far more likely to look to Bangkok or Marrakesh for ideas than to Paris or Lyons.

'Probably I'm biased, but I do believe that this is the only training which really allows a full mastering of cuisines, probably because French people have been writing on cuisines for the past five hundred years,' André Cointreau, Chairman of Cordon Bleu, told me when I put this objection to him. France is

Our chefs are so responsive to suppliers, the environment and to products. They tend not to have the constraints of their contemporaries in Europe, who are more bound by tradition. They are more free-wheeling than in the US, as they are bound by public relations spin. Our blend is open and rewarding, and the customers are treated very well.

JOHN SUSMAN

Philippe Mouchel and his chefs cooking at the theatrical open stove at Langton's Restaurant.

the focal point at which many national cuisines meet, he told me, and in its capital they are synthesised and codified: 'So I do believe that French cuisine is really a cuisine which is at the service of worldwide cuisine.'

I wondered at the time how, say, the sushi chefs of Japan would welcome the glad tidings that French cuisine was at their service—and I still wonder—but there's no doubt that the French way, and more specifically the *Cordon Bleu* way, has international appeal and that it was something of a coup for Sydney to be only the fifth city in the world (after Paris, London, New York and Tokyo) to have its own Cordon Bleu school.

And what would Australian cooks learn at the school? According to M. Cointreau, they would learn how to bring French technique to bear on Australian ingredients: 'Ten or fifteen years ago, I would have thought that New York or California would probably have had the leading role in this kind of fusion cuisine. Today, I believe that Australia is where things are happening, blending this kind of European traditional feeling with this kind of modern cuisine and Asian flavours. But, I would add, with a kind of—and that's very French—full respect not only of balance, but also of the taste of what you have in the recipe.'

So can this possibly mean that Sydney is the world's next great city, now that it, too, like Atlanta, will host the Olympics? One hopes not: only parvenu metropolises worry about their ranking in the world order. The mere possibility that Sydney, in particular, or Australia in general, might worry about questions like this is, perhaps, an uncomfortable reminder of how far we have to go before we acquire the French virtues of balance, moderation and calm confidence in a technique which can safely be placed at the service of the world.

Balance, moderation, calm confidence—above all else, these are adult virtues, and what, in the face of such maturity, can a younger culture offer? Well, of course, what we have is that adventurous eclecticism, that 'blending,' that 'fusion,' of which M. Cointreau speaks. But, as I've said, the trouble is, we're not the only ones. So does this mean that the undoubted glories of modern Australian cuisine are just the local variant of a global phenomenon of eclecticism, melding, fusion and confusion?

To some extent, this is exactly what it means: the Australian table changed because everything else changed—the world shrank, distances meant less and you could learn in Brisbane what somebody had eaten in New York a minute or so after they'd eaten it. But this cannot be the whole story. Cuisine today is global not just because Ronald McDonald embraces the world, but because chefs in fine restaurants, whether in Melbourne or in Massachusetts, approach their work in quite similar ways. The Australian contribution to global cuisine, however, is particularly inventive and particularly lively. Why is this so?

Before we can answer that question, we need to remind ourselves of what things used to be like. CONTINUED ON PAGE 16

Vic Cherikoff

Native Australian Flavours

'In years to come, it will be as natural to reach for a lemon myrtle leaf as it is to use a lime or kaffir lime leaf. Creative, innovative cooks are seeking outlets for these unique ingredients—try them, you will be impressed with these new flavours.'

Vic Cherikoff has been credited with pioneering the development of authentic Australian ingredients through his commercialisation of bush food species which were once eaten only by Aborigines. His company, Bush Tucker Supply Aust., was the first to provide indigenous foods through speciality food stores, supermarkets, direct marketing and over the Internet. Some products are creeping into supermarkets as ingredients, or are found in ice creams, teas and breads, and many are already available in overseas stores such as Sainsbury's in the United Kingdom.

Vic originally worked as a research scientist analysing wild foods for their nutritional composition—this fuelled his interest and he developed a network of Aboriginal collectors who now add to the national spread of farmers who grow the commercial supplies for today's native Australian food industry.

Vic has spread his enthusiasm for indigenous food flavours to professional growers, home gardeners, foragers and foodies, home cooks and chefs. He hopes to inspire Australians, as well as the rest of the world, to appreciate these wild flavours so they might be a unifying influence in our contemporary multicultural cuisine.

ABOVE LEFT: From left to right, the herbs to rear are raspberry leaves, native mint and lemon myrtle. In the front are warrigal greens, native raspberries, Illawarra plums (the darkest fruits), lemon aspen fruit, quandongs, Kakadu plums and bunya bunya nuts—all displayed on paperbark.

LEFT: Vic in his Sydney backyard, a paradise of edible native Australian plants, trees and shrubs.

RIGHT: Native raspberries ripening in Vic's backyard.

For complete descriptions of the authentically Australian ingredients mentioned in this book, refer to www.bushtucker.com.au

ABOVE: Clockwise from top left, Davidson's plums, aniseed myrtle, wild rosella flowers, native pepperberries, small wild limes, mountain pepper (leaves) and munthari berries displayed on paperbark.

The authentic Australian flavour of our bush foods will undoubtedly soon become world flavours, just like coriander and tomatoes which both, incidentally, come from South America.

VIC CHERIKOFF

The Land

We wanted to call the restaurant Narmaloo—the name of a special place, a waterhole at Balgo Hills. The Aborigines there had given us special permission for the name to be used even though it was a sacred place … It didn't occur to us that there would be a stumbling block. You can imagine our disbelief when we were told by the building's managers that we couldn't use that name—it was too 'ethnic.' This is Australia at the latter end of the twentieth century!

My stuffing in the Sicilian Stuffed Red Mullet recipe is an essential part of this mullet dish and it is also another example of how we Australians can combine different cultures in our cooking. Alone it would have been a Greek dish, but with the stuffing it creates a different dimension—one that we celebrate in Australia.

JANNI KYRITSIS

The managers, it seems, would have been quite happy with a French name, which somehow would not have been 'ethnic.' This is Jennice Kersh's account, in her book *Edna's Table*, of the opening of Edna's Table II, a very fine bush food restaurant hidden away in a leafy corner of the resolutely unethnic and international MLC Centre in the Sydney business district.

In 1998, after three years at Edna's Table II, Jennice Kersh and her brother Raymond (who is also her business partner and chef) published a book of recipes utilising Australian native ingredients. The foreword was by Mike Carlton, star of Radio 2UE, and he wrote in waggish mood: 'Even the greatest cooks have their recipe disasters and Raymond's was the Chocolate Chicken,' said Carlton, 'God knows how or where he came by it, and when I first saw it on the menu at the old Edna's Table, I assumed it was some sort of practical joke.' Unpersuaded by Jennice's observation that this was a famous Mexican delicacy, Carlton failed to enjoy his Chocolate Chicken: 'You got chook and you got chockie, all stuck together, and it was awful: the Easter bunny meets KFC.' As it happens, this is indeed a famous Mexican delicacy—though it's more properly made with turkey than with chicken—and herein lies a lesson for the cooks of Australia, a lesson to which I'll return shortly.

One of the most remarkable phenomena in the history of food is the speed with which the produce of the Americas went round the world. No European and no Asian knew anything about the place until 1492 and yet—in an age of mule carts and sailing ships—there were turkeys on the dining tables of Spain by the 1520s and potatoes in the soil of Ireland by the 1590s. And it is not the speed alone which is remarkable, but also the thoroughness with which these new ingredients were incorporated into culinary cultures that were already old and established. It is almost impossible now to imagine Italian food without tomatoes or Indian food without chillies, yet tomatoes did not reach Italy until at least the 1520s and chillies were unknown in India until 1611 (having been brought from South America to Europe and then to Goa by the Portuguese).

The trade was not one way. At the same time as tomatoes, turkeys, chillies and chocolate were enlivening the cuisines of the Old World, so the New World was being transformed by European livestock: cattle, sheep and pigs. On the cold, inhospitable Atlantic coast of North America, the Puritan settlers, struggling to eke subsistence out of an alien land, evolved a new culinary culture that incorporated the produce of their new home—corn, for example, which the Indians taught them how to grow—with the foods they already knew.

'And I suppose the same thing must have happened in Australia,' the American food writer Raymond Sokolov said to me when we were discussing this process (which he describes beautifully in his book *Why We Eat What We Eat*). Well, no, actually, it didn't. Until very recently, the only unique native Australian ingredient to be exploited commercially was the macadamia nut, and that had to be exported to Hawaii before anybody thought to do anything useful with it.

Why should this have been so? Sokolov suggested to me that it might have been because systems of global communication were already in place at the time Australia was settled by Europeans, so the new inhabitants could safely count on imports from home. This is a good guess, but it's not the whole story. The invaders could, more or less, rely on food from the old country, but the convicts and their guards who had arrived with the First Fleet in 1788 grew very hungry indeed while waiting for the Second Fleet to turn up.

Abandoned farm cottage near Daylesford, Victoria.

The first white settlers of this continent set about the task of feeding themselves with boundless ignorance and unjustified optimism. Fulsome accounts by the likes of Captain James Cook and the botanist Joseph Banks had led them to expect a green, fertile place, full of agricultural possibilities. Even before the First Fleet was dispatched, Evan Nepean, a British civil servant who had never been to Australia and was never to go there, was misleading himself and the government he served with seductive tales of 'a Country peculiarly adapted for a Settlement, the Lands about it being plentifully supplied with Wood and Water, the Soil rich and fertile, and the Shores well stocked with Shell and other Fish.' None of this was untrue, but the convicts and their overseers were very ill-equipped to take advantage of what the land had to offer. They had few draught animals, poor tools and, what was worse, they knew little about agriculture and next to nothing about the environment in which they intended to farm. The idea was that the new colony would become self-sufficient in less than three years: the inevitable result was three years of hunger. They tried their hands at farming, but they failed to persuade their European crops to take in Australia's unfamiliar soil and beneath its harsh sun. Supplies ran low and rations were reduced—flour, less than a kilogram each of salt pork and rice (not much protein, not much energy, no vitamin A or vitamin C)—which naturally meant that the amount of work that got done was also reduced.

Of course, there was another way of looking at the landscape: not as a place where food might just possibly be produced after much effort and expenditure, but as a place already rich in edible resources. This was the way the original inhabitants looked at it, so why did the newcomers not learn, as the early settlers of America had learned, from the native population? I suspect that one reason is that the Aborigines were not, like some of the indigenous people of America, farmers. They hunted and they gathered, which means that they had a deep knowledge of the culinary resources of their land, even though to Europeans they didn't seem to be doing anything at all *with* that land. To European eyes, land is being exploited when it can clearly be seen to be exploited: when it's under the plough or when sheep and cattle are being grazed upon it. 'The Land naturally produces hardly anything fit for Man to eat, and the natives know nothing of Cultivation,' wrote Captain Cook in 1770. You needed to know the territory to know what it could feed you and they certainly didn't know the territory. Besides, how could an urban or agrarian people learn to look at the land in the way that hunter–gatherers did? It would be rather like learning to read Japanese, only not quite as easy.

In time, sheer lack of food forced the new colony to turn to the indigenous flora. The leaves of the palm *Livisticus australis* were found to resemble cabbage; sweet trails left by insects on gum trees could be used in tea; tea itself could be made from the creeper *Smilax glycophyllia*. You see a pattern emerging here? Local plants are eaten only when they're all that's available, and they're seen as

BELOW: Chillies and bitter melon on display at a street market in Hobart, Tasmania.

CENTRE: Tomatoes arrive at Simon Johnson's Quality Foods.

FAR RIGHT: A First Fleet garden reconstructed in Sydney's Royal Botanic Gardens. *'I have, also, enclosed a spot of ground for a garden and make the cultivation of it one of my amusements. I put peas, and broad beans in, soon after I arrived (February) the peas podded in three months, the beans are still (June) in blossom, and neither of the plants are above a foot high, and out of five rows of the peas each three feet in length, I shall not get above 20 pods. If there are any plants that flourish better than others, these are yam, pumpkin, and the turnips are very sweet, but small ... it is evident that from some cause or other, though most of the seeds vegetate the plants degenerate in their growth exceedingly.'* SURGEON WHITE IN 12/11/1788.

substitutes for something else ('a kind of beans, very bad, a kind of parsley and a plant something resembling spinach …' noted an unenthusiastic explorer). This is an attitude that still persists. I remember a few years ago being given a cup of 'wattleccino'—a hot, frothy brew made from native wattle—and finding it fairly horrible, but perhaps I would have liked it if I'd been allowed to taste it on its own terms and not as a substitute for coffee.

We make a big thing of eating kangaroo and emu these days after years of ignoring them as sources of protein, but perhaps it isn't as important as we sometimes think. Historically, this neglect of the local vegetation—this failure to enjoy it for what it is and not for what it reminds you of—has probably had more effect on Australian food habits than neglect of the local fauna.

Only recently, and very slowly, have things started to change. 'Bush food' restaurants began to emerge in the 1980s, encouraged by the enterprise of suppliers like Vic Cherikoff (first an academic and then the owner of Bush Tucker Supply Aust.) and restaurateurs such as Jean-Paul Bruneteau, Alistair

Cattle graze on the fertile plains of the southern tablelands in New South Wales.

Punshon, Andrew Fielke and, of course, Jennice and Raymond Kersh. In seeking inspiration from Mexico and its chocolate-coated poultry, Raymond Kersh knew what he was doing.

Pavo in mole poblano is a dish which could have come about only from a fusion of two cultures: the colonial Spanish and the native Aztec. The Spanish would never have encountered chocolate if they had not come to the New World and, left to themselves, the Aztecs would never have used chocolate as a sauce for their native bird, the turkey: 'The idea of using chocolate as a flavouring in cooked food would have been horrifying to the Aztecs,' write Sophie and Michael Coe in their *True History of Chocolate*, 'just as Christians could not conceive of using communion wine to make, say, *coq au vin*.' This is, then, an essentially colonial, hybrid dish. Not only does it combine indigenous ingredients (tomatoes and several kinds of chilli, as well as chocolate and turkey) in a way which would never have occurred to the indigenous population, but it also combines them with produce from the Old World, such as salt, black pepper and garlic.

No such imaginative fusion of the new and the familiar occurred in Australia. As soon as they were able to, after the hungry years of the late-eighteenth century, Australians became great meat eaters and the meat which they ate came from animals which had been imported from Europe. But you can't found a cuisine on meat alone. Imaginative use of vegetables is what makes a cuisine, and, as we shall see, colonial conditions favoured neither vegetables nor imagination.

The Era of Meat and Cakes

To this day, there are many Australians of English or Irish ancestry (not very old ones, at that) who can remember their first encounter with olive oil. Their first serious encounter, that is, their first realisation that olive oil, instead of being kept in a cupboard for vaguely medicinal purposes and left there to go rancid, could be allowed to flow in all its unctuous, green-gold splendour. For some of them, it remains a symbol of change, of an awareness that something lay beyond the baked dinners of their childhood.

Vince Barbuto proudly displays a black forest cake in the Acland Cake Shop, St Kilda, Melbourne. Vince arrived in Australia as a child and now he and his brothers own this well-known shop specialising in famous cakes from many different food cultures.

Not that there's anything wrong with the baked dinner, of course. Baking—or 'roasting,' as the rest of the Anglophone world, not altogether accurately, calls it—is a fundamental cooking process the world over and it's a perfectly right and proper thing to do to a joint of beef or lamb. Nor is there anything wrong with boiling vegetables, decorating cakes or doing any of the other things that were enjoined on generations of Australian housewives by the Country Women's Association cookbook (nor, it goes without saying, is there anything wrong with the Country Women's Association cookbook). The real problem was the rigid monotony with which these rules were followed: baked dinner (or, to be more precise, lunch) on Sunday, cold meat on Monday, shepherd's pie on Tuesday. Dinner (or, as it tended to be called, tea) was at six o'clock, and it consisted of meat, often mutton, and two or three vegetables that had been cooked much more than was good for them. This was a joyless round of consumption, enlivened only, perhaps, by the cakes that were brought out on Sunday, upon whose preparation and decoration much love and skill had been devoted.

Meat, especially beef, has long been valued in this country, and beef is shared at a very familiar social ritual which almost every observer of Australian culture sooner or later finds it necessary to mention. Here, for example, is Gabrielle Carey, in pursuit of a national identity and its symbols:

But what is an Australian ritual? If you ask the person in the street, the first response is almost always the same: the barbecue. Anyone can outline the ritual of an Australian barbecue: the man cooking, usually with a tinny in one hand and tongs in the other; the woman preparing salads in the kitchen.

This is absolutely spot on. Recently, I posed the question 'What is an Australian ritual?' to a lecture hall full of students in the hospitality industry and the barbecue was the first thing they mentioned.

A sociological tour of the Australian backyard, published in 1987 in a book called *Myths of Oz,* introduces the matter with due solemnity: 'At one end of the outdoor living area is a space to be filled by a barbecue, the high altar in the ritual of outdoor living that signifies more than any other single item.' The authors of this account find it necessary to drag on the heavy intellectual artillery in the form of the French anthropologist Claude Lévi-Strauss (who said that the application of fire to our food is what distinguishes us from the animals) and suggest that the barbecue embodies a racial memory of the ways of our hunting ancestors. Given that Australia is not the only place in which the barbecue is a masculine preserve, some such very general account of its origins may well be necessary. Nor is it surprising that people living in warm climates should enjoy eating in the open air. There are, however, some specifically Australian elements to the ritual.

Gabrielle Carey's article on the subject, published in 1995 in the *Good Weekend* supplement of the *Sydney Morning Herald*, prompted a response from a reader who suggested that the barbecue was a phenomenon that had first appeared as recently as the early 1950s: 'It was an urban entertainment and many of the participants were men who, to their surprise, missed the open air (and alfresco meals?) that had been part of army life.' The same writer recalled that, before this time, the popular open-air ritual had been the bush picnic with, 'if time permitted,' grilled chops and tea boiled in the billy.

Whether or not this account of the origins of the Australian barbie is accurate, it does, with its mention of billy tea, recall one reason for the potency of the barbecue as a symbol of Australian life. The national myth, formed in the late-nineteenth century and codified in the pages of the *Bulletin* magazine, is an image of the open-air life: bushmen, bushrangers and shearers, doing it tough in the bush, cooking over an open fire and boiling their tea in a tin can. Meat is an essential part of this image, partly because meat is one of the principal products of the landscape in which the image is situated and partly because an obsession with meat and pride in animal husbandry had been exported by the English to their colonies.

This carnal love went first to America—where Al Bundy, lumpen star of the sitcom 'Married with Children,' once let out the heartfelt cry, 'I'm so hungry I could eat a vegetable!'—and then to Australia (and who can blame those Britons who were lucky enough to exchange English poverty for Australian warmth and wealth if they became addicted to something that had been so difficult to obtain in their native land?). The early settlers of New South Wales wanted fat cattle—'lean' was not, for them, a term of approbation—and lots of meat: they showed a marked disinclination to grow vegetables unless forced to do so by the governor.

In fact, the Australian fondness for animal flesh was so pronounced that, by 1893, Sydney physician Philip Muskett was complaining that, in New South Wales, 'the consumption of butcher's meat by each inhabitant is greater than in any other country in the world.' Muskett disapproved of a diet that seemed so unsuited to the Australian climate. He thought that if Australia was to have a national dish, it should be 'a macédoine of vegetables, or a vegetable curry, or some well-concocted salad.'

Given the importance of the 1890s for the self-image of Anglo-Australia, it is worth asking why it should ever have occurred to Muskett that Australia ought to have a national dish. After all, the distinguishing marks of a great nation used to be wealth and military victories, not the quality of its spices. Of course, wise rulers have always wanted their people to be well nourished—which is why

Australian cuisine exists in the same way multiculturalism does. We have evolved from this and it is what gives Australia the cutting edge. We have been used to so many different cuisines that our palates are broader, so we can taste more in a dish. We didn't stay with the traditional way of doing things because suddenly there were so many different cuisines. Our cuisine is evolving and not standing still. For many years, chefs kept their recipes secret, but now most people are sharing their information so that there is an explosion of knowledge.

GARY COOPER

Henri IV of France famously promised every peasant a chicken in his pot on Sundays—but nobody has ever thought of cooks as the vanguard of national glory. Muskett, though, was writing at the mid-point of that period which the historian Eric Hobsbawm has identified as one which saw newly invented traditions 'spring up with particular assiduity …'

This was the end of a century of nationalism: Germany and Italy had been unified, many of the nations of South America had won their independence and movements for national self-determination were already appearing like hairline cracks in the granite façades of the world's great empires. The new spirit of

nationalism sought embodiment not just in politics, but also in culture. Even nations long unified or long free—such as France and the United States—needed to provide their citizenry with a focus for its loyalties. It was now the state that directed people's destinies at the highest level, and not, as might have been the case in earlier times, some much smaller unit of political or even ecclesiastical government. As a consequence, nation states, new and old, needed to enlist the affections of a large and varied public. This was the period which saw the inauguration of Bastille Day as a public holiday in France and of Thanksgiving Day and the Fourth of July in the United States. It was the period which saw the pledge of allegiance to the flag become a daily ritual in American schools and, throughout Europe, it was the period in which team sports became institutionalised.

Hobsbawm's list of examples can easily be extended into the kitchen. It was also in this period that Pellegrino Artusi wrote *La Scienza in Cucina e l'Arte di Mangiare Bene* (*Science in the Kitchen and the Art of Good Eating*), the first cookery book to deal with the food of the whole of Italy. Artusi tried to do for Italy's food what Garibaldi and Mazzini had done for its political structure: to form unity out of diversity. In Greece, Nikolas Tselementes tried something similar, although with less success. (His book, published in 1910 and still hugely popular in Greece, represents an attempt to purge Greek cuisine of all those elements which its author saw as Turkish. Unfortunately, much that he thought of as Ottoman was

I think Australian cuisine is defined by an approach to food and service, by a style of eating, by the way we handle ingredients. It's the friendly way of serving—we like to learn from the waiter. Our food embraces multiculturalism—it's one of the cornerstones of this country. We're living it every day. I think, in the future, we'll develop regionalism within the Australian cuisine, that is, there will be different styles throughout the country.

GEOFF LINDSAY

genuinely Greek and much that he introduced was French: out went olive oil, garlic and a lot of spices, and in came the béchamel sauce that dominates restaurant moussaka to this day.) France had to wait just a little longer for her food to become a truly national treasure. As the sociologist Stephen Mennel has observed in his book *All Manner of Food*, the vogue for French regional cooking had its origins after World War I and was born out of an alliance of gastronomy and the tourist industry. Appropriately, its midwives were tyre companies such as Michelin and Kléber-Colombes, who published guides to the restaurants and hotels of France.

There is still something very pleasing about a home-cooked roast chicken dinner, fresh scones and cup cakes, the aroma of billy tea and a slab of charred steak.

So the idea of national cuisine was in the air when Muskett made his suggestions about an Australian national dish. The very vagueness, however, of his suggestions—almost anything would do, providing it was made of vegetables—seems to indicate that he did not feel the pressure of any existing model. Although he inveighed against the unimaginative way in which his compatriots served their meat, Muskett's real enemy was excess of animal flesh pure and simple, not animal flesh prepared in any particular way.

A few years later, he might have noticed a few rivals to the macédoine of vegetables, the vegetable curry and the salad as potential national dishes. There was the meat pie, for example, and there was the decorated cake, edged and piped with delicate icing, served up on beautiful plates with lacy doilies in a room specially set aside for afternoon tea. It was the decorated cake and not the salad that looked like becoming the national dish.

To some extent this is still true. You can see the truth of it every year at the Royal Easter Show held in Sydney by the Royal Agricultural Society: row after row of cakes, the winners and the runners-up, formal cakes rising tier after tier, cakes hung about with swags and lace and flowers of piped icing, cakes shaped like famous people, cakes shaped like cars or aeroplanes, even the odd cake shaped like a portable stereo (a sort of gâteau blaster).

This is a homely art, but it has an aristocratic ancestry in the work of Antonin Carême, the great French chef, who claimed that: 'The fine arts are five in number: painting, sculpture, poetry, music and architecture, whose main branch is confectionery.' At the beginning of the nineteenth century, Carême pleased his wealthy patrons with spectacular set pieces, temples and towers, elaborately carved in lard and decorated with spun sugar. The modern Australian cake is covered with a fondant or plastic icing (consisting mostly of glucose, glycerine and gelatin) and decorated with flowers and lacework made of piped royal icing (egg white, sugar and acetic acid). The result is less pretentious than Carême's fantasies and more edible, but equally architectural. Indeed, Don Dunstan, former Premier of South Australia and (as we shall see) a keen cook, has seen in confectionery a counterpart of the domestic architecture of the 1940s:

Australian society was much concerned as usual with putting on a social face. The houses of the time regularly had expensive façades, the decoration not being repeated on the side wall, and corrugated iron 'lean-tos' at the back … At afternoon tea, the best face was put forward, as in the building of façades. Elaborate cake-making is where the artistry went … Cake decoration classes predominated in what adult education classes in cookery there were at the time.

And, of course, there was, or soon would be, the barbecue, lyrically evoked in recent years by Graham Pont—philosopher, musicologist and a pioneering theorist of Australian gastronomy—in terms of 'delicious memories of burning gum, over-done sausages and chops and powerful red wine …' Pont argues that, although the culinary methods employed in the barbecue are of great antiquity, the Australian version of them is made unique by the abundance in this country of excellent fuel and by the availability of good, inexpensive wine and meat.

In recent years, some Australian culinary patriots have tended to ignore the barbecue, perhaps in the way that genteel Australians used to ignore those of their ancestors who had worked their passage here by stealing a few spoons or rustling sheep. Thus the folklorist Warren Fahey has remarked on the unremarkable fact that Australia's climate is ideal for outdoor eating, but in describing a suitable menu, he passes silently over the grilled chop in favour of a seafood antipasto, stuffed snapper or chicken and a papaya salad. Our leading culinary patriot, Cherry Ripe, reassures us that steak and chips—a sort of indoor equivalent to the barbecued chop—will continue to be available on Australian menus, but 'will happily coexist side by side with all manner of once-foreign food, from polenta to couscous, as well as Asian dishes and flavours.'

In fact, this neglect of the barbecue isn't altogether surprising: meat cooked over naked flame may once have furnished a powerful symbol of national identity, but it hardly amounts to a cuisine, or even to the beginning of one. As food historian Barbara Santich points out, quoting with approval an unnamed Frenchman, '*La cuisine, ça se prepare*' (a cuisine is something that is prepared). In the case of barbecued meat, the degree of preparation involved, the degree to which the raw ingredients have been transformed by art, has been too slight for the results to be called the product of a cuisine. So, the Australian kitchen entered the twentieth century with most of the artfulness and ingenuity of its best

Australian cuisine is the best in the world with its mixture of food cuisines. The surge of bush food is like the days of nouvelle cuisine—unless you understand these products, they should never be touched. Australian cuisine has taken on the world in its search for its roots, in which the basics of French cuisine and Asian fusion have proved very successful, but only from chefs who understand their craft.

RAYMOND CAPADLI

domestic cooks concentrated in one small area of culinary endeavour—the decorated cake. Otherwise, it was laden with the charred bodies of dead animals and animal fats. And, of course, there was no olive oil, which is curious because South Australia was at the time producing excellent olives. Why were they not being picked in quantities, pressed and then pressed into service in the kitchens of Australia?

To answer that question is to move closer to finding out why Australian food was as it was, and also why it changed.

Les Nouveaux Paysans

In the Barossa Valley of South Australia one crisp spring afternoon, I tasted some extraordinary olives. They were small and dark things, and they seemed to be almost all stone, yet their flavour was full and thoroughly fruity.

Fruity—this ought not to be a rare experience, but it is. Accustomed to olives that taste of salt and oil that tastes of nothing in particular, we forget sometimes that the olive is a fruit and that olive oil is fruit juice. 'This is typical of the wild olive,' I was told by Maggie Beer, renowned cook and Barossa Valley patriot, who was in charge of the food that day. 'They're really tiny as a general rule.' For a meal that would celebrate wildness, she had chosen several varieties of wild olive. After the fruity olive hors d'oeuvres, we—sixty or so of us seated at a long trestle table beneath the vats of the St Hallett's winery—were to taste riper, more mellow olives with some Murray cod and a very green olive oil with some asparagus: all supplied by Michael Burr, a former medical man who now devotes his time to the olive and the study of its history.

The olive tree, as the Roman poet Virgil observed, does not require cultivation: it just digs itself in and relies upon the Earth herself to provide all the moisture it needs. He was right: in South Australia, far beyond the farthest boundary of his world, the descendants of the trees he knew have dug themselves in so efficiently that they are now regarded as pests. 'There's argument as to whether it invades primary sites or only places that have already been turned over,' Michael Burr told me as we drove past a few wild olive trees on the way to the winery and Maggie's food. 'There are places in the Adelaide Hills where it's rampant.'

It was never supposed to turn out like this. The olive trees, most of them imported from Marseilles, were intended to be the basis of a local olive oil industry (for export only, of course: nobody expected locals to want the stuff) and at first the signs were very promising. As early as 1851, South Australian olive oil was winning prizes at the Great Exhibition in London, which was not bad going, considering that the olive tree had been introduced to the colony only fifteen years before. But labour was always too costly and soon the encroaching suburbs had swallowed up many of the groves (which were worth more as real estate than as a source of food). What little was left of the commercial operation hung on until the 1950s, but, by then, it was hopeless. Meanwhile, though, the olive tree had gone feral. Local councils now want to clear it away and there are certainly

The Australian cuisine is less eclectic than before, still innovative—it's more directional these days. The quality of produce is supreme. It's not showing off as we did in the experimental stage. It's more confident, with greater recognition—it's coming to maturity. Australian cuisine has come a long way very quickly.

MARTIN WEBB

Spring lambs grazing on lush pasture near Albury, New South Wales.

areas where the tenacious Mediterranean interloper will have to go, although, as Michael Burr pointed out to me, nothing should be removed without being inspected first: there could be genetic gold in those Adelaide Hills.

In most of Europe, the olive tree has until very recently been propagated asexually: by cutting, grafting and similar vegetative techniques. Although these methods ensure consistency—they guarantee that the new plant will be just like its parent—they also ensure that nothing will ever change. But the wild colonial trees have been going at it sexually for decades, and something of value may well have arisen from all this unsupervised crossbreeding. 'If there's anywhere in the world where you'd find a new crossbred variety, it would have to be Australia,' said Michael. The dexterous use of genetic material from the Barossa—duly patented, of course—may give us trees that can withstand disease, frost and drought; that are compact and small enough to be suitable for mechanical harvesting; and that give a high yield of good-quality oil.

Paradoxically, then, the olives trees of South Australia would not be so interesting had they been properly cultivated. They were not, however, totally ignored during their years of commercial insignificance. On the way to the winery, Michael and I stopped at the house of Rosa Matto, a teacher of cooking who also instructs a class of enthusiasts on how to turn olives into oil. We had arrived on bottling day and Rosa's front yard was full of recycled glass—clear bottles, green bottles, brown bottles—and fragrant with pressed olives. I don't recall handling much at all of the olive oil that lay all around me, but I still left with that clean, smooth feeling on my face and hands which comes from close contact with the stuff. Rosa's family—her parents immigrated from the Campania region of Italy in the 1950s—used to do this themselves: they picked their own olives from the trees that industry had by now abandoned.

But why were the Adelaide Hills not thick with locals, all availing themselves of the free olives? Well, the Anglos didn't like olives, of course, and they weren't particularly interested in olive oil (except, perhaps, as a laxative). According to one very influential view of the history of Australian food, however, there is more to it than this. We can probably best explore this aspect of the story by leaving South Australia and heading north to the Orange district of New South Wales.

Since the early 1990s, the people of Orange have been celebrating their local produce in an annual food festival. Each festival culminates in a big dinner and the first of these was cooked by Phillip Searle (then a Sydney chef, now painting and cooking not far from Orange, in the Blue Mountains). At forty dollars a ticket, a place at the festive board cost much more than many of the older inhabitants of the district had ever thought of paying for a single meal. Nonetheless, after much persuasion, one local farmer allowed his grown-up children to take him and his wife. The experience, as the children later told me, was a revelation to him. It had never occurred to him—a man who had lived his whole life surrounded by food in its raw, living form—that anything he ate could ever be this good. Suddenly, it seems, he began to look at farming in a different way. He had thought of himself as a producer not of food, but of raw commodities which were shipped off for somebody else to deal with. Now, at last, in his retirement, he began to see the possibilities of being in the food business rather than an extractive industry.

'There has never been the creative interplay between society and the soil,' says the food historian Michael Symons. 'Almost no food has ever been grown by the person who eats it, almost no food has been preserved in the home, and, indeed, very little preparation is now done by a family cook.' In other words, most white Australians have seen the land not as Rosa Matto's family saw it, but as it was seen by the farmer from Orange until he discovered what food could taste like.

The famous thesis of Symons's book *One Continuous Picnic* (first published in 1982) is that Australia's lack of a peasant, agrarian society has had a profound effect on its food. All developed societies, Symons argues, progress through three stages. The first is the hunter–gatherer stage, in which the population hunts or forages for its food; the second stage is the agricultural stage and the third industrial. It is at the second stage—in which production is dominated by peasants tilling the soil—that cuisine develops. Australia, says Symons, missed out on this fruitful middle passage: having for millennia been populated solely by hunter–gatherers, it acquired an industrial proletariat overnight when the convicts arrived in 1788, but it never had any peasants.

The convicts weren't peasants. Many had been city dwellers in the old country. Some, it's true, had been farm labourers, but a labourer is not a peasant: labourers are paid a wage and they move from farm to farm in search of work, but

BELOW: Marinated table olives from South Australia, typical of the wild olives growing rampant in the Adelaide Hills.

ABOVE: The green virgin olive oils are grown and pressed in South Australia, while the yellow oil is cold-pressed mustard seed oil grown and pressed in southern New South Wales.

peasants are deeply attached to the little patch of land which they and their forebears have worked for centuries and which provides them with their subsistence. The convicts, however—and the free settlers who came after them—were the children of a new industrial age. They saw a farm as a sort of low, flat, open-air factory. For many of them, farming, like mining, was just another way of getting money out of the ground.

Whatever the validity of Symons's historical argument—and it's certainly very plausible—much of its appeal to many of his first readers must have been romantic. He seemed resolutely to have turned his face against the modern and the urban: 'How people can live and work in skyscrapers, I don't know,' he wrote in a later work. 'They inhabit a corporate rather than a human landscape. Little wonder that the better Australian restaurants shift out to the suburbs, if not the countryside.' This was wishful thinking—most of the best Australian restaurants are slap-bang in the middle of big cities and few are in the suburbs or the countryside—but a lot of people seemed to share Symons's wishes.

Nobody wanted to infuse Australian society with the dark, intense passions of peasant life, but quite a few wanted food production that was less corporate, more regional, more local. The olive-oil bottling in Rosa Matto's backyard was a symptom of this, as was the food festival in Orange, and so, too, was the publication in 1991 of a very significant book about food in this country, *Stephanie's Australia*, by the distinguished Melbourne restaurateur Stephanie Alexander. This was a celebration of Australia's smaller food producers, people such as the Victorian cheese maker Richard Thomas; Gabrielle Kervella, a Western Australian maker of goat's cheese; Tony Lehmann, who produces milk-fed lamb on his property at Illabo in New South Wales; John and Mary Walker, who make chutneys and tracklements on their farm in Tasmania; and Michael Symons himself, who at the time was co-owner of a small restaurant in the Adelaide Hills where the dishes were simple and the produce was local. It was providores such as Will Studd and Simon Johnson, and the support of national stores such as David Jones, who helped these small specialist producers to flourish.

Stephanie Alexander, however, is no dewy-eyed romantic: she pays due attention to the politics and economics of her subject and she knows that it's not enough just to produce something wonderful down on the farm—somebody has to distribute it and somebody has to tell the world. Accordingly, she devotes space to food writers, such as Joan Campbell of *Vogue Entertaining*, and to distributors such as John Susman, who at the time she wrote was partner in a swashbuckling fish wholesalers called the Flying Squid Brothers.

Anybody depressed by *One Continuous Picnic*—with its tale of opportunities lost and of the Gothic horrors that have emerged from Australian kitchens—would be much cheered by *Stephanie's Australia*, which evokes a network of local food producers and of the cooks they serve. These people are not peasants—their crops are cash crops, produced with careful regard to the market—but with their passionate devotion to what they do and to the land on which they do it, they are as close as we can get, or need to get, to the sort of agrarian cultivators from whose labours great cuisines arise.

It was a lucky day for lovers of cheese when Will Studd, a cheese providore born and trained in England, set up business in Melbourne. It was a revolution when he began flying in fresh traditional cheeses from Europe and marketing them so they reached the consumers in peak condition. It also stimulated growth of Australia's embryonic farmhouse cheese industry, giving the cheeses distribution and promotion. Will made sure the best Australian cheese and the best traditional cheese from around the world were available to Australians.

Will is dedicated to the love and care needed to look after cheese and committed to passing that on to all who work with him. Cheese needs to be matured until it is just right for selling. This enables the customer to experience cheese at its best and to understand the extra dimension of flavour that is achieved only when the cheese is stored at the correct temperature (this varies between cheeses).

A Feed at the Chinese and Other Places

'Are your prawns fresh?' There's a stranger in town. He's from the big city (from Brisbane, in fact) and he's asking some awkward questions.

Albert, who runs a tiny restaurant, The Emperor's Palace, all by himself—with the help of an incompetent waitress—probably knows that it must be a trick question: this is an inland country town that we're in, so how fresh can the prawns ever be? But he knows how to play the game, too: yes, of course, the prawns are fresh—they were fresh when they were frozen, so how could they possibly not be fresh?

The scene is from Shirley Barrett's movie *Love Serenade*, which in 1996 brought to the screen an aspect of their national life which most Australians knew about, but which is seldom celebrated: the Chinese restaurant in a country town. Just about every settlement bigger than a village seems to have one (although few, it's to be hoped, are quite as bad as Albert's place) and the pattern is pretty much the same everywhere. I went to one recently—let's call it The Bamboo Garden—in a small town (population about 7000) in the grazing country of southwest Queensland. Like the shops in the strip of which it is a part, The Bamboo Garden faces the street with plate-glass windows stretching from floor to ceiling, although lace curtains protect the diners from the gaze of passers-by. Not that there are often many passers-by: if you dine in The Bamboo Garden at eight, you will walk to it along a largely empty main street (and you may not be popular with the staff, because the place closes at nine). Within, plush carpet, auspiciously coloured red, covers the walls to about waist height, after which wood veneer panelling takes over. Glass lanterns hang from the walls and the air is filled with the bland jangle of Chinese muzak. Your table is protected by functional brown leatherette over which white linen has been laid: at your right hand as you sit down is a pair of chopsticks, at your left a spoon.

The façade of the well-patronised Ho's Palace at Blackheath, in the Blue Mountains to the west of Sydney, New South Wales.

Aside from the starters (here called 'appetisers') and the soups, the printed menu is divided simply by basic ingredients: beef, pork, duck, fish and prawns—which cannot be fresh, because we are many kilometres from the coast—and these are further subdivided into battered and non-battered. If you order the roast duck with barbecue sauce and your companion orders the sweet and sour pork, then a plate of duck will be placed in front of you and a plate of pork in front of your companion. You are not expected to eat from dishes placed in the centre of the table and, in fact, any attempts at a Chinese style of eating are made difficult by the fact that all the plates are flat: there are no bowls which you can hold up to your mouth while you shovel the rice in with your chopsticks. While steamed rice is available, the menu is set out in such a way that it seems to assume that fried rice—perhaps decked out with a few frozen peas and some of those fresh prawns—is what you're going to eat. The prices are very reasonable.

CONTINUED ON PAGE 32

RIGHT: High-quality Coffin Bay scallops with their dramatic purple shell with a bright magenta-purple roe. John persuaded the chefs to serve them on their exquisite half shell.

ABOVE: You don't get much better than this mulloway or jewfish, caught on the line at Brooklyn on the Hawkesbury River to the north of Sydney.

RIGHT: Just-opened Sydney rock oysters. John convinced restaurants to open their own oysters correctly in-house and serve them in their own juice. 'I've explored all the native species and the regional differences, the growing techniques and the difference of quality in the seasons.'

John Susman

Waterbound Ambassador

'Coffin Bay scallops might have been sold in 2-kg (4-lb) frozen blocks if we hadn't convinced people to try for quality,' John Susman, high-flying fish providore concluded. The scallop story is an example of how dramatically seafood marketing has changed in the past ten to fifteen years. John had heard that, on the west coast of the Eyre Peninsula in South Australia, there were fantastic scallop beds that had been closed down due to overfishing with nets. He persuaded the government to let him undertake a hand-collection program. The divers were trained to collect only mature scallops. John then set up a processing plant nearby to prepare and pack the scallops carefully for market. Only salt water was used, with no chemical additives. Chefs such as Neil Perry,

Stefano Manfredi and Tetsuya Wakuda were delighted with these fine-quality scallops and they quickly became the darlings of the fine dining sector.

John's background is hotel management, but he felt drawn to the food industry. After a stint in Neil Perry's kitchen, he went to Paris and worked for a fishmonger who specialised in seafood from Brittany, supplying the top restaurants. Here he learnt all about the quality of fish and how it should be handled. He returned to Sydney and formed the Flying Squid Brothers. Travelling around Australia talking to commercial fishers, John realised there was an opportunity to supply higher quality seafood. He persuaded fishermen to catch quality fish on lines instead of nets and spent a lot of time perfecting the harvest-to-plate process.

'Chefs are now becoming species aware— seasonally and regionally. I was lucky to be part of the expansion of awareness of quality food. There are no boundaries. Now there is almost an

aggressive expectation for the food industry. The chefs are constructively driving the suppliers and the suppliers drive the growers—it's symbiotic. Everyone in the chain is clearly focused on high quality and there is a lot of passion. The harvesters and fishermen are the unsung heroes. I now work at developing export markets for specialist seafood products. You could describe me as a waterbound ambassador of Australian seafood.'

ABOVE: Oysters are farmed in the tranquil waters of the Hawkesbury River. Sydneysiders claim the small, sweet rock oysters are the finest in the world. Middens of ancient shells along the shore are evidence that Aboriginal peoples enjoyed them long before Europeans came across this delicacy..

There is such a great mixture of great restaurants and great ingredients here. People are very open-minded about trying new things. Like wine, it's a young industry catching up very quickly with the old traditions of France and Italy. The waiters are now professional and there are much better providores. It's great team work—chefs, providores, growers—and the food is better handled all along the line. For example, fish are now caught on lines instead of nets. Now we get the best.

GUILLAUME BRAHIMI

While in town, I spoke to an old inhabitant, now well into his seventies, whose father was Chinese and who remembers a racy past when even this modest conurbation had its own Chinatown with opium dens and lavish celebrations at the New Year. In those days, the Chinese population of the town were market gardeners, as most of the Chinese in Australia had been ever since they first came here in the goldrush years of the mid-nineteenth century. ('We know the Chinaman better than most people …' sneered the *Bulletin* magazine in 1890. 'He produces two things—vice and vegetables.') The vegetables that the old man's father and his friends produced were for the local market: nothing that would alarm the sensibilities of a conventional Anglo-Australian cook of the 1920s, 1930s or 1940s. For themselves, they grew or imported other things, and it is the absence of authentic Chinese vegetables from the menu at the Bamboo Garden that disappoints the old man, who never goes there.

But this very absence is a tribute to the adaptability of the Chinese. They, unlike the French, have been prepared to compromise their great cuisines, and so, from the 1960s onwards, places such as the Bamboo Garden have been offering the peoples of small Australian towns a version of Chinese food that they are prepared to accept. (This is in marked contrast to the United Kingdom, where Chinese restaurants were long concentrated in the capital and where, according to the food historian Christopher Driver, some smaller towns were getting their first taste of Chinese takeaway as late as the mid-1980s.) Once, this was the only Chinese food available in Australia to any but the most adventurous diners. Oliver Shaul, a Sydney restaurateur who arrived here as a refugee from Europe in 1939, recalls the role that Chinese food played in those days, the days of the 'six o'clock swill,' when pubs closed early and drinking had to be done in a hurry. 'A feed at the Chinese, as it was called, was mostly done by fellows who'd had a lot to drink,' he once told me. 'They were drinking like crazy from five to six and then they went to the Chinese—or, as they so terribly called it, "the Chow's"—to have a feed.'

To be more precise, the tradition that is being so cheerfully compromised here is Cantonese, the most exported of Chinese regional cuisines, with its fine-chopping, its steaming and its stir-frying. On the whole, to experience diversity in Chinese food—to taste the food of Beijing, for example, or Sichuan—you need to go to a big city where the Chinese community has grown sufficiently large to accommodate restaurants that don't need to look beyond that community for their customers. You won't find pig's blood on the menu at the Bamboo Garden, although it and much other exotica are easily available in the Chinatowns of Melbourne and Sydney, and even in some outlying suburbs of those cities:

Cabramatta is the only place worth eating at. It is the only place where you are not expected, *where the restaurant owner does not smile to welcome you. He doesn't want you there. He thinks you're a nuisance. When I go into a restaurant like this, I know am going to eat well. I know I will be eating the real thing.*

This is a lawyer from the inner city Sydney suburb of Enmore talking to Ghassan Hage, a lecturer in anthropology at the University of Sydney, who quotes him in a fascinating essay on food and the migrant experience. The lawyer clearly sees himself as a bit of an explorer. Boldly, he makes his way out to distant Cabramatta (all of 25 kilometres to the west of Enmore) so that he can be a tourist in his own country and congratulate himself on the purity of a gastronomic enthusiasm that pursues good food with no thought to those things that the less resolute of us tend to look for in a restaurant (like the feeling that we are welcome and a menu that we can understand). But, Hage remarks, the Vietnamese restaurateurs of Cabramatta are not so unbusinesslike as to behave in a manner that will turn potential customers away: 'As one restaurant owner revealed through his son, who was interpreting, many of the restaurant owners know that the absence of signs in English is a good way to attract Anglo customers!'

There is a game going on here. The name of the game is authenticity, and authenticity, like sincerity, is a thing well worth faking. In restaurants like those frequented by the lawyer from Enmore, authenticity seems to have become a commodity for knowing restaurateurs and unknowing customers. On the other hand, to dismiss the Bamboo Garden for its lack of authenticity, or even of any pretence to authenticity, would be both snobbish and inaccurate: it would be like asking Albert whether his prawns are fresh when you know they can't be, but that they're on the menu because his customers want them. What the Bamboo Garden offers may be good or it may be bad, but it is authentically what it is, and what it represents is a genuine model of a multiculturalism that is truly interactive: the customers will take only so much 'foreignness' in their food and no more; the restaurant is careful to give them only so much of it as they will take. So, both sides are exercising pragmatism and both, presumably, are happy.

But, I put it to you (as I can imagine the lawyer from Enmore saying) that someone venturing out in search of whatever uncertain welcome is to be found in the Vietnamese restaurants of Cabramatta is at least trying to educate his palate. Surely we want to taste what the Vietnamese eat and not just what they think we'd like to eat? Well, yes, but I suspect that new and interesting culinary developments emerge out of compromise. We're often told that it was the migrants who arrived here from Southern Europe after World War II—the Greeks and Italians, with their love of wine, olive oil and garlic—who transformed the Australian palate. Of course, their contribution was enormous, but we do them little justice if we think of them as just carrying on here what they'd done in the old country. There was something else going on, as Stefano Manfredi, Italian-born chef and restaurateur, acknowledges in his book *Fresh from Italy*:

And it all started in the ethnic ghettos of the outer suburbs of the great cities. In Cabramatta, right now, the future stars of Australian cuisine are growing up, doing what Franca, my mother, did in Blacktown in the 1960s—adapting, inventing, gathering, swapping. I can still remember walking through Blacktown shopping centre with Franca and being stopped in our tracks outside a pet food shop. There, on a tray, was a juicy slab of horsemeat. What luck! We bought it, took it home, sliced it wafer thin, soaked it in olive oil and lemon juice, cracked black pepper over it, and ate it, raw. It had been a long time since we'd had horsemeat carpaccio.

Australian cuisine is still a pimply, gangly youth—but with boundless, limitless energy, clumsy and enthusiastic as it still thinks all things are possible—it shows some signs of starting to mature.

DAVID THOMPSON

ABOVE: Gilbert Lau, owner of the Flower Drum, Melbourne, seated at a Chinese banquet set in the traditional way. Gilbert serves the finest quality Cantonese food in Australia. He and his chef are inspired by fine fresh ingredients such as the shiitake mushrooms and the freshwater Murray cod shown above. They regularly go back to China for inspiration as well.

Gilbert likes to make the sort of food he grew up with—Cantonese cooking is a contrast of flavours and textures. With each meal, the Cantonese traditionally like to eat a bit of seafood, some meat, rice and vegetables. Served this way, you don't have to have the dishes you don't like. Gilbert recommends eating with your fingers—it's more enjoyable.

The key phrase here is 'adapting, inventing, gathering, swapping'—these people didn't just arrive here with packets of dried pasta and get to work. In fact, they arrived here with very little and had to make do with what they could—picking wild fennel from suburban paddocks, as the young Manfredi did, or swapping with their Greek and Maltese neighbours.

And we would be wrong if we thought that the compromise and the adaptation went in one direction only. Any domestic cook of, say, the early 1970s, who owned a copy of the *Margaret Fulton Cookbook* (first published in 1968) and had worked through its chapters on pasta and on 'international' food would have been introduced not only to olive oil, ghee and the use of a wok, but also to noodles, lasagne, Greek lemon soup and five-spice chicken—all to be prepared without shortcuts or cheating. So perhaps the established population was prepared to meet the newcomers halfway.

Ghassan Hage tells a story from the western Sydney suburb of Westmead, where a Lebanese family introduced their Anglo neighbours to *lahmeh w'snoobar*, a mixture of minced meat, onions and pine nuts. The woman of the house thought that this was the best minced meat she had ever tasted, so she used it in making meat pies. This is a very Australian story, not just because the meat pie is supposed to be one of Anglo-Australia's culinary totems, but also because it implies that different cuisines need not stand in proud isolation from one another. This is a domestic version of what has happened in so many Australian restaurants and it's worth asking ourselves why this sort of thing should have happened in this place, at this time and with such conspicuous success.

ABOVE: Victoria Street, Richmond, in Melbourne is the hub of the Vietnamese shops and restaurants.

ABOVE RIGHT AND RIGHT: Bundles of chives and carrots, proudly organic and freshly harvested.

ABOVE LEFT: Barbecued ducks decorate the window of a Chinese butcher's store in Sydney's Haymarket.

LEFT CENTRE: Asian stalls at a street market in Hobart, Tasmania.

LEFT: Chinese gardeners have been using their traditional gardening techniques to cultivate this fertile market garden in Kyeemagh, near Sydney's international airport, for more than a hundred years.

Eat Like an Australian

Some time in the early 1980s, I remember, there was a comedy sketch on an Australian television show which featured a couple of blokes in overalls doing something strenuous with a piece of heavy machinery in the heat of the midday sun.

'Jeez,' said one, wiping his brow, 'I'm as dry as a …' He paused for thought. 'As dry as a …' He tried again: 'As dry as a …' He gave up. 'It's no good,' he said at last. 'I just can't manage that colourful Aussie slang.'

If only the people at Sheila's Bar Barbie had been similarly lost for words, we would have been spared a wine list which tells us that Brown Bros' Bin 60 Dry Red is 'as soft as a koala's belly' and that Penfold's Koonunga Hill is 'as stylish as a kookaburra's tail.' We might also have been spared a menu which commences with the following colourful Aussie rubric: 'When me and Bruce came over after the caravan was repossessed, it stood out like a snag in your cornflakes that there was nothing to eat worth an empty Esky …' As you may have gathered, Sheila's Bar Barbie is in London.

Situated in Covent Garden, close by such time-honoured eateries as Bertorelli's and Rules, Sheila's, though a relative newcomer, does its bit for tradition. It caters to the venerable, Pythonesque prejudices with which your Everage British diner approaches all things Antipodean. The floorboards are rough and bare, low beams hang from the ceiling and corrugated iron covers the walls. Hubcaps constitute a major motif in the decorative scheme and so do road signs telling you how far it is to the Black Stump or to somewhere called 'Ayres'

Rock. The salad bar is housed in the chassis of a ute, Australia's particular version of the American pick-up.

The staff wear Akubras and moleskins, and, although only one of three who served me seemed to be Australian, they all say 'No worries.' (Good coaching from management? Or is that colourful Aussie slang just so contagious that everybody who works there catches it?)

Trying hard not to look like a regular, I settled myself on a bench in the corner, decided against a cocktail (Dingo's Breakfast, Surfer's Lifesaver or Sex on the Beach) and chewed thoughtfully on an *amuse-geule* consisting of dry little scones served in a frying pan. Colourful Aussie slang was all over the menu like a swarm of blowies round a dead dingo (this stuff really is catching). Instead of starters, there was 'Tucker to get you goin',' including Down Under Soup, Chook Wings ('Removed by Bruce and fried by me') and Pommie Skins ('spuds with the middle thrown out'). For main courses, there were steaks in various shapes, sizes and degrees of negritude, pies, sausages and bonza chops topped with cinnamon apple chunks ('taught to me by a silvertail with too much time on his hands').

None of it, I have to admit, proved to be in any way offensive: the Pommie Skins broke between the teeth with an agreeable snap and the steak was done, as they say, to a turn. So it should have been, because Sheila's isn't an Australian restaurant at all: it's a steak house, like many another steak house. Add some chilli and it would be a Tex-Mex steak house; add some paprika and it would be Hungarian.

The point about Sheila's is that it is a theme restaurant whose theme has nothing to do with food. The management clearly know an Australian theme when they see one—it's all to do with Paul Hogan and memories of the Barry Mackenzie comic strip from the yellowing pages of old copies of *Private Eye*—but there are no real culinary clichés upon which they can hang their theme. In the days when Philip Muskett was worrying about Australia's lack of a national dish, this might have looked like a weakness; now it looks like a considerable strength. It is not easy to say who first spotted that we might turn this state of affairs to our advantage, but perhaps Don Dunstan and Cheong Liew might stand as representative midwives in the birth of new Australian cuisine.

In 1976—while he was still Premier of South Australia and when South Australia looked as though it might represent the bright future of the entire country—Dunstan published a cookery book which was unusual amongst celebrity cookery books in that it had actually been written by the person whose name was on the title page. Here, the Premier introduced the reader to his garden, his kitchen and his wok ('You should have one') and mused thoughtfully on Australian food.

Conceding that Australia had no distinctive cuisine of its own, he nonetheless looked forward to the development of 'an Australian cuisine which is inevitably derivative, but which will take the best from elsewhere; which will use our resources to the full and adapt to the Australian kitchen and social conditions the cooking techniques of our Asian neighbours, incorporating them with the European traditions which are more familiar to us.' This was visionary stuff.

Cheong Liew is one of Australia's most influential chefs. He pioneered the fusion of European and Asian cuisines and ingredients—his food has its own unique flavour, texture and visual appeal with the subtlety of a master chef.

Australian cuisine is about fresh seasonal produce and the thing that makes it so very exciting is the cosmopolitan influences from around the world. That makes it what it is today—one of the great food destinations in the world.

SIMON JOHNSON

One of the many fascinating stalls at the Queen Victoria Markets in Melbourne.

Inspired, perhaps, by what he called 'the Malaysian synthesis,' Dunstan offered his readers far more than the sort of additive multiculturalism that involves cooking pasta with a Chinese sauce.

And, even as he wrote, the Malaysian synthesis was already well represented in his city of Adelaide in the person of Cheong Liew—born in Kuala Lumpur, resident in Australia since the age of twenty—who, with his wife and some friends, had opened a restaurant called Neddy's in 1975. Cheong's work, which exerted huge influence on a whole generation of Australian chefs, reflected his experience in Greek, Indian, Southeast Asian, French and Chinese kitchens.

Greek, Indian, Southeast Asian, French, Chinese—the more conventional vision of how these cultures might coexist can be found in *Tucker in Australia*, a collection of essays edited by Beverley Wood and published the year after Dunstan's book. The various contributors to this volume describe the multitude of cuisines to which Australia was now playing host, but usually with reference principally to their country of origin and with no suggestion that synthesis might be just around the corner. Indeed, there was at the time no particular reason for anticipating such a synthesis. For example, the United States of America, whose culinary history might have been expected to be a model for Australia's, has never been a true melting pot of cuisines (or, at least, not until very recently). The American ethnologist Susan Kalcik remarks that, 'The plurality of American food … is such that we may cook and eat a variety of ethnic foods, if we so choose, because ethnic food traditions remain strong and viable in their isolation.'

In this respect, the comparison between the United States and Australia is revealing. Although both are pluralist, multicultural societies, one has a history of welcoming outsiders and the other does not. The result has been a curious paradox: on the one hand, there are no statues in Sydney Harbour or at Port Melbourne inviting in the huddled masses yearning to be free; on the other, there are no rules for becoming an Australian. In America, it is, or was, fairly simple: you worked at becoming an American by mugging up on the Constitution and learning to recite the list of presidents. In Australia, no such rules applied: you could learn to enjoy cricket, if you liked, you could take to calling people 'mate,' but nobody asked you to, and the reason that nobody asked you to was that nobody had really worked out what to do with you beyond using your labour.

In this state of affairs, there are curious consequences for food. Just as migrants to the United States had to learn to speak the language of American civic life, so they had to learn to eat American, too. Public cuisine had to be bland so as not to offend anybody, and culinary migrants, such as the hot dog and the pizza, were quickly made bland as well. If your name was Roselli or Kwan, you could still enjoy your native cuisine, but you did so at home or in restaurants which catered exclusively to interests like yours.

At one time, it looked as though this was the way that Australia was going. Ghassan Hage quotes an article published in the Sydney *Sun-Herald* in 1950. The author is enthusiastic about the food 'our new compatriots' have brought to town ('I've had a salami myself'), but finds that this 'peaceful invasion' is not officially sanctioned:

An official of the Department of Immigration became quite indignant at the suggestion that New Australians might be introducing their food habits into Australia: 'That's not the idea at all,' he said. 'What we want is for these migrants to become absorbed into the Australian community, not to bring their own habits with them.'

But, in fact, there was nobody telling these migrants how to become absorbed into the Australian culinary community, there was nobody telling them how to

ABOVE AND RIGHT: Vignettes from Stefano Manfredi's bel mondo restaurant in The Rocks district of Sydney.

FAR RIGHT: Robert Castellani's Naked Ravioli with Ricotta (page 64). The title is a play on words—it is ravioli without the skin. Very simple to make—serve with a crisp white wine.

eat like an Australian. Their children brought noodles or salami to school and were duly mocked by Anglos feasting on fish paste and white bread, but in the main it was indifference rather than hostility that had to be overcome. As soon as it was overcome, Australians could look with amazement at what had been all around them for a long time: a varied landscape capable of producing just about any foodstuff and a varied culture bursting with culinary skills and techniques. Out of the marriage of the two—effected, perhaps, by the Aussie spirit of brilliant improvisation—Australian cuisine was reborn.

Eating Australia

Of course, people who say that Australia has no cuisine of its own, that you don't get a national cuisine just by fiddling with the labels in a few restaurant guides, have a point. But it's a good point only if you're looking at cuisine from the perspective of the *commencement* rather than the *fin de siècle*.

At the far end of the troubled twentieth century, cuisines came, as they had for centuries, in just two forms: there were the local and particular—each of them unimaginable without its own peculiar combination of starchy staple and whatever was used to flavour the starchy staple—and there were those cuisines (notably, if not solely, the French and the Chinese) whose technique was so

powerful and adaptable that it could go around the world. But things have definitely changed.

There are few cooks today like the English chef Marco Pierre White, who has devoted his life to French cuisine, has no time for any other, yet has not spent more than a day in France. For good or ill, this sort of lonely dedication to a cuisine that exists largely in the mind is a thing of the past. Most modern chefs travel, and even those who don't can hardly ignore the supermarket of styles on their own doorsteps: the ethnic restaurants, the shops with their spices and banana leaves, not to mention the television shows and the books.

ABOVE: Three flavours of biscotti displayed on the bar at bel mondo restaurant.

And just as the number and variety of influences upon the chef have increased, so has the chef's importance in the scheme of things. In former times, restaurants and other public eating places exerted little influence over the home. Some offered a version of what was already being cooked in the domestic kitchen, others offered something which depended for its success upon a degree of technical competence and a scale of operation far exceeding anything that could ever happen there. For home cooks, it was unnecessary to emulate the former and impossible to emulate the latter (which is not to say that professional advice was of no use to them, hence books like *Ma Cuisine*, published in 1934 by the great French chef Escoffier). These days, however, we—that's to say, we, the home cooks of the English-speaking world—look to chefs to tell us what to do and how to do it. Where once we had mothers, where once some of us had faithful family retainers, now we have chefs and professional food writers. For us, a cuisine is not what it once was, the best combination of starch and flavour that circumstances would allow: instead, a cuisine is simply the point at which various culinary influences meet.

In this world of fast-moving, constantly changing culinary collage, Australia has a unique role to play: meeting place of cultures, with a vigorous restaurant industry in which there is not, and never really has been, any dominant tradition. This book, then, is a snapshot of a body in motion, its speed so great that even with the rapid exposure of the best cameras, the edges are blurred.

What does the camera reveal? Surprisingly, one the clearest parts of the image is French. We have actual French chefs, such as Jacques Reymond and Philippe Mouchel in Melbourne, and those who, born far from France, take their inspiration from the culinary traditions of that country. These include Liam Tomlin, Damien Pignolet, Peter Doyle, Diane Holuigue and Tony Bilson. Then there's Paul Merrony, author of a book whose title, *The New French Cooking in Australia*, might suggest that French cooking, although in Australia, is never really of Australia. Fortunately, it has never been like that; wherever they might have been born, our French chefs have always been alive to what this country has to offer: nobody has had a greater or more beneficial influence on local food producers than the French-Canadian Serge Dansereau, former executive chef at The Regent Hotel in Sydney and now chef at the new Bathers Pavilion.

Oddly, the other great exportable cuisine doesn't get much of a look in here, even though its native land is so much nearer to Australia than France is. In Adelaide, Cheong Liew can certainly be called a Chinese cook (although, as we have seen, he can be called much else besides), but otherwise the Chinese influence on Australian cuisine seems not to be as direct as that of France. The Middle Kingdom simply does not appear to have enchanted any Australian-born chefs in the way that Thailand has clearly enchanted David Thompson, who approaches Thai food with a devotion and scholarly attention that few native Thais bring to it. On the other hand, we have some truly excellent Chinese restaurants here, like the Flower Drum in Melbourne, and Asian restaurants—not just Chinese, but also Thai, Vietnamese and Japanese—are so much a part of the daily experience of eating in this country that our food tastes of Asia even when we're not trying to be authentically Asian. So, Asian flavours crop up here not only where you might expect them—in the work of Tetsuya Wakuda, say, or that of Neil Perry, who has written eloquently of his 'love affair with Chinese food and all things Asian'—but even in the work (which, honestly, I just mistyped as 'wok') of chefs whose influences are mostly European. Thus we find Stefano Manfredi mixing his pasta with abalone and shiitake mushrooms, Ralph Potter flavouring his crispy chicken with star anise, five-spice powder and Szechuan peppercorns, Mietta O'Donnell roasting her baby snapper with ginger, soy sauce and coriander (Chinese parsley).

But when we learn that one of Philip Johnson's recipes is for a salad of wild rice, hazelnuts and Peking duck, some might think that warning bells should sound. Philip Johnson has a restaurant in Brisbane called 'here it is'—or e'cco, as they almost say in Italy. And what is e'cco? It's a bistro, as they don't say in Italy. So the chef at an Australian version of a small French restaurant specialising in Italian cuisine offers us a recipe using Peking duck. Can it be that we have reached the level of desperate experimentation which, in 1990, the American food writer Jeffrey Steingarten found in the restaurants of the Pacific Northwest, where the ingredients are excellent, but nobody can agree on what to do with them?

'An odd combination known variously as Pacific Rim, Pan-Pacific, or Pan-Asian is spreading fast; it typically combines every known Oriental cooking method and ingredient, minus India and Japan,' Steingarten complains. 'One restaurant dishes up, simultaneously, the food of Mexico, the Caribbean, Brazil, Santa Fe, and someone's fantasy of Native American.' A local restaurant guide calls this sort of thing 'post-ethnic mélange' or 'pre-post Columbian,' but Jeffrey Steingarten calls it just plain cultural confusion and he's right. It's not what's happening here, though. Just a short walk from the wittily named e'cco will take you to Brisbane's Chinatown, where good barbecued duck—the finest form of takeaway known to humankind—is plentifully available, so what is more natural than using it in a salad?

Besides, it's not as though we don't have plenty of recipes here that provide what one food writer, quoted by Steingarten, sums up as 'one nationality,

BELOW: Back stage in a busy restaurant such as Banc, in the heart of the city of Sydney, is really hard work.

When I grew up in Italy, there were special small producers for fresh basil or fish—it wasn't at all like that when I first came to Sydney. Now in Sydney young people are excelling in specialised produce. The fresh ingredients are very exciting. Sydney is a mecca for some of the most inventive chefs in the world. I like being part of the Australian cuisine. And it's possible because the diners are adventurous.

LUCIO GALLETTO

ABOVE: Paul Merrony's Roast Salmon with Eggplant Purée, Zucchini and Sage (page 132). Paul likes to couple a purée with fish—it makes a nice contrast. The warm vinaigrette infused with sage adds a final touch.

indivisible, per plate at a time.' There's Marieke Brugman's Tomato Tarte Tatin (page 94), for example, Robert Castellani's Naked Ravioli with Ricotta (page 64), André Chouvin's Bouillabaisse (page 48) and much more besides. But then there's Greg Malouf's Salmon Kibbeh Tartare with Cracked Wheat and Garlic Cheese (page 149)—what are we to make of that sort of thing? Can it really be Lebanese, given that the Atlantic salmon is a cold-water fish unknown in those warmer Mediterranean climes where Malouf's ancestors learned to cook? But we're not in Lebanon, are we? We're in Australia, where the Atlantic salmon is very good, and what Lebanese cook of any era—what Greek, Chinese or Italian cook, for that matter—would have turned his or her back on a good ingredient that was close at hand and readily available?

And that, ultimately, is what this book is about: an Australian response to Australian ingredients. It's true that most of the ingredients haven't been here for more than a couple of centuries, but they've taken root, made themselves at home, and so have the varied culinary traditions of which this book is testimony. The flavour of Australia is the flavour of change, adaptation and—in the very best sense of the word—compromise.

Chapter 1
Soups and Starters

Alan Saunders

Soups and Starters

WHAT DOES A WOMAN REALLY NEED when she's living in the bush? A stockpot, of course. 'A kerosene can makes an excellent stock pot,' wrote Mrs Lance Rawson, purveyor of helpful domestic hints at the end of the nineteenth century. During her own time in the country, Mrs Rawson—'a lady of wide Australian experience in town and bush,' reads the introduction to her *Australian Enquiry Book of Household and General Information*—invented a somewhat superior stockpot and had it made up by a local tinsmith. Once your stockpot was ready (it would only cost you a few shillings, Mrs Rawson assured her readers), it could be in constant use: any scraps of meat or bone could be thrown into it, though you had to be careful with vegetables, which could go sour in the summer months unless you were on a cattle or sheep station, where the fire would be banked up at night rather than put out.

For Mrs Rawson, it was worth taking trouble with your stock because soup was such a useful thing to have in a hot country: 'The business man comes home in the middle of the day, tired, hot and hungry, yet with a disinclination to eat meat, vegetables, etc., but the very thing he feels he could enjoy is a plate of soup or a basin of broth.' Failing that, according to her, he'd probably turn to drink, take an extra glass of whisky or brandy with his midday meal (an extra glass?) and return to the office feeling a little the worse for wear.

Not surprisingly, the idea of a cold soup does not seem to have occurred to her—not even for the hot months, not even for Queensland, where she lived—although there are few things more refreshing than a chilled cucumber and yoghurt soup, such as the one Mietta O'Donnell (right below) provides here. In fact, all the soups here have a light touch: they are based on chicken or fish stock, and go easy on the cream—although Ralph Potter's Wild Mushroom Soup (page 49) and Liam Tomlin's Velouté of Potato and Oyster with Oyster Beignets (right above) are hearty and substantial enough to please Mrs Rawson.

Soup aside, there's no shortage of traditional starters here—tarte, terrine, tartare. Much of the rest of what's on offer reflects the tendency of modern restaurant menus to blur the distinction between starters and main courses. Often, these days, there's not so much as a ruled line or a space between the two: price alone indicates where one ends and the other begins, and often enough a first course will come tagged with two prices in case you want to have it as a main. So, plenty of these salads and pasta dishes could be expanded (or served to fewer people) as a main course, or any one of them could form part of a selection of dishes placed in the centre of the table in the manner of Spanish tapas or Greek mezze. Or, of course, you could just have one of them for lunch instead of that extra glass of brandy.

PREVIOUS PAGE: Liam Tomlin's Velouté of Potato and Oyster with Oyster Beignets. This dish is all about fresh oysters—something more adventurous than simple, fresh-shucked oysters.

Liam Tomlin, chef

Velouté of Potato and Oyster
with Oyster Beignets

INGREDIENTS

POTATO AND OYSTER VELOUTE

45 g (1½ oz) butter

750 g (1½ lb) potatoes, peeled and cut
  into even-sized pieces

300 g (10 oz) leek, finely sliced

300 g (10 oz) onion, finely sliced

7 cups (1.75 litres/3 imp. pints)
  chicken stock

1¼ cups (310 mL/10 fl oz) light
  (single) cream

16 freshly shucked oysters

salt and freshly ground black pepper

OYSTER BEIGNETS

½ cup (60 g/2 oz) plain (all-purpose)
  flour

1½ tablespoons water

2½ tablespoons warm beer

1 teaspoon olive oil

1 egg, separated

16 freshly shucked oysters (reserve juices)

flour for dusting

salt and freshly ground black pepper

A light, very Australian dish to serve in winter. The soup is rather like a vichyssoise finished with fresh oysters—it tastes and smells of the sea. The accompanying oysters are warm, creamy and coated with crisp batter.

To make the velouté, melt the butter in a heavy-based saucepan and sweat the potato, leek and onion without colouring. Pour in the chicken stock and simmer for 20 minutes, then add the cream. Bring back to the boil, reduce the heat and simmer for 10 minutes. Transfer the velouté to a blender or food processor, and purée before passing through a fine sieve. Add the oysters and their juices (including the extra juices reserved from the beignets) to the velouté and, using a hand-held blender, blend into the velouté. Taste and adjust seasoning, then pass through a fine sieve one more time. Keep warm.

To make the oyster beignets, mix the flour, water, beer, olive oil and egg yolk together to form a batter. Cover with plastic wrap and rest for an hour, before whisking the egg white to a stiff peak and folding it through the batter.

To serve, heat a small pot of oil—it is ready for cooking when a cube of bread rises straight to the top. Place the oysters on a kitchen cloth and gently pat dry before lightly dusting with flour. Dip half the oysters into the batter and gently mix with your fingertips until well coated. Pick them out and cook in the hot oil until crisp and golden brown. Remove with a slotted spoon and drain on a clean cloth or absorbent kitchen paper, and lightly season with salt and pepper. Cook the remaining oysters in the same way. Pour the hot velouté into warm cups placed on serving plates. Serve the fried oysters on the side in a warm oyster shell.

Serves 8 Recipe: medium complexity

Mietta O'Donnell, restaurateur and food writer

Chilled
Cucumber and Yoghurt Soup

INGREDIENTS

6 small Lebanese (continental)
  cucumbers, peeled and finely diced

salt and freshly ground white pepper

3 cloves garlic

4 cups (1 litre/1¾ imp. pints) sheep's
  milk yoghurt

1 bunch of fresh mint, stalks removed
  and finely chopped, plus extra mint
  leaves for garnish

Experiment with other herbs in this soup. Mint is the most refreshing, but dill is also very good. It is stronger than mint, however, so use less.

Sprinkle the cucumber with salt and leave for 1 hour in a colander to drain. Crush the garlic with a little salt. Mix a few spoonfuls of the yoghurt with the garlic and season with salt and pepper. Rinse and dry the cucumber and combine with the garlic yoghurt mixture and the remaining yoghurt. For a smooth texture, the cucumbers can be blended first. Add the chopped mint and chill well. Serve in chilled bowls garnished with the extra mint leaves.

Serves 6 Recipe: easy to make

Guillaume Brahimi, chef

Blue Swimmer Crab Soup
with Black Mussels and Aïoli

INGREDIENTS

1–1½ kg (2–3 lb) blue swimmer crab

1 cup (250 mL/8 fl oz) olive oil

2 small onions, finely diced

1 leek, finely diced

½ Florence fennel bulb (finocchio), finely diced

1 clove garlic, diced, plus 1 clove extra

5 tablespoons white wine

1 teaspoon saffron threads

1¼ cups (310 mL/10 fl oz) mussel juice

2 cups (500 mL/16 fl oz) fish stock

2 cups (500 mL/16 fl oz) water

pinch of tarragon

salt and freshly ground black pepper

12 black mussels, steamed and kept in shell

2 small, ripe tomatoes, diced

12 scallops, roe removed and lightly sautéed

freshly snipped chives to garnish

A light, clean dish suited to any time of the year. Use scallops to garnish if there are beautiful ones available, otherwise keep it simple.

Clean the crab and chop the meat. Heat some of the olive oil in a frying pan or skillet, and add the crab meat, onion, leek, fennel and diced garlic, making sure the crab meat does not stick to the pan.

In a separate saucepan, quickly boil the white wine to evaporate the alcohol. Add to the crab mixture with the saffron, mussel juice, fish stock, water, tarragon, garlic and salt and pepper to taste. When the soup begins to boil, remove from the heat and pass the liquid through a strainer after resting for 20 minutes.

To serve, put 3 mussels on the bottom of each shallow soup plate with some of the crab meat and tomato, and pour the hot soup over the top. Garnish with 3 scallops per plate, if liked. Sprinkle with chives and serve immediately.
Serves 4 Recipe: medium complexity

RIGHT: Blue Swimmer Crab Soup with Black Mussels and Aïoli. Use fine-flavoured crab—one from South Australia, for instance—you don't need to do much with it. The fennel matches it perfectly and the saffron adds visual drama.

Michael Lambie, chef

Artichoke Soup

INGREDIENTS

45 g (1½ oz) butter

1 tablespoon olive oil

2 kg (4 lb) Jerusalem artichokes, peeled and finely sliced

1 leek, white part only, finely sliced

1 onion, finely sliced

8 cups (2 litres/3¼ imp. pints) chicken stock

4 cups (1 litre /1¾ imp. pints) heavy (double) cream

2 pieces confit of duck or rabbit, warmed and divided into 10 serves

truffle-infused olive oil

Jerusalem artichokes have a fairly short winter season, so it is great to use them when they are available and particularly in this fresh, light soup. The addition of the truffle oil at the end gives it an interesting character.

In a large saucepan, melt the butter and olive oil over medium heat. Add the artichoke, leek and onion, and sweat the vegetables until softened. Set aside.

In a separate saucepan, bring the chicken stock to the boil, then pour it over the vegetables. Bring the stock back to the boil, then reduce to a simmer. Cook until the vegetables are tender, about 20 minutes. Add the cream and return to the boil once more. Purée the soup in a blender or food processor, then pass through a sieve for a smoother texture.

To serve, place some confit and a drizzle of truffle oil in the centre of each warmed, flat soup bowl. Place on the table and pour the soup over from a jug.
Serves 10 Recipe: easy to make

André Chouvin, chef

Bouillabaisse
Fish Soup

INGREDIENTS

ROUILLE

1–2 slices white bread, crusts removed

1 clove garlic, crushed

pinch of paprika

1 egg yolk

1 teaspoon saffron threads

1 cup (250 mL/8 fl oz) olive oil

8 slices thick white bread or baguette

olive oil

½ Florence fennel (finocchio), diced

4 ripe, red tomatoes, halved

4 cloves garlic, chopped

1 onion, diced

½ leek, diced

1 carrot, diced

1 bay leaf

1 sprig thyme

1 kg (2 lb) baby John Dory or any
   fine-textured white fish

1 kg (2 lb) red rock cod or rascasse

1 tablespoon tomato paste (purée)

1 teaspoon saffron threads

assorted fish and shellfish of choice

A celebrated seafood stew from Provence, originally made by fishermen with the leftovers from the catch of the day. The soup is ladled over thick slices of toasted bread and served with rouille. For special occasions, use lobster as the final seafood garnish.

To make the rouille, make a paste with the bread and garlic by mashing with a fork, then add the paprika and stir through before adding the egg yolk and saffron. Whisk in the olive oil gradually—drop by drop at first, and faster as it coagulates into a texture resembling a thick mayonnaise.

Make the croutons by toasting the thick slices of white bread and cutting them into squares or toasting baguette slices.

To make the base of the soup, heat a little olive oil in a frying pan or skillet, and pan-fry the fennel, tomato, garlic, onion, leek, carrot, bay leaf and thyme slowly over low heat, stirring often. Do not allow to brown. When they soften, add the fish and tomato paste. Stir through, then add enough water to cover the fish. Bring to the boil and let simmer for 15 minutes. Add the saffron and simmer for 20 minutes more. Pass through a sieve to make a thick soup.

To serve, poach your seafood of choice in the soup for a few minutes, until opaque and lightly cooked, then arrange on deep serving plates. Pour the thick soup over the seafood and serve with the rouille and the croutons.

Serves 6 Recipe: medium complexity

Matthew Moran, chef

Roast Tomato and Basil Soup

INGREDIENTS

2 kg (4 lb) ripe egg (Italian plum)
   tomatoes

salt and freshly ground black pepper

6 cloves garlic, unpeeled

5 tablespoons finest virgin olive oil

½ cup freshly chopped basil leaves

4 small pita breads

tapenade

Preheat the oven to 220°C (425°F). Slice the tomatoes in half lengthwise and place on a greased baking sheet. Season with salt and pepper to taste. Roast the tomatoes and garlic in the oven for 20 minutes. Slip the garlic cloves out of their skins and purée in a food processor with three-quarters of the tomato. Strain the tomato purée through a fine sieve and chop the remaining tomato. Place the puréed tomato in a bain-marie or in a bowl over a pan of simmering water. Whisk in the olive oil to add flavour. To serve, add the chopped tomato and basil as a garnish just before serving. Spread the pita bread with tapenade and serve with the soup.

Serves 4 Recipe: easy to make

Luke Mangan, chef

Cauliflower Soup

with Truffle Oil and Chives

INGREDIENTS

1 onion, finely sliced

1 tablespoon butter

1 medium cauliflower, cut into florets

2 cups (500 mL/16 fl oz) milk

2 tablespoons light (single) cream

1 tablespoon truffle oil

freshly chopped chives

salt and freshly ground black pepper

Silky smooth, rich yet subtle and sweet, this soup is cooked in milk to keep the whiteness of the cauliflower. The truffle oil blends into the soup, adding the finishing touch. It's a sexy dish.

Sweat the onion in the butter, making sure it does not brown. Add the cauliflower and sweat for a further 5 minutes over low to medium heat. Cover with the milk, bring to the boil and simmer for about 20–30 minutes, until the cauliflower is soft. Purée in a blender or food processor, then pass through a fine sieve. Pour into a clean saucepan, add the cream and bring just to the boil once more. Spoon the soup into bowls, drizzle with truffle oil and sprinkle with the chives. Season to taste with salt and pepper, and serve immediately.

Serves 2 Recipe: easy to make

Ralph Potter, chef

Wild Mushroom Soup

with Horseradish Cream

INGREDIENTS

1 onion, chopped

2 stalks celery, chopped

1 leek, chopped

½ clove garlic, chopped

200 g (7 oz) unsalted butter

500 g (1 lb) saffron milkcap
  mushrooms, sliced

6 cups (1.5 litres/2½ imp. pints) chicken
  stock

300 g (10 oz) potatoes, peeled

2 tablespoons freshly grated horseradish

4 tablespoons sour cream

salt and freshly ground white pepper

155 g (5 oz) cèpes or slippery jack
  mushrooms, sliced

1 tablespoon chopped parsley

This is a classic regional dish. Wild mushrooms are so plentiful when the sun has come out after it's been raining for a few days in autumn, why not be indulgent and make a special soup out of them and celebrate the seasons.

In a frying pan or skillet, sweat the onion, celery, leek and garlic in some of the butter over low heat until soft. Add the saffron milkcaps to the pan. Continue to cook over low heat for 5–6 minutes. Add the chicken stock and potatoes to the saucepan and bring to the boil. Simmer for 45 minutes. Purée the soup in a food processor or blender. Don't be tempted to thin the liquid down too much as the finished soup should be fairly thick. Keep hot.

Make the horseradish cream by mixing the horseradish with the sour cream and some pepper.

Melt a little butter in a frying pan and quickly fry the cèpes. Add the parsley, toss together and then strain through a fine-mesh sieve to drain off the butter.

To serve, adjust the soup's seasoning with salt and pepper, and serve in deep bowls with some of the sautéed cèpes and a dollop of horseradish cream in the middle.

Serves 4–6 Recipe: easy to make

Joan Campbell
and Sue Fairlie-Cuninghame

Inspirations: Media and Regionalism

Joan Campbell

'Few individuals have had a more powerful influence on contemporary Australian food than Joan,' wrote Cherry Ripe, food writer. Joan Campbell has been a cookery teacher, caterer and food journalist, and, as Food Director for the Vogue food publications in Australia, she has contributed to Australia's culinary tastes and styles for more than thirty years. Joan has been in a unique position to promote the sort of food and the chefs in which she really believed. She has done this without fear or favour.

It is a source of great joy to Joan that her daughter Sue shares her passion for food. Their food is elegant and simple. They both style food evocatively for photography in a quintessentially Australian casual style that has established a benchmark for fine food photography in Australia and internationally. Australian chefs have been helped tremendously by their visual skills in portraying their food.

'We used to entertain a lot in the country, but when I came to the city I had to earn money. Friends said, you can cook—why don't you cater? I really enjoyed it. When I look back, it was so much work I can't believe I did it. I gave cooking classes, which spread by word of mouth and we were packed out every time. I did restaurant reviews in the Sunday Telegraph as well. I started at Vogue twenty years ago and gradually gave up the catering classes.

'I've called myself a bush cook, and I've frequently said that I admire simplicity with fresh ingredients, but, apart from that, I don't think I have a style at all … the most important thing to me is just to cook a good dish or a good meal, and have everyone say it's delicious.'

ABOVE: Barbecued Duck Curry (page 121). This dish is really, really easy to make. It has a multi-purpose sauce that you can make with any sort of fresh fish, shellfish or white chicken, instead of the rich duck. Cook the sauce quickly to save it splitting. All the ingredients are available from supermarkets. Use a steamed chook if you can't get a Chinese barbecued duck. The duck makes it a gala occasion dish.

FAR RIGHT: Deep-fried Squid Rings (page 56)—crunchy and light, and perfumed with basil. Serve with side dishes of kecap manis, sweet chilli sauce and lime quarters.

Sue Fairlie-Cuninghame

'Mum and I are both self-taught cooks. We believe that measurements are just a guide—you should never stop tasting. To get the finest flavour, you need the best ingredients you can afford. Simplicity is best. My two benchmarks are perfectly made vanilla ice cream and mashed potato.'

After ten years as Vogue Entertaining and Travel Executive Editor: Food and Wine,

Sue Fairlie-Cuninghame resigned to pursue a freelance career. She still contributes regularly to Vogue while pursuing other interests. 'I am passionately committed to regionalism. I grew up on the land and this agricultural background has produced everything I focus on. I know what "tough in the bush" means. In the committees I work on, we encourage producers to think laterally, to grow things such as lavender, tomatoes and organic lamb, and to value-add. We encourage them to market locally and, as the product succeeds, providores such as Simon Johnson will pick them up.' Sue works with communities across Australia focusing on food trends—how we will eat in the future. She is also a member of the Culinary Advisory Committee of Tourism NSW, which works to assist the quality of food and hospitality in country regions. Sue and her husband are weekend farmers in Mudgee, growing cattle and grapes.

'As a farmer, I believe in the integrity of my industry—the integrity of the produce and the people I work with. The generosity of the top chefs supporting and educating me has contributed significantly to my success.'

Michael Moore, chef

Crisp Skin Quail

INGREDIENTS

2½ cups (625 mL/20 fl oz) water

1 tablespoon maltose (malt sugar)

1 teaspoon salt

3 tablespoons white vinegar

4 large quails, about 140 g (4 oz) each

5 tablespoons frying oil

sea salt

2½ tablespoons olive oil

1 tablespoon balsamic vinegar (8 years
old or finest quality)

4 thin slices ventreche or bacon

4 ripe black figs

12 wild rocket (arugula) leaves

Place the water, maltose, salt and vinegar into a saucepan and bring to the boil. Plunge the quails into the boiling liquid for 20 seconds, remove and place onto a wire rack to drain.

Heat the frying oil in a saucepan. Test the heat by dropping in a cube of bread—when it rises to the surface immediately, the oil is ready. Put a whole dry quail in and fry for 2 minutes, or until the quail is golden and crispy. Remove the quail from the pan and place on absorbent kitchen paper to drain, then season with sea salt. Cook the remaining quails in the same way.

Make a dressing by mixing the olive oil and balsamic vinegar together. Grill the ventreche or bacon until crisp.

To serve, cut each quail in half using a large chopping knife. Cut through the back of the ribs and place 2 halves one on top of the other on each serving plate. Dress with a little of the dressing. Cut each fig into 6 segments and place next to the quail. Now toss the rocket leaves with the remaining dressing and place with the ventreche on top of the quail. Season and serve while warm.

Serves 4 Recipe: medium complexity

Mietta O'Donnell, restaurateur and food writer

Goat's Cheese Salad

INGREDIENTS

⅔ cup (100 mL/3½ fl oz) heavy (double)
cream

2 tablespoons freshly chopped chives

1¾ cups (185 g/6 oz) chopped walnuts

90 g (3 oz) butter

625 g (1¼ lb) ciabatta bread, cut into
2-cm (¾-inch) slices

625 g (1¼ lb) goat's cheese

salt and freshly ground black pepper

2½ tablespoons olive oil

mesclun with herbs to garnish

2 heads witlof (Belgian endive), finely
sliced

1 tablespoon red wine vinegar

Preheat the oven to 200°C (400°F). Make the chive cream by mixing together the cream and chives. Roast the walnuts in the oven for a few minutes until crisp, but do not allow to darken. Mix the butter with half of the walnuts. Spread onto the bread slices. Slice the goat's cheese and lay on top of the walnut butter. Season with salt and pepper to taste and dribble over a little of the olive oil.

Put the mesclun onto the serving plates. Place the witlof on top and dress with a vinaigrette of the remaining oil and the wine vinegar. Put the bread slices in the oven for 3–5 minutes. Arrange the toasts on the plates and spoon the chive cream beside it. Scatter the remaining walnuts over, season and serve.

Serves 4–6 Recipe: easy to make

Cheese Impressions

As I'm a cheese maker, naturally my whole world revolves around cheese. I have put together a few food ideas here, which, although simple, have made lasting impressions. Perhaps it was just their simplicity, who can say?

A dear friend who was working in the Italian Alps, right up against the French border, introduced me to some mountain cheese makers with whom I subsequently was lucky enough to work for a few days. They were producing butter with an extreme richness of flavour and a wide range of cheeses—soft and fresh, waxy and sweet, old, hard and bitter, blue and wild.

One day, lunch was bread smeared with honey in which truffle peelings and scraps were embalmed. It was accompanied by what could only be described as a slab of mountain Gorgonzola. We washed it down with a good half litre of red wine, followed by a snooze. Elegant in its simplicity, it was one of the most complex flavour experiences of my life.

That experience set me looking for simple things to eat that can be made in a moment with what is around us. In Australia, we may not always have the best the world has to offer, but, overall, our ingredients are so very good.

Olive oils, though not as refined as the Spanish, are full of flavour just the same—a spill of good local oil over one of our good pecorino or Romano cheeses made by an Italian producer is pretty special. Eat it with a nashi pear and enjoy the wet and crunchy texture.

I recently spotted an old Italian couple, 'weeding the roadside' in the Yarra Valley. It was rucola, or rocket or arugula as we call it, a weed for which the Italians have found a virtue. Wild rocket is so peppery, but when blanched and pushed through a fresh acid goat cheese, it presents us with an extraordinary flavour, one very different to our expectations. Serve with chillies stuffed with anchovies and drizzle with olive oil.

A special dessert can be made with a stack of falwasser-type wafers. Top one with two egg-sized pieces of Meredith Blue cheese, scooped from the cheese. On this, place a slice of nashi which has been lightly poached so that it retains its crunch in a dessert wine, such as De Bortoli Noble One Botrytis Semillon or Brown Bros Noble Riesling. Repeat the stack, and top with a wafer and a spoonful of mascarpone. Warm some truffled honey and circle the stack with it.

Other surprising favourites of mine are Gruyère with Grey Poupon mustard; the now well-known quince or sweet potato paste with blue cheese; Tokay drunk when eating a mature farmhouse cheddar; and feta marinated overnight in olive oil with crushed raw garlic.

Paul Merrony, chef

Goat's Cheese Terrine

INGREDIENTS

500 g (1 lb) very firm goat's cheese, at
    room temperature
⅔ cup (155 mL/5 fl oz) natural (plain)
    yoghurt
⅔ cup (155 mL/5 fl oz) sour cream
1 tablespoon olive oil, plus extra
salt and freshly ground white pepper
pinch of ground nutmeg
4 tomatoes
1 red capsicum (sweet pepper)
Tabasco Sauce
5 tablespoons vinaigrette, plus a little
    more
½ telegraph cucumber, peeled and
    julienned
small bunch of chervil, picked over, or
    chives, chopped

The day before, pass the softened goat's cheese through a food mill using the fine grill or mash with a potato masher into a large bowl. Thoroughly mix the yoghurt, sour cream and olive oil into the goat's cheese using a wooden spoon. Season with pepper and a little nutmeg. Put into a small terrine mould lined with plastic wrap. Push well into the corners and tap on the bench or work surface to compress the ingredients. Cover with plastic wrap and refrigerate.

On the day, blanch the tomatoes, remove the skin and cut the outside flesh off and chop into ½-cm (¼-inch) dice. Set aside. Reserve the middles of the tomatoes. Roast the red capsicum in a little oil in the oven and then peel under running water. Liquidise the capsicum flesh in a blender or food processor with the tomato middles, then pass through a fine sieve. Season with salt and pepper, and a few dashes of Tabasco. Whisk in the vinaigrette. This sauce should coat the back of a spoon, but if it is a little thick, thin with chicken stock or water.

Sprinkle the cucumber with salt, put in a colander and drain. After about 20 minutes, rinse the cucumber well and drain again.

To serve, spoon the capsicum sauce over the plates, leaving about a 3-cm (1-inch) border. Arrange the cucumber julienne in the border. Sprinkle the cucumber with the tomato dice and season with the extra vinaigrette. Slice the terrine into 1-cm (½-inch) slices (a warmed knife will make it easier) and place on the sauce. Season and sprinkle the chervil over the cucumber and tomato.

Serves 12 Recipe: medium complexity

Robert Castellani, chef

Poor Man's Soup

INGREDIENTS

1 kg (2 lb) cannellini beans, soaked
4 carrots
4 red onions
2 stalks celery
1 small bunch of silverbeet (Swiss chard)
2 tablespoons virgin olive oil, plus extra
1 head garlic, peeled
1 loaf sourdough bread
2 x 800-g (26-oz) cans peeled tomatoes
1 bunch of flat-leaf parsley
rind of Parmesan cheese
500 g (1 lb) fresh borlotti (cranberry)
    beans
handful day-old sourdough bread, torn

Rinse the soaked cannellini beans and place in a saucepan. Cover well with fresh water, bring to the boil and cook until the beans are soft, about 40 minutes. Preheat the oven to 180°C (350°F).

Cut the carrot, onion, celery and silverbeet into rough shapes and sweat in a large, ovenproof saucepan with the olive oil until they are soft. Add the garlic and cover the pan with a lid. Remove the crust from the sourdough loaf and discard. Soak the bread in water until it is mushy or porridge-like in consistency. Drain the tomatoes and reserve the juice, then purée the tomatoes with three-quarters of the cannellini beans in a mouli or food processor, and add to the vegetables. Reserve the remaining beans. Add the soaked bread, reserved tomato juice, parsley, Parmesan cheese and borlotti beans to the soup, and just cover with water. Cover the saucepan and transfer to the oven for 2 hours.

To serve, add a chunk of day-old bread to each soup bowl, ladle in some soup, garnish with the reserved cannellini beans and drizzle some olive oil over the top.

Serves 6–8 Recipe: easy to make

LEFT: Goat's Cheese Terrine. Delicious with crusty toasted bread, this easy-to-make terrine can also be a great addition to a cheese plate. The recipe is for twelve people because a terrine for four is not really practical. Note that moist goat's cheese is nearly impossible to mould—decreasing the sour cream and yoghurt will help.

ABOVE: Poor Man's Soup. This is a true one-pot meal, a real family dish. Originally, it would have been slowly cooked on the hearth or in a wood-fired oven. A nurturing dish, it has deep, satisfying flavours which combine with the soft texture of the beans and bread.

Joan Campbell, food writer

Deep-fried Squid Rings

INGREDIENTS

500 g (1 lb) small to medium squid
    rings
1 tablespoon Thai fish sauce (nam pla)
2–3 cloves garlic, crushed (to taste)
3 tablespoons freshly chopped basil
coarsely ground black pepper
4 cups (1 litre/1¾ imp. pints) peanut oil
cornflour (cornstarch) for dredging

TO SERVE

kecap manis
sweet chilli sauce
2 limes, quartered

A light summer starter, this is also a delicious dish to serve as drink food with a beer before lunch in the summer.

Rinse and drain the squid rings. Mix the fish sauce, garlic, basil and pepper together, turn through the squid rings, cover and marinate at room temperature for 1 hour, stirring occasionally.

Shake the excess marinade from the squid rings and heat the peanut oil in a wok or deep-fryer until hot, but not smoking. Test with a small cube of bread—when it rises immediately to the surface, the oil is hot enough. Dredge the squid rings lightly in cornflour, shaking off any excess, and deep-fry a few at a time, for about 2 minutes. Drain on crumpled absorbent kitchen paper, repeating the process until all the squid is fried.

Just before serving, reheat the oil and fry the squid rings again for about 30 seconds or until golden brown. Drain as before and serve immediately with side dishes of kecap manis, sweet chilli sauce and lime quarters.

Serves 4 Recipe: easy to make

Leo Schofield, food critic

Small Casserole of Shellfish

INGREDIENTS

6 large mussels, cooked (reserve liquor)
6 scallops
6 large oysters
250 g (8 oz) fish fillets cut into round
    balls, preferably snapper or any other
    fine, white-textured fish
60 g (2 oz) unsalted butter
½ cup (125 mL/4 fl oz) reduced fish or
    mussel stock
1¼ cups (310 mL/10 fl oz) fine sparkling
    white wine, methôde champenoise
1 egg yolk
salt and freshly ground black pepper

Warm 6 tiny casseroles or ovenproof dishes (8 cm/3 inches in diameter). In each one, place a mussel, the coral from the scallop and an oyster.

Poach the scallops and fish roundels in the combined butter, stock and wine until just cooked, 2–3 minutes. Drain the scallops and fish, and reserve. Put the liquid in a heatproof bowl over simmering water and amalgamate the sauce with an egg yolk (or, if preferred, a little hollandaise sauce). Whisk well until the sauce is thick enough to coat the back of a spoon. Season with salt and pepper to taste.

Divide the scallops and fish among each casserole and mask with the sauce. The sauce should be hot enough to heat the casserole right through.

Serves 6 Recipe: medium complexity

Philippe Mouchel, chef

Sauté of Calamari
Served on a Compôte of Ratatouille

INGREDIENTS
RATATOUILLE
1 kg (2 lb) ripe tomatoes or 200 g (7 oz) semi-dried

1 tablespoon sugar

salt and freshly ground black pepper

4 cloves garlic

1 red capsicum (sweet pepper)

olive oil

1 medium zucchini (courgette)

1 medium eggplant (aubergine)

2 fresh basil leaves, finely julienned

300 g (10 oz) fresh calamari (squid), cut into thin strips

3 teaspoons butter

1 tablespoon soy sauce

salt and freshly ground black pepper

1½ tablespoons extra virgin olive oil

4 whole basil leaves, plus 5 extra, very finely chopped

There is such good calamari around in summer that I was inspired to make this dish by lightly sautéing the calamari rather than producing the heavier taste of deep-frying.

To make semi-dried tomatoes, preheat the oven to 100°C (200°F). Blanch the tomatoes in boiling water, then refresh in iced water and remove the skins. Cut into quarters and place on a greased baking sheet. Sprinkle with the sugar and salt to taste. Chop 3 of the garlic cloves and sprinkle over the top. Cook in the oven for about an hour, depending on the quality of the tomato. When cooked, reserve the tomato and increase the oven temperature to 180°C (350°F).

Wrap the capsicum in foil with a little olive oil and water. Cook in the oven for 20 minutes, then set aside. When cold enough to handle, remove the skin, discard the seeds and cut the flesh into large strips.

Wash the zucchini and eggplant and cut into ribbons. Lightly sauté in a little olive oil in a frying pan or skillet, season with salt and pepper, and cook for about 2 minutes longer. Finely chop the remaining clove of garlic. Add the reserved tomato and capsicum to the pan, mix through and season with the garlic and the julienne of basil. Reserve at room temperature.

Pat the calamari dry and quickly sear in a very hot frying pan brushed with olive oil. Add the butter and soy sauce to caramelise the calamari, then season with salt and pepper to taste. Remove from the heat and reserve. Deep-fry the 4 whole basil leaves and drain.

To serve, place the vegetables in the centre of 4 large plates and arrange the calamari nicely on the top. Blend the extra chopped basil and extra virgin olive oil in a food processor. Sprinkle the basil oil over and around the food, and garnish with the fried basil leaves. Serve immediately.

Serves 4 Recipe: medium complexity

Martin Webb, chef

Rock Oysters

with Red Onion Salsa

INGREDIENTS

RED ONION SALSA

6 ripe egg (Italian plum) tomatoes

2 small red onions

2 red chillies, finely chopped

½ cup freshly chopped coriander
  (Chinese parsley)

2 tablespoons lime juice

2 tablespoons olive oil

freshly ground black pepper

24 oysters, well-scrubbed and
  unopened, if possible

2 limes, halved crosswise

LEFT: Rock Oysters with Red Onion Salsa. A refreshing start for an alfresco summer lunch washed down with a Margaret River Chardonnay. The clean, sea flavours combine with a hint of Asian ingredients to create a simple starter, made with minimum fuss.

Australians are great oyster lovers and are blessed with an enviable supply of rock oysters. Salsa and oysters form a felicitous partnership of tastes and textures. Ideally, prepare the salsa 30–40 minutes before eating. This gives sufficient time for the flavours to mingle. If left longer than an hour, water exudes from the tomato and onion, giving a watery finish, while the coriander becomes limp and loses its aroma.

To make the salsa, remove the eyes from the tomatoes with a small, sharp knife and cut a small cross on each end to help skinning. Blanch in boiling water for 10–15 seconds, then transfer immediately to a bowl of iced water and leave for 1 minute. Remove the skin and cut each tomato into 4 pieces. Scoop out the seeds and pulp, and discard. Cut the flesh into small dice and set aside.

Peel the onion and cut into similar-sized dice. Add the onion, chilli and coriander to the tomatoes with the lime juice and olive oil. Season to taste with pepper, stir and leave to stand while opening the oysters.

To open the oysters, put each oyster on a flat surface with the flatter shell upwards and hinged end towards you. Hold the other end firmly in a cloth with one hand and ease the tip of a knife into the small opening in the hinge with the other. Wiggle the tip until the muscle gives. Once inserted, twist the knife to lever open, taking care not to let any shell fragments fall on the flesh. Sever the muscle attaching the oyster to the shell. Don't wash the oyster or discard the liquid. Arrange the opened oysters on 4 plates of crushed ice and put a teaspoon of salsa on each. Place a lime half on each plate and serve.

Serves 4 Recipe: easy to make

Richard Thomas, cheese maker

Squid Ink Tagliatelle

with Things Mediterranean

INGREDIENTS

500 g (1 lb) dried squid ink tagliatelle

2 red chillies or 2 red capsicums
  (sweet peppers) preserved in oil

6 anchovy fillets in oil, drained and
  broken into pieces (reserve oil)

2 tablespoons tapenade

1 teaspoon caperberries

200g (7 oz) firm, semi-matured
  goat's cheese

This dish can be garnished with greenery and splashed with garlic oil made from freshly crushed garlic marinated in good oil and kept refrigerated for these occasions.

Cook the tagliatelle in plenty of boiling water until al dente and drain all but a tablespoon of water off (this will evaporate, leaving the surface of the pasta moist). Cut the chilli into fine strips or dice, then add to the pasta with the anchovy, tapenade and caperberries. Pour some of the reserved anchovy oil over the pasta and roughly mix all the ingredients together. Serve the pasta in 4 warm bowls, with largish chunks of the cheese broken over the top of each serving.

Serves 4 Recipe: easy to make

Neil Perry, chef

King Prawn Cake and Scallops
with Spicy Prawn Sauce

INGREDIENTS

PRAWN STOCK

5 tablespoons olive oil

1 kg (2 lb) green prawn (shrimp) shells

½ small onion, finely diced

1 small carrot, finely diced

2 cloves garlic, minced

½ small leek, washed and finely diced

6 tablespoons brandy

6 tablespoons port

1 cup (250 mL/8 fl oz) dry white wine

1 cup (250 mL/8 fl oz) chicken stock

4 vine-ripened tomatoes, blanched,
    peeled, seeded and finely chopped

leaves from ½ bunch of fresh thyme

leaves from ½ bunch of fresh tarragon

MOUSSE

3 cloves garlic

2 red shallots

3 coriander roots

10 white peppercorns

2 teaspoons sea salt

1¼ cups (310 mL/10 fl oz) heavy
    (double) cream (35% butterfat)

1 cup (250 mL/8 fl oz) coconut cream

750 g (1½ lb) fresh king prawns
    (shrimp), to yield 375 g (12 oz) flesh
    (reserve the heads and shells)

2 egg whites

1 egg yolk

PRAWN SAUCE

8 cloves garlic

6 red shallots

2 stalks lemon grass, chopped

1 slice galangal, peeled and chopped

2 slices fresh turmeric, peeled and
    chopped, or ¼ teaspoon ground
    turmeric

I guess you could call this dish a meeting of East and West—it is a blend of French mousse-making technique and Asian flavours. The coconut cream makes the mousse a little heavier than one would normally expect, and the resulting cake is somewhere between the softness of a French mousse, the texture of which I sometimes find a little disconcerting, and the firmness of fish cakes, which give resistance to the bite. The mousses can be made in advance and gently steamed again when needed.

To make the prawn stock, place a heavy-based saucepan over high heat and heat the olive oil until very hot. Add the prawn shells and stir for 5 minutes, or until coloured. Add the onion, carrot, garlic and leek, and cook for a further 5 minutes. Add the brandy and reduce until it almost disappears. Add the port and reduce, then the white wine and reduce until it has almost gone. Pour in the chicken stock and add the tomato, thyme and tarragon. Lower the heat and don't allow the stock to boil again. Cook for 20 minutes. Push through a food mill and then through a fine strainer, and reserve.

To make the mousse, spray 6 dariole moulds with a light vegetable oil. Preheat the oven to 150°C (300°F). Using a mortar and pestle, crush the garlic, shallots, coriander roots, white peppercorns and sea salt to a fine paste. Chill the bowl of a food processor in the freezer. Mix the cream and coconut cream in a jug or pitcher, and place in the freezer as well. Make sure the prawns are very cold. This is all necessary so the mousse will not split.

Place the bowl on the food processor and add the prawns and garlic paste. Turn on the motor and add the egg whites, one at a time, followed by the egg yolk. Add the cream mixture in a thin stream, making sure the processor isn't running for more than 2 minutes in all. Spoon the mousse into the greased moulds and tap them on the bench or work surface to knock out any air bubbles. Fill a bain-marie with hot water and place the moulds inside—the water should reach halfway up the moulds. Place in the oven for 25 minutes.

To make the prawn sauce, using a mortar and pestle, crush the garlic, shallots, lemon grass, galangal, turmeric, lime zest and chilli to a fine paste. Dry-roast the peppercorns, fennel seed and coriander seed, and when cool, grind in a food mill. Add to the paste and combine.

In a saucepan, heat the peanut oil until almost smoking. Add the reserved prawn shells from the mousse and the paste and fry, stirring continuously, until the paste is fragrant, the shells red and the oil takes on the colour of the prawns. Add the whisky and cook until it evaporates, then add the stock and fold through the tomato. Once the chicken stock hits the shells, the sauce must not boil or it will become slightly bitter. Reduce the heat and leave the sauce on the stove, without boiling, for 20 minutes. Remove and strain through a fine sieve, pressing on the shells to extract the flavour.

1 strip kaffir lime zest, chopped
8 wild green chillies, chopped
1 teaspoon white peppercorns
1 teaspoon fennel seed
1 teaspoon coriander seed
½ cup (125 mL/4 fl oz) peanut oil
5 tablespoons whisky
1¼ cups (310 mL/10 fl oz) chicken stock
2 tomatoes, blanched, peeled, seeded
   and chopped

1⅔ cups (405 mL/13 fl oz) prawn stock
6 kaffir lime leaves, julienned
1 large knob of fresh ginger, julienned
10 fresh water chestnuts, sliced
6 slices fresh bamboo shoots, julienned
5 tablespoons coconut cream
palm sugar (jaggery), to taste
Thai fish sauce (nam pla), to taste
18 sea scallops
10 Thai sweet basil leaves, julienned
3 tablespoons roasted peanuts, crushed

To finish the dish, bring the prawn stock to the boil in a stockpot. Lower the heat so that the stock is just simmering. Add the lime leaves, ginger, water chestnut, bamboo shoot and coconut cream. Season with palm sugar and fish sauce to round out the flavour. Make sure the mixture doesn't boil again as the coconut cream splits easily.

In a heavy-based saucepan or on a grill, cook the sea scallops until golden brown on both sides, but still translucent and succulent in the middle.

Turn out the mousses into 6 large, white bowls by running a paring knife around the rim and turning out gently onto the plate. A little shake should be enough to dislodge them.

Spoon the prawn sauce over the top of the mousse, about 4 tablespoons per person, making sure each person gets some of the solids. Top with the sweet basil and sprinkle over some peanuts. Place the scallops around each mousse, and serve immediately.

Serves 6 Recipe: complex

Philip Johnson, chef

Saffron and Leek Risotto
with Scallops and Vodka

INGREDIENTS
2 tablespoons olive oil
½ onion, sliced
2 leeks, washed and sliced
3 cloves garlic, sliced
large pinch of saffron threads
1½ cups (280 g/9 oz) Arborio rice
6 cups (1.5 litres/2½ imp. pints) chicken
   stock, hot
500 g (1 lb) scallops
¾ cup (100 g/3½ oz) grated Parmesan
   cheese
2 tablespoons crème fraîche or sour
   cream
juice of ½ lemon
salt and freshly ground black pepper
fresh basil leaves, torn
vodka

Heat the olive oil in a heavy-based saucepan over medium heat. Sweat the onion, leek and garlic until transparent. Add the saffron and rice, stirring until the rice is well coated with the oil.

Increase the heat and add the hot chicken stock, a cup at a time, as the liquid is absorbed (keep the stock simmering in a saucepan throughout this process). Continue cooking and stirring, adding stock as required until rice is al dente. Now add the scallops, Parmesan cheese, crème fraîche and lemon juice. Season with salt and pepper to taste. Fold the basil leaves through the risotto. Spoon into warm bowls and drizzle with vodka. Serve immediately.

Serve 6 Recipe: easy to make

FAR RIGHT: Just a few of the fine cheeses created by Richard Thomas. All are matured and are just right for eating. It is important to taste cheese at its best. From left, Meredith Blue, matured caprini (little goat's cheese), ashed goat pyramid, white mould sheep's milk cheese (Camembert-style), Meredith Blue and an Australian pecorino (made from sheep's milk).

ABOVE: Richard Thomas contemplates the fruits of his labours.

RIGHT ABOVE: A slice of matured Meredith Blue, a sheep's milk cheese served with truffled honey and crusty bread. Make your own truffled honey—just slice off some truffle peelings or paste, and infuse them in a quality honey. The Cameron family of Meredith Cheeses, Victoria, went from being typical Western District farmers to highly innovative farmhouse cheese producers—one of the most important in the country.

RIGHT: A fresh farm goat's cheese served with rocket leaves, marinated chillies stuffed with anchovies and crusty bread, and drizzled with a fine olive oil.

Richard Thomas

Artist as Cheese Maker

'I made Meredith Blue the first time with a bucket of sheep's milk in the back room of a restaurant. I used a Gorgonzola mould from the mountains of northern Italy, in preference to the sharper Roquefort mould. It came out right the first time and it has never been changed—that was eight years ago. It was the first time sheep's milk blue cheese was made in Australia that we know of.'

This was only one of several 'firsts' for Richard Thomas, cheese maker and consultant. Richard has developed many of Australia's finest classic farmhouse cheeses—Gippsland Blue, Yarra Valley Chèvre, Yarra Valley Persian Feta, Milawa Washed Rind, Milawa Fromage Frais, Milawa Chèvre, Milawa Blue, King River Gold, Meredith Blue and Meredith Goat cheeses.

He originally worked in the dairy industry as a chemist before deciding to combine his love of good food with the art of cheese making.

'Gorgonzola inspired me! I was naive and couldn't see why we couldn't make decent cheeses instead of cheddar. I didn't want to let food technology get in the way of making a fine cheese. I have a distaste for the arrogance of science. Because cheese making doesn't happen in Australia naturally—we're not a cheesemaking continent—we have to make things happen. We have all these flavour experiences so we can be inventive and do non-traditional things. There is no reason why any type of cheese can't be made in Australia.

'I'm presently working on getting maximum flavour into cheese. We don't just eat food for nourishment—we eat for flavour. The milk quality is important, as well as the way we ripen the milk. I'm currently working on pecorino-style cheese and some of the harder Italian varieties of Parmesan as well.'

The market in Australia is now sophisticated enough to appreciate and sell these wonderful farmhouse cheeses. When Richard began, he was making his first great cheese, Gippsland Blue, by hand (six tons in 1984). It was the only blue cheese made in the country. At first he couldn't sell it for more than $5.00 per kilogram, then Will Studd, a cheese providore newly arrived from London, began airfreighting in French cheese and Richard asked him to help. Will Studd says that Gippsland Blue looked and tasted as good as anything he was bringing in from Europe ... and so the first Australian fine farmhouse cheese was born.

Victoria Alexander, restaurateur

Warm Tart of Blue Cheese
and Caramelised Onions

INGREDIENTS

scant cup (225 mL/7 fl oz) oil

4 onions, peeled and sliced very thinly

185 g (6 oz) blue cheese

60 g (2 oz) mascarpone

1 egg yolk

500 g (1 lb) puff or shortcrust pastry

½ cup packed, shredded spinach leaves

tomato chutney to serve

This is one of the most successful dishes from the first Bathers Pavilion and one which I continue to serve by popular demand.

To caramelise the onions, heat the oil in a medium saucepan over low heat. Add the onions and cook slowly until they are a deep golden brown and very soft, about 30 minutes. Drain off any remaining oil and set the onions aside.

To make the tart, mix together the blue cheese, mascarpone and egg yolk in a bowl. Roll out the pastry on a lightly floured board to a thickness of 7 mm (¼ inch) and use to line 8 loose-bottomed tart pans (10 cm/4 inch in diameter and 1.25 cm/½ inch deep). Place in the refrigerator for 30 minutes to allow the pastry to rest.

Preheat the oven to 200°C (400°F). Place baking parchment in the tart shells and line with pastry weights or dried beans. Bake blind in the oven until they are pale gold, about 8 minutes. Remove the weights and baking parchment.

Place a little caramelised onion in the bottom of each tart shell, then a little spinach and top with the cheese mixture. Bake the tarts for about 10–12 minutes. The tops should be puffed and golden, but with the centres still creamy. Remove the tarts from the pans—place each pan on a small, upturned mould so that the outer ring drops down, then slide a spatula between the pastry and the base, and lift off the tart. Serve with a dollop of tomato chutney on the side.

Serves 8 Recipe: medium complexity

Robert Castellani, chef

Naked Ravioli
with Ricotta

INGREDIENTS

750 g (1½ lb) fresh spinach

750 g (1½ lb) silverbeet (Swiss chard)

340 g (11 oz) Parmesan cheese

500 g (1 lb) fresh ricotta

5 egg yolks

salt and freshly ground black pepper

½ teaspoon grated nutmeg

1 cup (125 g/4 oz) plain (all-purpose) flour

2 tablespoons butter

8 fresh sage leaves or baby spinach leaves

Put the spinach and silverbeet into a large bowl. Blanch for 5 minutes with boiling water, then refresh in cold water. Squeeze out excess moisture until very dry. Reserve the spinach and finely chop the silverbeet leaves and place in a bowl.

Grate two-thirds of the Parmesan cheese and add with the ricotta and egg yolks to the silverbeet. Shave the remaining Parmesan and reserve. Season the ricotta mixture with salt and pepper, and add the nutmeg. Mix together well and form into walnut-size balls. Roll the balls in the flour, making sure they are uniformly floured before poaching them. Poach for 30 seconds in plenty of boiling water in a large saucepan.

At the same time, reheat the reserved spinach in the butter and place in warm, flat bowls. Add the ravioli balls, garnish with the Parmesan shavings and fresh sage leaves, and serve immediately.

Serves 6 Recipe: easy to make

Suzanne Gibbs, food writer

Sweet Potato Gnocchi
with Burnt Butter Sauce

INGREDIENTS

750 g (1½ lb) red sweet potato (kumera), peeled and roughly chopped

30g (1 oz) unsalted butter

1¾ cups (225 g/7 oz) plain (all-purpose) flour

1 egg yolk

salt and freshly ground black pepper

fresh sage leaves

a little oil for frying

fresh Parmesan cheese shavings, optional

BURNT BUTTER SAUCE

100 g (3½ oz) butter

1 clove garlic, crushed

1 tablespoon chopped sage leaves

Place the sweet potato in a saucepan with just enough water to cover. Cover the pan with a lid and boil until the potato is tender. Drain and mash the sweet potato, then rub through a metal sieve using the bottom of a glass or jar to help. Return the sweet potato to the saucepan and add the butter, stirring over gentle heat and, as soon as the purée is cool enough to handle, start beating in the flour and egg yolk, then season with pepper. Stir until the dough is soft but elastic.

Roll small walnut-sized pieces of the dough in the palm of your hand. Press each piece of dough gently around your finger to curve it, using a fork to make ribbed grooves. The shaping is not just decorative, it serves to thin out the centre of the gnocchi so they cook evenly, and the grooves and centre trap the sauce.

To make the burnt butter sauce, melt the butter in a small saucepan with the garlic and sage, and cook gently until the butter begins to turn golden brown, but take care not to burn it. Remove from the heat and keep warm.

Drop the gnocchi in batches into a large saucepan of boiling, salted water. When ready, they will float to the top. Cook just another 10 seconds, then remove with a slotted spoon to a warm serving dish.

To serve, quickly fry the sage leaves in a little oil until crisp. Spoon the burnt butter sauce over the gnocchi and toss lightly. Sprinkle with shavings of Parmesan cheese, if liked, and garnish with the crisp-fried sage leaves. Serve immediately.

Serves 4 Recipe: easy to make

Stefano Manfredi, chef

Veal Shank Salad

INGREDIENTS

1 veal shank, trimmed of fat and skin

1 carrot, cut into chunks

1 onion, cut into quarters

2 stalks celery, cut into 2-cm (¾-inch) lengths

1 leek, cleaned and trimmed

3 golden shallots, peeled and sliced

1 Florence fennel (finocchio) bulb, cleaned and sliced

large handful of fresh parsley, chopped

1 tablespoon extra virgin olive oil

balsamic vinegar

sea salt and freshly cracked black pepper

This salad can be a meal or part of an antipasto. The veal shanks are really tender—the meat just falls away.

Place the shank in a saucepan and cover well with cold water. Add the carrot, onion, celery and leek. Simmer for at least an hour, or until the shank is tender. When it is done, take the shank out of the broth and allow to cool. Strain the broth, allow to cool and keep in the refrigerator as a soup base.

Once cooked, the shank is thinly sliced and placed in a salad bowl with the shallots, fennel and parsley. Add some olive oil and toss. Add a few drops of balsamic vinegar and season with salt and pepper to taste. Toss once again and serve.

Serves 6–8 Recipe: easy to make

Robert Castellani, chef

Seared Scallops,
Black Orrechiette and Mascarpone

INGREDIENTS

200 g (7 oz) mascarpone

¼ cup (30 g/1 oz) grated Parmesan cheese

salt and freshly ground black pepper

20 scallops, trimmed

2 tablespoons olive oil

200 g (6½ oz) black orrechiette or other small black pasta

freshly snipped chives to garnish

freshly chopped basil leaves to garnish

This is one of my favourite summer dishes. Use imported pasta that has been air-dried if possible—it has a rough, pitted surface to which the sauce can cling. Machine-dried pasta, in contrast, cooks the flour and smooths the surface.

Melt the mascarpone over low heat and, when hot, add the Parmesan cheese. Season with pepper, then remove from the heat and keep warm.

Season the scallops with salt and pepper, then quickly sear them in half the olive oil. Cook the pasta in plenty of boiling, salted water until al dente, drain and put into a warm bowl. Toss the remaining oil through the pasta, add the mascarpone mixture, scallops, chives and basil, and serve immediately.

Serves 4 Recipe: easy to make

RIGHT: Seared Scallops, Black Orriechette and Mascarpone. This dish can also be made using chargrilled octopus or squid stuffed with a little garlic and parsley, and then sliced.

LEFT: Warm Black-Lip Abalone, Shiitake and Corzetti Salad. It's a really nice combination of textures and visually appealing. The abalone is chewy, the corzetti is soft but al dente, the shiitake is soft—the dish's earthy flavours are not masked.

Stefano Manfredi, chef

Warm Black-Lip Abalone,
Shiitake and Corzetti Salad

The abalone is basically a large muscle contained in a beautiful, ovoid shell. The black-lip abalone has a jet black trim around the sides of the muscle. To prepare, the muscle must be first cut away from the shell. To do this, run a small, sharp knife around the edge of the lip, cutting away from the shell. You should be able to feel just where the muscle is attached with the blade of the knife. Once free, slice the muscle very thinly with a sharp, wide-bladed knife and marinate the slices in extra virgin olive oil and a little lemon juice.

CONTINUED ON PAGE 68

INGREDIENTS

SAFFRON CORZETTI

2 cups (250 g/8 oz) plain (all-purpose) flour

2 eggs, infused with ½ teaspoon saffron threads

2 tablespoons olive oil

1 cup (125 g/4 oz) freshly grated Parmesan cheese

extra virgin olive oil

200 g (7 oz) shiitake mushrooms, thinly sliced

2 cups cooked corzetti (as above)

8 cloves garlic, minced

1 live abalone (see introduction)

salt and freshly ground black pepper

some young salad leaves

Sift the flour into a bowl, make a well in the centre and add the eggs. Stir with a knife, adding a little cold water (about 3 tablespoons), and form into a firm dough with your hands. Turn out onto a floured board and knead, turning and pushing with the heel of your hand for about 15 minutes, or until the dough is smooth and pliable. The dough will be stiff at first, but will become more pliable as you knead. Shape into a ball and cover with plastic wrap. Leave to rest for 20 minutes.

To make the saffron corzetti, take small pieces—about the size of a thumbnail—off the large lump of pasta dough. Keeping your fingers well floured, press each piece onto the work surface with your thumb so that it is roughly round (similar in shape to a coin). Cook the corzetti in an abundant amount of rapidly boiling, salted water until al dente. Drain and dress with some of the olive oil so that they don't stick to one another. Mix in the Parmesan cheese. Heat the remaining olive oil in a frying pan or skillet, and toss in the corzetti. Sauté until golden, about 5 minutes. Remove from the heat.

Heat the olive oil in a large frying pan or wok. When it has begun to smoke, add the shiitake, corzetti, garlic and abalone. Toss for a minute, season with salt and pepper to taste and serve on the salad leaves.

Serves 8 Recipe: medium complexity

Dany Chouet, chef

Parfait de Foie de Canard et sa Salade
Salad of Duck Liver Parfait

INGREDIENTS

LIVER PARFAIT

200 g (7 oz) unsalted butter

500 g (1 lb) duck livers

3 sprigs fresh thyme

salt and freshly ground black pepper

sunflower oil

1 tablespoon each brandy and port

DRESSING

2½ tablespoons sherry vinegar

5 tablespoons grapeseed oil

5 tablespoons virgin olive oil

salt and freshly ground black pepper

250 g (8 oz) baby lettuce mix

1–2 bunches of thin green asparagus

200 g (7 oz) white button mushrooms

juice of 1 lemon

1 bunch of spring onions

1 bunch of fresh chervil

To make the parfait, dice the butter and keep in a warm place until soft and creamy, but not melted. Preheat the oven to 200°C (400°F). Clean the livers, place on a greased baking sheet and marinate with the thyme, pepper and a drizzle of sunflower oil. Leave at room temperature for 30 minutes. When the butter is ready, quickly cook the livers in the oven for 3–4 minutes. Keep them very pink. When they have cooled a little, purée in a food processor and, whilst they are still lukewarm, push through a fine sieve before returning to the cleaned food processor. Add the creamed butter, brandy and port. Season with salt and pepper to taste, and blend very briefly. Place the mixture in a porcelain terrine to set in the refrigerator for 2–3 hours. Make the dressing by combining all the ingredients and mix well. Set aside until ready to use.

To make the salad, wash and dry the lettuce. Trim the asparagus, using mainly the tips, and steam for 4 minutes. Slice the button mushrooms very thinly and toss in a little lemon juice so they stay white. Slice the spring onion very thinly.

To serve, arrange the lettuce on 4 serving plates, sprinkle the mushrooms around, arrange the asparagus and sprinkle the spring onion all over. Shape 4 scoops of liver parfait with a stainless steel spoon dipped into hot water. Place the parfait in the middle of each salad. Dress the salad with the dressing, using a clean pastry brush dipped into the dressing. Arrange some chervil sprigs on top of each salad and serve.

Serves 4 Recipe: medium complexity

Ralph Potter, chef

Oyster and Braised Baby Squid Noodle Salad

with Soy, Rocket Oil and Ginger

INGREDIENTS

SQUID

450 g (14½ oz) baby squid

salt

3 whole cloves garlic

1 brown onion, peeled and halved

3 thick slices fresh ginger

1 lemon, halved

300 g (10 oz) fresh egg vermicelli

1¼ cups (310 mL/10 fl oz) extra virgin
   olive oil

36 rocket (arugula) leaves, washed and
   dried

2 tablespoons balsamic vinegar

3 tablespoons fresh ginger, finely
   julienned

6 tablespoons low-salt soy sauce

18 oysters, shelled

½ teaspoon ground lemon myrtle leaves

freshly cracked black pepper

ROCKET OIL

handful of rocket (arugula) leaves

⅔ cup (150 mL/5 fl oz) top-quality extra
   virgin olive oil (choose a green,
   peppery-flavoured oil)

A contemporary Australian dish—simple, fresh and summery. Use only small squid for this dish—reject any that are larger than 15 cm (6 inches) as they will be too thick. Ideally, the cut squid should be a similar size to the noodles. As an alternative to fresh egg vermicelli, use dried rice vermicelli.

Clean the squid by removing the head, taking out the beak and guts, and cutting the body down the side. Lay it flat and scrape the skin off with the back of a knife. Strip the suckers off the tentacles with your fingers. Cut the tentacles from the head and thinly slice the tubes lengthwise. They should be no wider than 2–3 mm (about ⅛ inch). Wash and place the squid in a large saucepan, cover with cold water and bring to the boil. Skim and add the salt, garlic, onion, ginger and lemon, and simmer for 45–50 minutes, or until the squid is tender.

Cook the vermicelli in plenty of boiling water for 5 minutes and refresh in cold water. Set aside. Remove the squid from the water with a mesh spoon and discard the aromatics. While the squid is still warm, cover with some of the olive oil and leave to cool.

To make the rocket oil, purée a good handful of rocket leaves in the food processor or blender, and blend together with enough extra virgin oil to make an oily purée. Place in a container and reserve.

To assemble the dish, drain the excess oil from the cooked squid, leaving enough to keep it moist. Dress the rocket leaves with a little of the rocket oil and some of the balsamic vinegar, and place in the centre of each plate.

Mix the squid with the cold cooked noodles, then add 2 tablespoons of the ginger, soy sauce, the remaining balsamic vinegar and 12 of the oysters. Mix gently together and place on top of the rocket leaves. Each portion should have 2 oysters. Top each pile with a third oyster.

To finish, dribble some of the soy dressing from the squid mixing bowl onto the plate and then dollop some of the rocket oil purée around. Sprinkle the dish with the lemon myrtle and season to taste with pepper. Garnish each serving with a little of the remaining ginger.

Serves 6 Recipe: medium complexity

Raymond Kersh and Jennice Kersh, chef and restaurateur

Double-baked Lemon Aspen and
Goat's Cheese Soufflé

INGREDIENTS

LEMON ASPEN SALSA

juice of ½ orange

1 lime

125 g (4 oz) lemon aspen fruit, cleaned and finely chopped

2 small basil leaves, shredded, plus 1 tablespoon chopped basil leaves (extra)

¼ red onion, finely diced

1 small golden shallot, finely chopped

1 clove garlic, finely chopped

4 tablespoons honey

1 tablespoon white wine vinegar

1½ tablespoons white wine

salt and freshly ground black pepper

1 tablespoon chopped chives

WHITE SAUCE

1⅓ cups (330mL/11 fl oz) milk

½ small brown onion

1 bay leaf

pinch of ground nutmeg

2 tablespoons butter

2 tablespoons plain (all-purpose) flour

SOUFFLE

⅓ cup (60 g/2 oz) goat's cheese, crumbled, plus ½ cup (75 g/2½ oz) extra

3 lemon aspen fruit, cleaned, cored and finely chopped

2 egg yolks

1 tablespoon aspen fruit juice

4 egg whites

2 cups (500 mL/16 fl oz) light (single) cream

2 tablespoons chopped chives

To make the lemon aspen salsa, combine all the ingredients except the extra 1 tablespoon chopped basil and the chives in a saucepan and bring to the boil. Simmer for 20 minutes, adding a little water as needed so that it doesn't burn. Add the extra basil and chives after removing from the heat and mix through. Reserve.

To make the white sauce, slowly bring the milk, onion, bay leaf and nutmeg to the boil. In the meantime, make the roux by melting the butter in a saucepan and stirring in the flour. Cook, stirring, over medium heat for 2 minutes. When the milk has come to the boil, strain into the roux and whisk until the sauce is smooth and has thickened. Simmer, stirring occasionally.

To make the soufflé, preheat the oven to 180°C (350°F). Grease 4 dariole moulds or ovenproof cups. While the sauce is still hot, stir in the ⅓ cup (60 g/2 oz) goat's cheese, aspen fruit, egg yolks and aspen juice. Whip the egg whites and fold one-third of the egg white into the sauce. When mixed, gently fold in the remaining egg white. Spoon the mixture into the moulds and place the moulds on a baking pan with about 2 cm (¾ inch) water in the bottom. Bake in the oven for 15–20 minutes.

When cooked, remove the tray from the oven, but do not turn the oven off. Take the moulds off the tray and let stand on a wire rack to cool. The soufflés will collapse at this point, but will puff back up when rebaked. When cool, cut and remove from the moulds and place into ovenproof bowls. Mix the remaining ½ cup (75 g/2½ oz) goat's cheese and cream together, and put one-quarter of this mixture on each soufflé. Now put ⅓ teaspoon of the aspen salsa on top of each one and bake in the hot oven for 8–10 minutes. When brown, garnish with the chives and serve immediately.

Serves 4 Recipe: medium complexity

Chapter 2
Salads and Vegetables

Alan Saunders

Salads and Vegetables

There are two classic accounts of the Australian salad and both are more or less tragic. First, there was poor Philip Muskett, munching his unhappy way through the meaty menus of New South Wales in the 1890s and yearning for the gastronomic pleasures of France. Why couldn't his countrymen make salads like the French? Why did they have to follow the English method? The English, said Dr Muskett, cut their lettuce first into halves and then into quarters. Next, they place the pieces in water to soak and leave them on a plate to drain, a process which is supposed to be thoroughly cleansing, but which does absolutely nothing to disturb whatever minute insects might be lurking among the leaves. Then the whole thing is shredded and tossed with a few slices of hard-boiled egg and finally 'a mysterious mixture known as salad-dressing' is poured over it all: 'Thus is produced the orthodox English salad, which everyone, probably from patriotic motives, pronounces to be extremely nice.' It didn't get any better.

Seventy years later, Hal Porter was writing in his memoir *The Watcher on the Cast-Iron Balcony* of Sunday tea in the early 1920s. There were the green jellies, the sponge cakes, the macaroons and the lamingtons; there was the ham, crumbed and stuck with cloves; and, at his mother's end of the table, there were 'the highly peppered Sargasso of sliced cucumber, tomato, lettuce, onion and radishes sodden in Champion's Malt Vinegar which Mother imagines is a salad.' But things have at last changed, and you can learn how much they *have* changed by trying to find malt vinegar on the shelves of an Australian supermarket today. It will still be there (and so it should be, though I suspect that its virtues are now little appreciated), but its bulbous little proletarian flasks are likely to be outnumbered and outclassed by the aristocratic newcomers: tall, elegant bottles of red wine vinegar, white wine vinegar and balsamic vinegar, rice vinegars and distilled vinegars from Japan, not to mention those raffish and suspect bottles into which somebody has stuck a sprig of tarragon or other irrelevant foliage.

Actually, Dr Muskett seems to have approved of tarragon vinegar ('which is so admirably put up by Messrs Crosse and Blackwell'), but probably only because he found tarragon itself comparatively hard to come by. A good oil, a good vinegar and some salt were all that he really required for his salad dressings, although he was quite prepared to countenance more elaborate concoctions such as crayfish salad and herring salad with warm potatoes: he would probably have got on very well with Geoff Lindsay's Sugar-cured Beef with Miss Jane's Pesto Beans and Black Olive Oil (page 75) or Alain Fabrègues's Warm Salad of New Potatoes with a Julienne of Steamed Chicken and and Freshly Smoked Salmon (page 77).

It goes without saying that everything here would be beyond Mrs Porter's wildest imaginings of what a salad might be, although Peter Doyle's contribution (right) strikes an authentically Australian note with its use of beetroot (red beets)—they are, however, fresh, roasted and skinned. They really ought to come out of a can and bleed over the other ingredients.

PREVIOUS PAGE: Peter Doyle's Roasted Beetroot, Blood Orange, Red Witlof and Asparagus with Orange Oil. 'I wanted something complementary to the main ingredients—something a little bit bitter, so I added red witlof and frisée. The mâche adds a little bit of neutrality. The citrus oil lifts and combines the salad and brings it all together.'

Peter Doyle, chef

Roasted Beetroot, Blood Orange,
Red Witlof and Asparagus with Orange Oil

INGREDIENTS

ORANGE OIL

2 cups (500 mL/16 fl oz) strained
  orange juice
2½ tablespoons lemon juice
grapeseed oil

2 beetroot (red beets)
2 bulbs red witlof (Belgian endive),
  leaves separated, washed and dried
1 bunch of frisée (curly endive), washed
  and dried
corn salad (mâche) leaves
2 blood oranges, peeled and sliced into
  rounds
24 green asparagus spears, peeled,
  blanched and refreshed
2 tablespoons pine nuts, toasted

WALNUT VINAIGRETTE

1 tablespoon white wine vinegar
1 tablespoon walnut oil
4 tablespoons olive oil
salt and freshly ground black pepper

Blood oranges and asparagus have a real affinity. This dish is a play on Maltaise sauce, but in a lighter, fresher version more conducive to our climate. Beetroot goes really well with blood oranges and asparagus.

To make the orange oil, reduce the citrus juices over medium heat until syrup-like, then cool to room temperature. Whisk in or blend an equal amount of grapeseed oil and reserve.

Meanwhile, roast the beetroot. Preheat the oven to 180°C (350°F). Trim the stems of the beetroot, leaving 1 cm (½ inch). Wrap the stems in foil and roast the beetroot in the oven for 1 hour. Allow to cool, then peel and cut each beetroot into 12 wedges.

To make the walnut vinaigrette, whisk together the wine vinegar, walnut oil and olive oil. Season to taste with salt and pepper.

To serve, toss the witlof, frisée and corn salad in the walnut vinaigrette and place in the centre of the plate. Arrange the beetroot, blood orange, asparagus and pine nuts around and over the greens. Drizzle with orange oil and serve.

Serves 6 Recipe: easy to make

Geoff Lindsay, chef

Sugar-cured Beef
with Miss Jane's Pesto Beans and Black Olive Oil

INGREDIENTS

500 g (1 lb) eye fillet of beef, trimmed
   of fat
1 tablespoon chopped fresh thyme
100 g (3½ oz) freshly crushed white,
   black, and Szechuan peppercorns
⅔ cup (155 g/5 oz) sugar
1 cup (250 g/8 oz) rock salt
2½ tablespoons brandy

BLACK OLIVE OIL

5 tablespoons extra virgin olive oil
3 tablespoons Ligurian olives, pitted

MISS JANE'S PESTO BEANS

250 g (8 oz) baby green beans
2 tablespoons pesto
45 g (1½ oz) semi-dried tomatoes, cut
   into strips
45 g (1½ oz) pickled onions

An Italian-influenced dish, this starter is designed to stimulate the appetite. The beef is cured then flavoured with black pepper, and balanced by salty black olive oil.

To make the sugar-cured beef, roll the eye fillet in the thyme and peppercorns, making sure it is completely covered. Mix the sugar, salt and brandy together, then pack around the beef so it is completely enclosed. Cover and refrigerate for 48 hours. Turn every 12 hours. Remove from the brine and pat dry with absorbent kitchen paper.

To make the black olive oil, put the olive oil in a food processor with the olives and blend to a fine paste. Strain the olive paste through a fine sieve, pushing it through to form a thick oil.

To serve, blanch the beans in rapidly boiling water until tender, about 5 minutes. Mix with the pesto while still warm, then add the semi-dried tomato and pickled onion. Place a pile of pesto beans on each serving plate. Finely slice the cured beef and drape a few slices of meat over the bean salad. Drizzle the plate and meat with the black olive oil. Serve while the pesto beans are still warm.

Serves 4 Recipe: medium complexity

LEFT: Sugar-cured Beef with Miss Jane's Pesto Beans and Black Olive Oil. The texture in this dish is as important as the flavour—the fine slices of beef have a soft, luscious character; the oily beans are crisp and fresh, and the semi-dried tomatoes add sweetness.

LEFT: Borlotti Beans with Parsley and Garlic. A really simple dish reliant on borlotti beans at their best. The beans should be firm and not too mushy.

Stefano Manfredi, chef

Borlotti Beans
with Parsley and Garlic

INGREDIENTS

1 kg (2 lb) fresh borlotti (cranberry)
   beans, in their shells
3 tablespoons extra virgin olive oil
salt and freshly ground black pepper
½ cup roughly chopped flat-leaf parsley
2 cloves garlic, finely chopped

Serve as part of an antipasto—the beans say it all.

Shell the fresh beans. Place in a saucepan and cover with cold water. Bring to the boil and simmer until tender, but not overcooked, about 20 minutes. Strain off the excess water, then dress the beans with the olive oil and season with salt and pepper to taste. Add the parsley and garlic, and serve as part of an antipasto. This is also a good way to dress cooked green beans.

Serves 6–8 Recipe: easy to make

Tony Bilson, chef

Tomatoes Braised in Pernod
with Snails and Mussels

INGREDIENTS

TOMATOES

10 medium vine-ripened tomatoes

155 g (5 oz) canned snails

⅔ cup (155 g/5 fl oz) olive oil

100 g (3½ oz) butter

2 golden shallots, chopped

½ bunch of flat-leaf parsley, chopped

½ bunch of fresh basil, chopped

1 head garlic, peeled and smashed

1 tablespoon fresh ginger, chopped

3 pieces of star anise

salt and freshly ground black pepper

1 cup (250 mL/8 fl oz) Pernod

155 g (5 oz) cooked mussels or periwinkles

155 g (5 oz) poached eel

½ cup (60 g/2 oz) ground almonds

PARSLEY BUTTER

200 g (7 oz) butter

1 tablespoon chopped garlic

½ bunch of flat-leaf parsley, chopped

juice of 1 lemon

MIREPOIX

100 g (3½ oz) each onion, carrot, fennel
  and celery, finely chopped

1 tablespoon chopped fresh ginger

3 cloves garlic, chopped

zest of 1 orange

3 sprigs thyme and 2 sprigs tarragon

1 star anise

1 teaspoon coriander seed

2 tablespoons olive oil

1 cup (250 mL/8 fl oz) mollusc stock

5 tablespoons shellfish stock

5 tablespoons veal stock

2 tablespoons butter

girolle mushrooms or straw mushrooms

A dish designed for the summer menu—light and fresh tasting, it draws on Provençal flavours. Shellfish and mollusc stock can be replaced by a stock made with mussels, prawns (shrimp) or lobster heads.

Preheat the oven to 180°C (350°F).

To make the tomatoes, blanch them in boiling water for 10 seconds, plunge into iced water and then remove the skins. Slice the top off each tomato and reserve the tops to cover at the end. Seed the tomatoes, taking care to keep them whole.

Gently pan-fry the snails in a frying pan or skillet in some of the olive oil and butter over medium heat. Add one-third of the shallots, and the parsley, basil, garlic, ginger and star anise. Season with salt and pepper. Deglaze with one-quarter of the Pernod. Repeat this process with the mussels and the eel. Mix all together gently, add the ground almond and fill the tomatoes with the mixture.

To make the parsley butter, soften the butter and mix in the other ingredients. Shape into a sausage, wrap in foil and refrigerate. When hard, place one slice of the seasoned butter on top of the filling in each of the tomatoes, then place the reserved tops back on the tomatoes.

To braise in a frying pan, melt the olive oil and soften the mirepoix ingredients. Place the stuffed tomatoes on the bed of mirepoix and deglaze with the remaining Pernod. Reduce the liquid and then add the mollusc, shellfish and veal stocks. Place the pan in the oven for 15 minutes, basting the tomatoes regularly.

Remove the tomatoes from the pan, strain the braising liquid and add some butter to the strained sauce.

To serve, place the tomatoes on a serving plate and surround with some sauce. Garnish with the girolle mushrooms and serve immediately.

Serves 10 Recipe: medium complexity

Alain Fabrègues, chef

Warm Salad of New Potatoes

with a Julienne of Steamed Chicken and Freshly Smoked Salmon, Corn Salad and Herbs from Our Garden

INGREDIENTS

16 new season potatoes (such as Nadine
    or Foxton, or other best-quality waxy
    variety)
1 large chicken breast
5 tablespoons balsamic vinegar
3 tablespoons virgin olive oil
scant cup (200 mL/7 fl oz) sour cream
juice of 1 lemon
½ bunch of chives, finely chopped
½ bunch of fresh chervil, finely chopped
6 slices fresh-smoked salmon
Maldon sea salt and freshly ground
    white pepper
corn salad (mâche) leaves, washed and
    dried

Choose new season potatoes—the small ones with very thin skins—just dug out of the ground. They will still have that strong, nutty flavour.

Cook the potatoes in a saucepan of salted water. Remove the skins and keep warm by returning to the cooking water. Steam the chicken breast until cooked, about 35 minutes. Reduce the balsamic vinegar in a small saucepan over high heat. Allow to cool and reserve.

Mix half the olive oil with the sour cream, then add the lemon juice, chives and chervil. Remove the skin from the chicken breast and slice the chicken into strips about 3 cm (1¼ inch) long. Cut the smoked salmon the same way.

Slice the potato and fold into two-thirds of the sour cream mixture. Check the seasoning and season with sea salt and white pepper if necessary. Fold the chicken and smoked salmon into the remaining sour cream mixture.

In a separate mixing bowl, lightly mix the remaining olive oil, reserved balsamic vinegar and corn salad leaves.

To serve, place the potato salad in the centre of 4 serving plates, scatter around some corn salad leaves and spoon the chicken mixture on top.

Serves 4 Recipe: easy to make

Tony Bilson

A Celebration of the Senses

'Cooking is such a basic part of living; it is too important to leave up to others. For me, cooking is an expression of our life rhythms, a celebration of seasonality and sensuality. Great cooking celebrates our relationship with the earth and agriculture, and, with wine, is a fascinating part of our cultural heritage.'

Tony Bilson developed his unique Australian cooking style more than thirty years ago, combining classic French cuisine with Mediterranean flavours and local seasonal produce. The imaginative food ideally suited the Australian environment and lifestyle. 'I'm French and Japanese inspired; their cuisines are so compatible with wine. Cooking is transformed into a transcendental experience only through its marriage with wine. The flavours in my dishes are especially designed to be accompanied by Australian wines.'

Tony was one of the leaders of the food revolution in Australia, along with Cheong Liew and Phillip Searle. He began his professional career with Paul Harbulot at Johnnie Walker's Bistro in Angel Place, Sydney. His first restaurant, Tony's Bon Goût, was an immediate success. It was instantly recognised as fine cooking eminently suitable for Sydney. Since then, his style has continued to develop and grow.

With Gay Bilson, he created the iconic Berowra Waters and established new guidelines for fine food and dining. He went on with his distinctive style to Kinsela's, Bilson's (now Quay), Fine Bouche and the Treasury.

Tony has trained and influenced many of the best chefs around the country and educated, and been supported by, loyal patrons. His latest restaurant, Ampersand, opened in 1998 to great acclaim. The restaurant is set in a rooftop garden with superb views of Darling Harbour and is a celebration of Australia's food culture, local wines and produce.

'I like to celebrate the quality of the ingredients as a metaphor for the joy of existence.'

RIGHT: Chocolate Soufflé (page 201)—a classic dish. With a little bit of practice, a soufflé can become a standard dish in the repertoire of home cooks.

LEFT: Tomatoes Braised in Pernod with Snails and Mussels (page 76). By using very complex flavours in the sauce, the strength and clarity in the shellfish stuffing is emphasised.

Categorising cooking by nationality is always dangerous to me, but especially dangerous for Australian cuisine. The quality of cooking is more dependent on individuals.

TONY BILSON

Leo Schofield, food critic

Mussel Salad

INGREDIENTS

mussels (allow 6 per person)

1 bottle dry white wine

2 golden shallots, chopped

1 tablespoon chopped fresh parsley

salt and freshly ground black pepper

4 tablespoons extra virgin olive oil or
    truffle oil

1 tablespoon lemon juice

2 cos (romaine) lettuce

1 bunch asparagus

500 g (1 lb) zucchini (courgettes)

1 truffle, optional

This salad looks smashing on the plate, and makes a marvellous light luncheon dish if simply followed by cheese and fruit—or a very appealing first course at dinner. Much of it can be made in advance.

Scrub and de-beard the mussels. Place in a large saucepan and pour in the white wine. Add the shallots and parsley, and season to taste with salt and pepper. Bring to the boil and simmer for 5 minutes, or until the mussels just open—be careful not to overcook. Remove the mussels from the liquor, then from their shells. Reserve the mussel stock.

In a bowl, mix together the oil and lemon juice to make a mild dressing. Then toss the warm, shelled mussels lightly in it, season and place in the refrigerator.

Wash and dry the lettuce and separate the leaves into three sizes—small, medium and large. Reserve the largest leaves for another use.

Scrape and steam the asparagus until tender, but not overdone. Pass the zucchini through the slicing blade of the food processor or alternatively slice by hand into fine, even rounds. Strain the reserved mussel stock, return to the heat and bring to the boil again. Toss the zucchini pieces in for only a few seconds to blanch, then remove and run under a cold tap to refresh.

To assemble the salad, arrange 4 of the middling-size lettuce leaves in the form of a cross on each plate. Between each leaf, place an asparagus spear to make a star-like formation.

Toss the zucchini with the smallest of the lettuce leaves in a fine, light vinaigrette and place a mound of this salad at the centre of each star. On top, pile half a dozen mussels. For added luxury, a shredded truffle may be strewn over the mussels.

Recipe: easy to make

Luke Mangan, chef
Salad of Grilled Baby Corn,
Feta and Fresh Pear with Walnut Dressing

INGREDIENTS

1 tablespoon sherry vinegar

2 tablespoons walnut oil

pinch of sea salt

30 medium rocket (arugula) leaves

20 g (⅔ oz) Yarra Valley Persian feta or
   any other good-quality feta cheese

½ ripe pear (preferably beurre bosc)

6 fresh baby corn

A very autumny, summery salad—add barbecued prawns (shrimp) or scatter some walnut pieces over the top for more texture. I prefer to use Yarra Valley Persian feta from the Yarra Valley and very fresh baby corn.

Using a whisk, mix the sherry vinegar and walnut oil together, adding a pinch of sea salt. Place the rocket leaves in a bowl, splash a generous quantity of the dressing over and toss well. Place the rocket in the centre of each of 2 serving plates, keeping some height in the greens. Break up the feta cheese and place around and on top of the rocket. Cut the pear into 6 wedges and arrange 3 wedges around each plate. On a very high heat, chargrill the corn and place between the pear slices. Drizzle the remaining dressing over each plate and serve.

Serves 2 Recipe: easy to make

Simon Johnson, providore
Panzanella

INGREDIENTS

1 loaf of fresh sourdough

2 bunches of asparagus, sliced

10 fresh broad (fava) beans, shelled

1 red onion, halved and finely sliced

1 avocado, roughly diced

1 cucumber, cut into bite-size pieces

good vine-ripened tomatoes, cut into
   bite-size pieces

1 bunch of fresh basil, roughly chopped

sea salt and freshly ground black pepper

1 cup (250 mL/8 fl oz) Joseph or other
   best-quality extra virgin olive oil

2 tablespoons Cabernet Sauvignon
   vinegar or other fine red wine vinegar

Panzanella is a classic rustic Italian bread dish. Make it with wonderful sourdough and the filling with whatever you have in the refrigerator or in the garden.

Preheat the oven to 200°C (400°F). Slice the top off the bread and scoop a little bit of the bread out to make a shell. Remove some from the lid also. Place in the preheated oven for 5–10 minutes to heat.

Blanch the asparagus and broad beans in simmering water for a couple of minutes, until al dente. Peel the beans.

Into a bowl, place the asparagus, broad beans, onion, avocado, cucumber, tomato and basil. Season well with sea salt and pepper. Pour some of the oil and the vinegar over, and mix well. Take the warm bread out of the oven and pour the remaining olive oil inside the bread shell and on the lid. Place the filling inside the bread shell and place the lid on top.

Serves 4–6 Recipe: easy to make

Peter Doyle, chef

Salad of Blue Swimmer Crab
with Avocado, Coriander and Mint

INGREDIENTS

TOMATO MOUSSE

10 very ripe egg-shaped (Italian plum)
   tomatoes, peeled and seeded
2½ tablespoons extra virgin olive oil
salt and freshly ground black pepper

DIPPING SAUCE

½ cup (125 mL/4 fl oz) Thai fish sauce
   (nam pla)
⅔ cup (155 mL/5 fl oz) cold water
½ cup (125 mL/4 fl oz) lime juice
2 tablespoons sugar
4 cloves garlic, finely minced
3–4 red serrano chillies
small bunch of mint leaves, finely
   chopped
small bunch of coriander (Chinese
   parsley) leaves, finely chopped

PRAWN OIL

6½ cups (1.6 litres/2¾ imp. pints)
   olive oil
450 g (14 oz) prawn (shrimp) shells
1 carrot, diced
1 onion, diced
1 stalk celery, diced
6 thyme stems
4 tarragon stems
1 bay leaf
4 parsley stems
1¼ cups (310 mL/10 fl oz) dry white
   wine
juice of 1 lemon
salt and freshly ground black pepper

INGREDIENTS CONTINUE ON PAGE 84

A nice, light summery dish.

To start the tomato mousse, begin at least 4 hours before using. Line a sieve or colander with a double thickness of muslin or cheesecloth, and set over a bowl. Purée the tomatoes in a food processor or blender until they are completely smooth. Scrape the purée into the lined strainer and place in the refrigerator. Leave the purée to drain for at least 4 hours or overnight, until it is very thick. Scrape the thick purée into a bowl and whisk in the oil. Season to taste with salt and pepper. Keep in a container until needed.

To make the dipping sauce, mix the fish sauce, cold water, lime juice, sugar and garlic together in a small bowl. Halve the chillies lengthwise, remove the seeds, chop finely and add to the sauce. Add the mint and coriander just before you sauce each serving of crab.

To make the prawn oil, preheat the oven to 220°C (425°F). Brush a few large baking sheets with oil and roast the prawn shells in the oven until they are a deep pink colour. Heat some of the olive oil in a large saucepan and colour some of the shells in a saucepan as well. Sweat the carrot, onion and celery in a little more of the olive oil in a separate saucepan, then add the prawn shells, thyme, tarragon, bay leaf and parsley. Add the wine and continue cooking for 15 minutes. Add the remaining olive oil, reduce the heat and cook about 30 minutes, stirring often to prevent burning on the bottom. Remove from the heat and, when the oil and ingredients stop steaming and have cooled quite a bit, cover the saucepan and let it sit at room temperature overnight. It is important to leave the mixture in the saucepan as this will intensify the flavour. Do not refrigerate.

Strain the oil in a fine strainer and keep in an airtight container in the refrigerator. Mix in lemon juice to taste and season with salt and pepper. This recipe makes more than is needed, but cannot be made in smaller quantities. The prawn oil will keep refrigerated for 3 months.

NOTE: Recipe continues on page 84

RIGHT: Salad of Blue Swimmer Crab with Avocado, Coriander and Mint. The combination of seasonal produce and the dipping sauce accentuates the flavour of the crab. The avocado, prawn oil and tomato add complementary complexity.

SALAD

450 g (14 oz) blue swimmer crab meat, shelled

1½ tablespoons lemon juice

⅔ cup (155 mL/5 fl oz) extra virgin olive oil

sea salt and freshly ground black pepper

1 avocado

½ telegraph cucumber, peeled, seeded and finely diced

30 coriander (Chinese parsley) leaves, chopped

20 mint leaves, chopped

12 corn salad (mâche) leaves, rinsed

1 frisée (curly endive), rinsed and picked

To make the salad, pick over the crab meat to remove all traces of shell and divide into 6 portions.

Make a lemon vinaigrette with the lemon juice and olive oil. Season with salt and pepper to taste to make sure it is not too acidic.

Peel the avocado, remove the seed and slice into even slices. If using a ring mould, place the avocado in the bottom of the mould and dress with a little lemon vinaigrette.

Place the crab meat in a bowl or bowls and add some of the cucumber, some coriander and mint, and 1 tablespoon of dipping sauce per serve. Toss all the ingredients together and place on top of the avocado in the ring moulds or shape into a ball.

Mix the corn salad and frisée together in a bowl and toss with a little lemon vinaigrette. If using the ring moulds, place the ring into the centre of each plate and slip the ring off the crab and avocado. If moulded by hand, simply place the crab and avocado mixture in the centre of each plate. Divide the salads into 6 portions and place neatly on top of the crab and avocado. Spoon a small quenelle of tomato mousse in front of the crab and drizzle a little prawn oil around the plate. Don't use too much, as the prawn oil is quite intense in taste and you don't want its flavour to dominate the crab salad, just enhance it. Serve immediately.

Serves 6 Recipe: complex

Genevieve Harris, chef

Tomato, Olive and Parsley Frittatas

INGREDIENTS

4 vine-ripened tomatoes, quartered, seeded and diced

20 kalamata olives, pitted and diced

½ small red onion, finely diced

1 cup parsley leaves, chopped

Parmesan cheese, grated

salt and freshly ground black pepper

6 eggs

This adaptation of the traditional frittata came from Frances Grundy, who works in the kitchen at Nediz Tu. We make them in mini muffin pans and serve them as a welcoming starter when guests arrive at the restaurant. The ingredients are placed in the pans individually to ensure an even mix of flavours.

Preheat the oven to 220°C (425°F). Lightly oil two 12-cup mini muffin pans with olive oil.

Divide the tomato, olives, onion and parsley evenly between the muffin pans. Sprinkle each one with Parmesan cheese and season with salt and pepper to taste.

In a stainless steel bowl, whisk the eggs then pour them into a jug or pitcher, and carefully pour the egg mixture into the muffin pans. Place the pans on a baking sheet and bake in the oven for about 18 minutes until set. Allow to cool in the pans. Turn out and gently heat before serving.

Makes about 24 Recipe: easy to make

Alain Fabrègues, chef

My Terrine of Eggplants
and Roma Tomatoes on a Tapenade Sauce

INGREDIENTS

TERRINE

6 small Japanese eggplants (aubergines)

salt and freshly ground black pepper

5 tablespoons good olive oil

24 ripe egg (Italian plum) tomatoes

PESTO

⅔ cup (45 g/1½ oz) pine nuts

⅔ cup (45 g/1½ oz) grated Parmesan
  cheese

2 cups fresh basil leaves

3 cloves garlic, crushed

⅔ cup (155 mL/5 fl oz) olive oil

TAPENADE

1⅔ cups (200 g/6½ oz) black olives,
  pitted

3 anchovy fillets

2 tablespoons capers, rinsed

2 cloves garlic, crushed

2 tablespoons olive oil

virgin olive oil

Maldon sea salt and freshly cracked
  white pepper

To make the terrine, the day before serving, peel the eggplant and slice lengthwise into strips 1 cm (½ inch) thick. Place in a layer on a baking sheet and sprinkle generously with salt. Allow to cure for 1 hour. Wash the salt away in plenty of cold water and pat the eggplant dry. Place the olive oil in a frying pan or skillet, and pan-fry the eggplant. Place on a clean baking sheet lined with baking parchment and keep, covered, until needed.

To make the pesto, place the pine nuts, Parmesan, basil and garlic in a food processor and blend. Add the oil gradually as the motor is running, until it forms a thick sauce. Set aside.

Preheat the oven to 150°C (300°F). Immerse the tomatoes in boiling water for a few seconds. Refresh in cold water, then peel and cut each tomato in half lengthwise. Remove and discard the seeds. Place the tomato halves on a baking sheet lined with a sheet of baking parchment.

Using a pastry brush, brush the tomatoes generously with the pesto. Season with salt and pepper, add a few drops of olive oil and place the baking sheet in the oven for 45 minutes. Put the eggplant in the oven at the same time. Remove the sheets from the oven and allow to cool.

Line the bottom of a terrine mould with plastic wrap and start layering—the tomato on the first row, then the eggplant, then the tomato. Keep layering until the terrine is full or you have run out of ingredients. Cover the terrine with plastic wrap and put a small board on top with a weight to compress the terrine. Leave to set in the refrigerator for 24 hours.

To make the tapenade, put all the ingredients in a food processor or blender, and blend for a few minutes, until it has made a fine purée.

Slide the terrine out of the mould and remove the plastic wrap. Using an electric knife, cut into slices 1 cm (½ inch) thick.

To serve, place a slice of terrine in the centre of each plate, and spoon a circle of tapenade around. Brush some virgin olive oil over the terrine to give it a shine. Put a few grains of Maldon sea salt and a couple of cracked white peppercorns on top. Olive bread or just plain toast will go very well with it.

Serves 10 Recipe: medium complexity

Liam Tomlin, chef

Mille-Feuilles of Potato
with a Ragoût of Wild Mushrooms and Fresh Truffle

INGREDIENTS

1 large baking potato

2 tablespoons olive oil

1 kg (2 lb) mushroom stalks or whole
   button mushrooms

125 g (4 oz) butter

1 onion, diced

2 cloves garlic

2 sprigs of fresh thyme

2 cups (500 mL/16 fl oz) milk

salt and freshly ground black pepper

250 g (8 oz) chilled butter, diced

750 g (1½ lb) selection of wild
   mushrooms, such as oyster, shimeji,
   morel, slippery jacks

julienne of flat-leaf parsley

freshly sliced truffles, optional

truffle oil, optional

The very light sauce is made from a stock of leftover mushroom stalks combined with water and milk, and frothed up like a cappuccino. Make this dish when fresh truffles are in from France or Italy, or whenever there are interesting mushrooms available. The potato crisps are more delicate than puff pastry.

Preheat the oven to 180°C (350°F). To make the potato mille-feuilles, slice the potato lengthwise as thinly as possible. Rub a baking sheet with 1 tablespoon of the olive oil and lay the potato slices on the sheet in a single layer. Cover with baking parchment and press another baking sheet on top so that the potato stays flat. Place in the oven for 15 minutes, then gently turn the potatoes over and cook for a further 5 minutes. Remove the sheet from the oven and carefully lift the potatoes onto a clean cloth or absorbent kitchen paper to absorb any excess oil.

To make the mushroom cappuccino, pour the remaining 1 tablespoon olive oil into a heavy-based saucepan and sauté the mushroom stalks until they are golden brown. Drain in a colander. In a clean saucepan, heat the butter and, when it has melted, add the onion, garlic and thyme. Cook until the onion is soft and translucent, but do not allow to brown. Add the mushroom stalks, cover with water and cook gently for 30 minutes. Pass the mushroom stock through a fine sieve, pour into a clean saucepan and reduce in volume by two-thirds.

Bring the milk to the boil in a separate saucepan, then pour it onto the mushroom stock over low heat. Season to taste with salt and pepper. Blend with a hand-held blender, gradually adding the chilled butter, until it is fully incorporated. Set aside in a warm place until ready to use, but do not reboil.

Sauté the wild mushrooms in a little olive oil until golden brown. Season with salt and pepper to taste. Add the parsley and a few drops of truffle oil (if using), and stir through gently.

To serve, place one of the slices of baked potato on a plate, spoon some of the mushrooms on top of the potato, then spoon over some of the mushroom cappuccino. Place another slice of potato on top, and then another layer of mushrooms and cappuccino, allowing the sauce to run down onto the plate. Finish with a slice of potato on top. Garnish the dish with the sliced truffle (if using) and a drizzle of truffle oil, if desired.

Serves 4 Recipe: medium complexity

RIGHT: Mille-Feuilles of Potato with a Ragoût of Wild Mushrooms and Fresh Truffle. A simple dish of earthy forest flavours—the crunchiness of the mushrooms, crispness of the potato and creaminess of the sauce are enhanced by the fresh truffle.

Janni Kyritsis, chef

Spinach and Mushroom Roulade

INGREDIENTS

SPINACH FILLING

750 g (1½ lb) spinach leaves, washed

1 red onion, finely chopped

30 g (1 oz) butter

1 teaspoon salt

freshly ground black pepper

pinch of ground nutmeg

2 teaspoons fresh thyme

½ cup (60 g/2 oz) freshly grated
  Parmesan cheese

MUSHROOM FILLING

405 g (13 oz) large mushrooms

3 tablespoons olive oil

1 clove garlic, crushed

½ teaspoon fresh coriander (Chinese
  parsley), chopped

2 teaspoons salt

1 teaspoon freshly ground black pepper

CAPER BUTTER

125 g (4 oz) butter

2 tablespoons salted capers, blanched

PASTA

2¾ cups (340 g/11 oz) plain
  (all-purpose) flour, sifted

½ teaspoon salt

2 eggs

5 egg yolks

200 g (7 oz) ricotta

Parmesan shavings to serve

I love the combination of these ingredients for lunch. The burnt butter and salted caper sauce gives an extra richness to the dish that can stand alone or with Parmesan.

To make the spinach filling, put the spinach leaves in a large saucepan and cook until just wilted, stirring constantly. Place in a colander and squeeze to remove the excess water. In a frying pan or skillet, cook the onion in the butter until soft, but not coloured. Season with salt, pepper and nutmeg. Add the thyme and Parmesan, and mix together. Remove from the heat and fold the spinach into the mixture. Reserve.

To make the mushroom filling, cook the mushrooms in the oil in a frying pan or skillet. When just soft, season with the garlic, coriander, salt and pepper. Remove from the heat and reserve.

To make the caper butter, melt the butter in a small saucepan and allow to brown. Add the capers, stir through, remove from the heat and keep warm.

To make the pasta, mix the flour and salt in a bowl. Make a well in the centre and add the eggs and egg yolks. Stir with a knife, adding a little cold water—about 3 tablespoons—and form a firm dough. Turn out onto a floured board and knead, turning and pushing with the heel of your hand for about 15 minutes, or until the dough is smooth and pliable. Shape into a ball, cover with plastic wrap and leave to rest for 20 minutes. Feed the dough through a pasta machine until the pasta is as thin as possible without breaking.

Cut the pasta sheets into 6 squares, the width of the sheet. Spread the reserved mushroom filling onto one half of each square, then the reserved spinach filling onto the other half. Place chunks of ricotta onto the spinach. Roll carefully and wrap and tie in a clean kitchen cloth. Have ready plenty of boiling, salted water in a large saucepan and poach the roulade for 20 minutes. Remove from the heat. The roulade can be kept in the refrigerator for a few hours before poaching—you will need to add an extra 5 minutes to the cooking time.

To serve, unwrap the roulade and cut into slices. Serve 2 slices per person, with the caper butter poured over the top and accompanied by a bowl of Parmesan shavings.

Serves 6 Recipe: medium complexity

Margaret Fulton, food writer

Globe Artichoke
and Bean Spaghetti Salad

INGREDIENTS

4 globe artichokes

1 lemon

3 tablespoons olive oil

3 cloves garlic, peeled and quartered

3 sprigs oregano or marjoram

1 bay leaf

1 cup (250 mL/8 fl oz) dry white wine

salt and freshly ground black pepper

4 kipfler potatoes or any other waxy
   variety

200g (7 oz) green beans

1 small carrot

balsamic vinegar

truffle or virgin olive oil

First prepare the artichokes for cooking. Remove the tough outside leaves and then cut one-third off the top of the artichokes. Trim the stalk and outer leaves, cutting the sharp points of each leaf with scissors and then halve or quarter them (depending on size); scrape out the choke, if any. As each artichoke is prepared, place in a bowl of cold water into which has been squeezed some lemon juice, to prevent the artichokes from discolouring. Drain thoroughly.

Heat the oil in a heavy frying pan or skillet. Add the artichokes and sauté for 1–2 minutes until golden, then add the garlic, oregano, bay leaf and wine. Season with salt and pepper to taste. Cover and simmer gently for 20 minutes, turning the artichokes several times during cooking.

Meanwhile, cook the potatoes in a saucepan of boiling, salted water until tender, about 15 minutes. Drain, peel and cut the potato carefully into slices. Bring a small saucepan of salted water to the boil. Add the beans and carrot, and cook for 3–4 minutes, or until tender crisp. Drain and refresh in iced water. Drain once more and cut the beans into matchsticks and the carrot into slices.

To serve, arrange 2 or 3 artichoke quarters per person on serving plates and scatter around the potato and carrot. Pile the green beans on top and drizzle a few dashes of balsamic vinegar and truffle oil over each serving.

Serves 6 Recipe: medium complexity

Richard Thomas, cheese maker

Goat's Cheese
with Roasted Whole Garlic and Croutons

INGREDIENTS

1 garlic bulb per serve and 1 extra for
   testing

really good olive oil (your favourite
   will do)

sourdough baguette, cut into 1-cm
   (½-inch) slices, generously painted
   with garlic oil

100 g (3½ oz) fresh goat's cheese per
   serve

natural (plain) yoghurt, optional

freshly ground black pepper

Going way back, I think it was Iain Hewitson who first exposed me to making a mousse of goat's cheese. We've come a long way since then, but I think Hewi would agree that our goat's cheeses are light enough to stand alone with perhaps just a little olive oil and black pepper whipped into them.

Preheat the oven to 180°C (350°F). Slowly roast the garlic bulbs in the olive oil, basting now and again. It can take 45–60 minutes until they are juicy and soft. Pull a clove off the extra bulb every so often to test.

In the last 20 or so minutes of cooking, place the bread slices onto a rack in the oven to crisp. Whip the goat's cheese with a little olive oil and, if liked, perhaps some yoghurt to make it lighter. Season with pepper to taste.

When the garlic is ready, serve with 2 or 3 croutons per person. I like to stack the garlic on a plate and put the goat's cheese in a deep, colourful bowl and let everyone help themselves. It also looks very elegant served on individual plates.

Recipe: easy to make

Vignettes from Simon Johnson's showroom at Pyrmont, Sydney. Olive oil tasting glasses on the far right are ready for a tasting, with the obligatory apple to cleanse the palate before proceeding.

Simon Johnson

Shopping for Quality

Bakers' sourdough, pure pork saucisson, clotted cream, Heidi Farm Gruyère, Latini spaghettini, Mariage Frères teas, Auschovies, sevruga caviar, fresh truffles and Valrhona chocolate—these are just some of the tantalising ingredients available from Simon Johnson's quality food store and delivery service. This treasure trove of some of the world's best food has been operating since the late 1980s, supplying restaurants, hotels, retailers and the public. The best of Australian olive oils and vinegars might sit beside the best from Spain, Italy and France; Western Australian anchovies rest alongside the Ortiz brand from Spain.

'Fifty to sixty per cent of my produce is Australian. If I can't source it here, I go elsewhere. My philosophy is simply the best quality—and quality of service.'

Simon is actually a trained chef. After working in various restaurants, however, he found himself teaming up with Barry McDonald to set up Paddington Fruit Market as a retail and wholesale trader. Richard Thomas and Gabrielle Kervella, two of Australia's leading farmhouse cheese makers, then approached him to distribute their cheese. He introduced a range of Italian products, including preserves, extra virgin olive oils and pasta. In 1991, he moved to a warehouse in Pyrmont and set up as Simon Johnson, Purveyor of Quality Foods. The range of produce has continued to expand and diversify due to Simon's commitment to purchasing food directly from the producers—both locally and

overseas. They are usually small, owner-operated businesses like his, run by people who share the same passion for excellence.

In 1998, Simon opened a store in Queen Street, Woollahra, and in Fitzroy, Melbourne, where there is a seminar room and fully equipped kitchen for the Talk, Eat, Drink seminars that have run so successfully in Sydney. They are hosted by well-known chefs and producers passionate and generous about sharing their knowledge. Simon also publishes a stunningly designed retail catalogue four times a year. Not only does it feature the food items, but it also contains fascinating editorial detail about the food, recipes, chefs and producers.

It has been a revelation for consumers—the difference between air-dried pasta and machine-dried, for instance; olive oil tastings; tea tastings;

cheese correctly stored in a humidified cool room and the marvellous flavour of cultured butter.

'I'm very fortunate because I love what I do—I'm driven by my stomach and stimulated by the people I supply to. I love meeting the small producers. I eat in their homes, learn about their food and their cultures. The job is always changing and never boring and I'm stimulated by quality.'

Marieke Brugman, chef and food teacher

Hara Kebab

INGREDIENTS

2 bunches of spinach, stalks removed
   and washed

500 g (1 lb) fresh ricotta

2 teaspoons garam masala

2 teaspoons ground mace

½ teaspoon freshly ground cardamom

¼ cup (30 g/1 oz) besan (chickpea) flour

2 green chillies, seeded

15 g (½ oz) fresh ginger, peeled

60 g (2 oz) roasted cashews, finely
   chopped

60 g (2 oz) shelled pistachios, finely
   chopped

pinch of sea salt

grapeseed or canola oil

These spinach cakes are inspired by a dish eaten at Dum Phukt, a restaurant in Delhi specialising in very delicate, steamed cuisine. The food in northwest India is fabulous and very different, as the chefs utilise all manner of indigenous winter desert plants.

Preheat the oven to 120°C (250°F). Blanch the spinach in small batches in boiling water until just wilted, then refresh in iced water. Drain and squeeze thoroughly to remove excess moisture. Weigh out 450 g (14½ oz) spinach.

Place a sheet of baking parchment on a wire rack set over a baking dish. Punch some holes in the parchment and place the ricotta on it. Make a foil-domed lid to seal the ricotta and place in the oven for 1½–2 hours, until it is dry. Weigh out 250 g (8 oz) ricotta.

Combine the garam masala, mace and cardamom with the besan flour and dry-roast in a non-stick frying pan or skillet over medium heat. The spices will smell aromatic and the flour will colour slightly.

In a food processor, blend the chilli and ginger to a fine paste. Add the spinach and blend into a fine purée. (Repeat the process in a blender for a very fine purée.) Add the ricotta and combine. Transfer the spinach mixture to a bowl. Add the roasted flour, cashews, pistachios and sea salt, and combine well.

Line a baking sheet with baking parchment. Using a 7.5-cm (3-inch) biscuit (cookie) cutter, lightly oiled, form the spinach cakes. Refrigerate for 1 hour to set.

Preheat the oven to 220°C (450°F). Brush a film of grapeseed or canola oil in a non-stick pan and heat. Carefully cook the spinach cakes on each side briefly until a light golden colour. Gently place the cakes back onto the baking parchment and place in the hot oven until heated through. Serve at once.

Serves 6 Recipe: medium complexity

Michael Moore, chef

Vine Tomato Salad with Bocconcini

INGREDIENTS

CAPER AND ANCHOVY DRESSING

100 g (3½ oz) Ortiz anchovies

2 tablespoons Italian capers

4 golden shallots, chopped

3 tablespoons olive oil

2 tablespoons vegetable oil

1 tablespoon red wine vinegar

grated zest of 2 lemons

1 teaspoon freshly ground black pepper

1 teaspoon fresh thyme leaves

8 vine-ripened tomatoes

100 g (3½ oz) bocconcini, made from
  buffalo milk

½ cup fresh basil leaves, torn

12 rocket (arugula) leaves

sea salt and freshly ground black pepper

For the maximum flavour from tomatoes, store them at room temperature. Add four extra, broken Ortiz salted anchovies and 2 tablespoons of capers for a more robust flavour if liked.

To make the caper and anchovy dressing, place all the ingredients into a blender or food processor. Purée for 2 minutes, or until smooth.

Plunge the tomatoes into boiling water for 5 seconds, then place immediately in cold water. Peel and discard the skins, and place the tomatoes on a cloth. Slice the tomatoes thickly and divide among 4 serving dishes. Cut the bocconcini into wedges and lay at random over the tomato. Sprinkle the basil and rocket leaves at random. Drizzle the caper and anchovy dressing over, and season with sea salt and pepper. Add some extra capers and anchovies, if liked.

Serves 4 Recipe: easy to make

Sue Fairlie-Cuninghame, food writer

Green Papaya Salad

INGREDIENTS

500 g (1 lb) green papaya (pawpaw),
  peeled and seeded

3 small green chillies, seeded and finely
  chopped

2 red shallots, peeled and finely sliced

1 small bunch fresh coriander (Chinese
  parsley) leaves, stems and scraped
  roots, finely chopped

DRESSING

5 tablespoons freshly squeezed lime juice

1 teaspoon soft palm sugar (jaggery)

2–3 trimmed inner hearts lemon grass,
  very finely sliced

2–3 teaspoons Thai fish sauce (nam pla)

1–2 teaspoons crushed fresh ginger

1–2 fresh kaffir lime leaves, shredded

Serve Green Papaya Salad with Barbecued Duck Curry (page 121) or fresh oysters or prawns (shrimp). The dressing is the highlight. It is important to shred every ingredient as finely as possible for this salad.

Very finely julienne the papaya or pass it through a Japanese mandoline. Toss the papaya into a bowl with the chilli, shallot and coriander.

To make the dressing, put all the ingredients into a screw-top jar and shake until well mixed, adjusting the flavour to taste.

To serve, pour half of the dressing over the salad ingredients and toss well. Serve while the salad is freshly made. The salt in the fish sauce may make the papaya limp and wet if it is left to stand.

Serves 4 Recipe: easy to make

Marieke Brugman, chef and food teacher

Tomato Tarte Tatin

INGREDIENTS

15 large egg (Italian plum) tomatoes

2 teaspoons sumak (available from Middle Eastern speciality shops)

2 teaspoons Maldon sea salt flakes

2 teaspoons freshly ground black pepper

4 teaspoons sugar

4 red onions, finely sliced

⅔ cup (100 mL/3½ fl oz) virgin olive oil

20 basil leaves, finely shredded

50 fresh French tarragon leaves or chervil or flat-leaf parsley

200 g (7 oz) Mt Emu Creek Romney Fresca sheep's milk cheese or creamy feta or firm goat's cheese

PASTRY

1 cup (125 g/4 oz) plain (all-purpose) flour

100 g (3½ oz) unsalted butter, finely cubed

¼ cup (60 mL/2 fl oz) sour cream

This is one of Howqua Dale's most popular dishes—it allows the flavours of summer to linger. It started as a way of increasing flavour with winter tomatoes. The lightly caramelised tomatoes harmonise with feta, buffalo mozzarella or goat's cheese, drizzled with fine olive oil and basil. The foolproof pastry is one we have used for twenty years and is always crisp.

Preheat the oven to 120°C (250°F). Split the tomatoes lengthwise and place them, skin-side down, in a single layer on a baking sheet lined with baking parchment. Evenly scatter the sumak, salt flakes, pepper and sugar over the cut surface. Place in the oven for about 4 hours, until the tomatoes have semi-dried and lightly caramelised. They should look like very plump apricots.

Combine the onion and olive oil in a large frying pan or skillet over medium heat. Cook until the onion is well caramelised and much reduced in volume. Strain through a sieve and reserve the oil for your vinaigrette.

To make the pastry, combine the flour, butter and sour cream in a food processor and pulse only, just until the mixture knots into a ball around the blade. Pat into a flat, circular disc. Cover with plastic wrap and refrigerate for at least 1 hour before rolling out.

To assemble the tarte, line a 28-cm (11-inch) non-stick circular mould, 4 cm (¼ inch) deep, with a circle of baking parchment—a Le Creuset frying pan works just as well. Place the tomatoes, flesh side down, in tight, concentric circles on the bottom of the mould. Scatter the basil and tarragon over the tomatoes. Distribute the drained onions evenly over the tomatoes. Slice the cheese finely and scatter over the onions.

Roll the pastry out into a circle 2 cm (¾ inch) wider than the mould. Place the pastry on top of the mould. Trim the edge with scissors and tuck into the sides of the mould to form a lip around the tomatoes. Return the tarte to the refrigerator for at least 30 minutes before baking.

Preheat the oven to 220°C (425°F). Bake the tarte in the oven for about 25 minutes, until the pastry is golden and crisp. Invert the tarte onto a large, flat plate and serve within 30 minutes. Accompany with a salad dressed with the reserved oil from the onions and some fine red wine vinegar and freshly ground black pepper.

Serves 10–12 Recipe: medium complexity

Chapter 3
Meat and Poultry

Alan Saunders

Meat and Poultry

The men who work the stockyards just outside the town of Roma in southwest Queensland rise early and have steak for breakfast. There are two long tables in the canteen with benches to sit on and you reserve your place by leaving your Akubra on the table while you go to the serving hatch to order something to eat. The steak is cut thin, grilled on a hot plate and served with toast.

Meat for breakfast, meat for dinner, meat for tea, meat three times a day—this used to be a way of life in Australia, just as it was (and still is) in other places where European cattle have transformed the landscape, such as Texas and Argentina. In this country, though, it's sheep as much as cattle that have fed the insatiable hunger for animal flesh.

Nowadays, though, Australians have lost some of their enthusiasm for these monotonous pleasures and, at the same time, have at last turned their attention to indigenous animals such as the kangaroo, which are good to eat and which do less harm to the Australian topsoil than the hard-hoofed imports.

All in all, then, a simple baked dinner, though very welcome from time to time, is no longer quite enough. (Incidentally, Australia seems to be alone in this use of the word 'baked'. It's quite accurate—roasting is done in front of an open fire, while what goes on in an oven is called baking—but it depends on a distinction which the rest of the world appears to have forgotten.)

Marieke Brugman's recipe for Pigeon Rice (page 116) is a good example of what has been happening with the use of meat in the best Australian cooking. This is a Portuguese dish (Arroz de Pombas Bravos, in the original) and it's offered here modestly in all its Portuguese simplicity: for the most part, it has not been adapted, modernised or otherwise tarted up for the Australian kitchen. On the other hand, Marieke is very clear as to what sort of bird is to go with the rice. 'My favourite poultry is squab from Ian Millburn at Glenloth in the Mallee,' she writes. 'He is one of many local heroes …'

In other words, we have learned to care about where our meat comes from and to value the people who prepare it for us. Even the simple pleasures of a good steak are now more refined: the best steak restaurants will tell you where the steak comes from and on what it has been fed. The cattle grower and the sheep producer are no longer just the custodians of vast, anonymous herds or flocks which they periodically ship off somewhere else to be butchered and sold. They're doing the value-adding themselves—and everybody is benefiting.

On Monday we've mutton, with damper and tea;

On Tuesday, tea, damper and mutton,

Such dishes I'm certain all men must agree

Are fit for peer, peasant, or glutton.

On Wednesday, we've damper, with mutton and tea;

On Thursday, tea, mutton, and damper,

On Friday we've mutton, tea, damper while we

With our flocks over hill and dale scamper.

PREVIOUS PAGE: Paul Merrony's Lamb Shanks with Red Capsicum, Black Olives and Tomatoes. 'Lamb shanks, when poached or braised, must rate as one of the most succulent cuts of meat around. It also rates as one of my favourite dishes. Here the shanks are served with sauce Basquaise. The sweetness of the red capsicums (peppers) and the spiciness of the olives contrast well with the fleshy and juicy shanks.'

Paul Merrony, chef

Lamb Shanks with Red Capsicum,
Black Olives and Tomatoes

INGREDIENTS

8 lamb shanks, about 8 cm (3 inches) long
1 small carrot, peeled
1 stalk celery
2 small onions, peeled
salt
10 black peppercorns

SAUCE BASQUAISE

1 tablespoon olive oil
18 ripe tomatoes, cored, blanched and peeled
155 g (5 oz) kalamata olives, pitted, blanched and quartered
2 large red capsicums (sweet peppers), peeled under running water after a quick roast in oil in the oven, then julienned
freshly ground black pepper
a little sugar, optional

2 tablespoons freshly chopped chives

Served with a steaming plate of floury potatoes and a green salad, this dish is great for lunch on a cold winter's day.

Cover the shanks with cold water in a large saucepan and blanch. Drain in a colander and wash the shanks and the saucepan to remove any resultant scum. Return the shanks to the saucepan, cover with cold water once more, bring back to the boil and then skim. Add the carrot, celery, one of the onions, salt to taste and peppercorns. Reboil and then simmer for about 1–1½ hours, or until the shanks are tender (test with a skewer after 1 hour), and leave in the cooking juice.

While the shanks are cooking, make the sauce Basquaise. In a large saucepan, sweat the remaining onion in the olive oil until translucent. Cut the tomatoes in half and squeeze out the seeds. If you do this under running water, you must then drain well. Next, chop but do not purée the tomatoes in the food processor or blender. Put this pulp into the saucepan with the onion, bring to the boil and simmer for 10 minutes. Add the olives and red capsicum, and season with salt and pepper. Add a little sugar if desired, to help remove some of the bitterness which cooked tomatoes can have. Cook gently for a further 15 minutes or until the sauce is thick, stirring occasionally.

To serve, heat 4 plates and put 2 hot shanks on each plate. Spoon the sauce over the shanks and sprinkle with the chives. Serve at once.

Serves 4 Recipe: medium complexity

Michael Lambie, chef

Braised Ox Cheek
with Winter Vegetables

INGREDIENTS

8 whole ox cheeks, about 200 g (7 oz), trimmed of any excess fat

2 carrots, roughly chopped

2 onions, roughly chopped

2 leeks, well rinsed and roughly chopped

½ head celery, roughly chopped

½ garlic bulb, roughly chopped

¼ bunch fresh thyme leaves, chopped

1 bay leaf, roughly chopped

4 cups (1 litre/1¾ imp. pints) Shiraz or other red wine

salt and freshly ground black pepper

20 cups (5 litres/8 imp. pints) beef stock

12 baby carrots, peeled

12 baby turnips, peeled

12 kipfler or other small, waxy potatoes, cut into barrels

12 golden shallots, peeled

butter

chervil sprigs to garnish

A favourite dish to eat in front of the log fire in the heart of winter.

Place the ox cheeks, carrot, onion, leek, celery, garlic, thyme and bay leaf in a bowl. Cover with the red wine and marinate for 24 hours.

Strain the meat and vegetables from the wine. First, pour the wine into a saucepan, place over high heat and reduce by half. While this is happening, pat the meat dry and season well with salt and pepper. In a very hot frying pan or skillet, seal the meat until it is brown and caramelised all over.

In a large saucepan, cook the marinated vegetables with a little cooking oil over medium heat. When the wine and meat are ready, add to the vegetables and then cover with the beef stock. Bring to the boil, then simmer gently for an hour or two until the meat is ready—that is, when the meat breaks apart easily.

Remove the meat from the cooking liquor and set aside. The cooking liquor can now be strained and placed back onto the stove to reduce over high heat. It is ready when it resembles a thick syrup.

While the sauce is reducing, the vegetables can be prepared. The baby carrots, turnips and potatoes need to be cooked separately, in boiling, salted water, until tender. Cook the shallots in a 50:50 water and butter emulsion until tender.

To serve, place the meat in the wine sauce and reheat gently over low heat. Warm the vegetables in a little butter, salt and pepper. Serve the meat and sauce surrounded by the vegetables in 4 large, flat bowls and garnish with the chervil.

Serves 4 Recipe: medium complexity

LEFT: Braised Ox Cheek with Winter Vegetables. A hearty winter dish, very rich and robust. The beef is cooked slowly until it is very tender and almost falling apart. Use a really strong Shiraz and, if beef cheeks are unavailable, use beef blade.

RIGHT: Peter Doyle's Slow-cooked Beef Cheeks with Celeriac and Field Mushrooms (page 100). 'We like to have a dish that is slow-cooked for most months of the year. Garnish with parsnip chips if liked.'

Peter Doyle, chef

Slow-cooked Beef Cheeks
with Celeriac and Field Mushrooms

INGREDIENTS

3 tablespoons olive oil

6 beef cheeks, trimmed of fat

5 tablespoons white wine

6 cups (1.5 litres/2½ imp. pints) veal
stock

1 onion, peeled and sliced roughly

2 carrots, peeled and cut into 2-cm
(¾-inch) rounds

2 stalks celery, cut into 3-cm (1-inch)
lengths

1 bouquet garni (thyme, parsley, bay
leaves and peppercorns)

1 bulb garlic, halved horizontally

2 bulbs celeriac, peeled, cut into rounds,
blanched and refreshed

100 g (3½ oz) broad (fava) beans, peeled
and shelled, or fresh green peas,
blanched and refreshed

6 field mushrooms, trimmed, cut into
rounds and roasted

Beef cheeks are a great cut for slow cooking because they hold up very well.

Preheat the oven to 160°C (325°F). Heat the oil in a large frying pan or skillet over medium heat and seal the beef cheeks on all sides until browned. Remove the cheeks and place on a rack over a baking pan. Pour any remaining oil from the frying pan and deglaze the pan with the white wine over high heat. Add the veal stock and bring to the boil.

Place the beef cheeks in a clean saucepan or braising dish just large enough to contain the cheeks. Surround with the onion, carrot, celery, bouquet garni and garlic. Pour over the hot veal stock and place in the oven to braise for 2–2½ hours, depending on the size of the cheeks. The meat should be very soft and falling off the bone.

Remove the cheeks from the oven and set aside. Strain the stock through a fine strainer and leave to settle for a few minutes. Ladle any fat off from the surface of stock, pour the stock into a clean saucepan and reduce by half. Keep warm until needed.

The cheeks can now be left to cool down to be reheated later or returned to the oven with a little veal stock to reheat at 200°C (400°F). While reheating, baste the cheeks every few minutes with some of the hot stock to give the cheeks a nice golden brown glow.

When the cheeks are warmed through, reheat the celeriac rounds and broad beans by steaming them and reheat the field mushrooms in the oven. To serve, place a field mushroom in the centre of each warmed bowl, top with a celeriac round, place a warm beef cheek on each celeriac round and spoon over the sauce. Scatter the broad beans around the beef cheeks and serve immediately.

Serves 6 Recipe: medium complexity

Jacques Reymond, chef

Lamb's Brains
with a Papillote of Celeriac
and a Warm Salad of Rocket and Baby Spinach

INGREDIENTS

1 celeriac, peeled and julienned

8 red shallots, sliced

4 cloves garlic

155 g (5 oz) roasted hazelnuts, crushed

4 sprigs fresh wild thyme

salt and freshly ground black pepper

2½ tablespoons hazelnut oil

5 tablespoons pure virgin olive oil

scant cup (100 g/3½ oz) Parmesan
   shavings

1 tablespoon balsamic vinegar

handful of rocket (arugula) leaves

handful of baby spinach leaves

pine nuts to garnish

fresh coriander (Chinese parsley) sprigs

2 red chillies, chopped

LAMB'S BRAINS

4 lamb's brains, soaked overnight and
   cleaned of all blood vessels

2 tablespoons olive oil

2 tablespoons butter

1 tablespoon blanched ginger, julienned

1 tablespoon diced tomatoes

1 tablespoon baby capers

1 tablespoon balsamic vinegar

5 tablespoons reduced veal juices (saved
   from a veal roast or use deglazed beef
   stock)

Lamb brains are a very rich offal, so it is nice to contrast them with the lightness and freshness of celeriac, rocket and spinach.

To make the papillote, preheat the oven to 220°C (425°F). Lay down a large sheet of foil and place the celeriac on the foil. Sprinkle with the shallots, garlic, hazelnuts and thyme, then season with salt and pepper. Pour the hazelnut oil and 4 tablespoons of the olive oil over the celeriac. Place the Parmesan shavings on top and cover with another sheet of foil. Seal tightly. Cook in the oven for 10 minutes.

Open the papillote, place the celeriac on warm serving plates and add the vinegar to the natural juices which are in the foil. Pour this juice over the celeriac. Use this as the base along with a warm salad of rocket and baby spinach, which has been tossed in a wok with the remaining 1 tablespoon oil until just wilted.

At the same time, cook the lamb's brains. Braise in the hot oven for 10 minutes in a heatproof dish with the olive oil and butter. Deglaze the natural cooking juices with the ginger, tomato, capers, balsamic vinegar and veal juices. Place the brains on top of the celeriac and salad, and pour the juices over. Top with the pine nuts, coriander sprigs and chilli. Serve immediately.

Serves 4 Recipe: Complex

Serge Dansereau, chef

Boiled Veal Shank
with Green Sauce

INGREDIENTS

VEAL SHANKS

4 veal shanks

1 carrot

1 onion

1 stalk celery

1 leek

1 bay leaf

fresh thyme

sea salt and 10 black peppercorns

5 litres (10 US pints/8 imp. pints) water

PASTA

250 g (8 oz) dried linguine

sea salt and freshly cracked black pepper

2 tablespoons butter

2 tablespoons grated pecorino or
Parmesan cheese, plus shavings to
garnish

GREEN SAUCE

1 bunch of rocket (arugula)

1 bunch of fresh basil

2 bunches of spinach

½ bunch of fresh flat-leaf parsley

1 roast onion (baked in its skin for
1 hour at 180°C/350°F)

6 cloves garlic (baked in foil for
80 minutes at 150°C/300°F)

juice of 2 lemons

scant cup (200 mL/7 fl oz) virgin
olive oil

sea salt and freshly ground black pepper

Italian cooking, in contrast to that of the French, can seem very disorganised. Out of that, however, comes a purity of ingredients. The Italians generally use fewer ingredients, but they understand the product and concentrate on enhancing the natural flavour.

To cook the veal shanks, place them in a tall saucepan and cover with cold water. Bring to the boil and simmer for 2 minutes. Discard the water and wash the shanks in cold water. Return to the saucepan, then add the vegetables, bay leaf, thyme, salt to taste and peppercorns. Cover with the water and simmer very gently for 3 hours. Remove the shanks carefully from the pan and strain the liquid and reserve to make a soup. If you are using the shanks later, wrap in plastic until ready to reheat, then place in the oven for 20 minutes at 150°C (300°F). Serve on the bone or, if preferred, pull the meat off the bones and serve without.

To cook the pasta, put plenty of salted water in a tall saucepan and bring to the boil. Cook the pasta until al dente. Drain well, place in a mixing bowl and add the butter, pecorino and pepper. Mix well in a swirling motion to achieve a nest of pasta.

To make the green sauce, quickly plunge the rocket, basil, spinach and parsley in boiling water, then immediately plunge into iced water. Drain and squeeze all the excess water out in a clean cloth. Peel the roast onion and chop in a food processor or blender with the spinach mixture, garlic and lemon juice. Transfer to a bowl and fold in the olive oil. Season with salt and pepper to taste.

To serve, roll a quarter of the linguine around a large serving fork to make a nice pasta mound. Place a mound on each warm plate beside a veal shank. Garnish with the pecorino shavings. Drizzle the shank with a touch of the green sauce and serve the rest on the side.

Serves 4 Recipe: medium complexity

RIGHT: Boiled Veal Shank with Green Sauce. The green sauce enhances the flavour and works to provide colour as well. A very homey dish made using a whole shank for a change.

Philip Johnson, chef

Lamb Rump

with Salad of Eggplant, Salted Lemon, Chilli and Watercress

INGREDIENTS

2 small eggplants (aubergines), cut into
   1.5-cm (¾-inch) slices
olive oil for brushing
salt and freshly ground black pepper
6 x 225 g (7 oz) lamb rumps, trimmed
   (leaving some fat)
1 bunch of watercress, picked, washed
   and dried
1 bunch of fresh coriander (Chinese
   parsley), picked, washed and dried
fresh chilli, to taste, seeded and chopped
1 red onion, sliced
2 teaspoons chopped preserved lemon

BALSAMIC VINAIGRETTE

1½ tablespoons balsamic vinegar
3½ tablespoons olive oil
pinch of sugar
salt and freshly ground black pepper
1 clove garlic, finely chopped
2 sprigs fresh thyme

Preheat the oven to 220°C (425°F). Brush the eggplant with oil and grill under a preheated hot griller (broiler) until cooked, about 5–8 minutes. Season the lamb and brush with oil. Place in a very hot, oiled ovenproof frying pan or skillet over high heat and seal on both sides. When the meat is a good colour, place the frying pan containing the lamb in the oven and cook for about 15 minutes for medium meat. Rest in a warm place for 10 minutes before slicing.

Meanwhile, make the balsamic vinaigrette by combining all the ingredients and whisking together.

To serve, combine the eggplant, watercress, coriander, chilli, onion and preserved lemon. Toss the balsamic vinaigrette through the salad, then place the salad on the serving plates and top with the sliced lamb rump. Drizzle a little vinaigrette over the meat.

Serves 6 Recipe: easy to make

Maggie Beer, food writer and producer

Polenta with
Smoked Kangaroo and Parmesan

INGREDIENTS

150 g (5 oz) Parmesan cheese

3 cups (750 mL/24 fl oz) chicken stock

185 g (6 oz) polenta

1½ teaspoons salt

butter

4 tablespoons extra virgin olive oil

200 g (7 oz) smoked kangaroo, very
thinly sliced

2 handfuls of rocket (arugula)

good-quality balsamic vinegar, optional

*This dish came from one of our Sunday nights with our restaurant 'family'.
I sometimes add goat's cheese as well.*

Preheat the oven to 150°C (300°F). Grate two-thirds of the Parmesan cheese and set aside. Heat the stock in a deep saucepan until simmering, then pour in the polenta and salt, stirring constantly. Stir the polenta over very gentle heat for about 20 minutes, until it begins to leave the sides of the pan, then add the grated Parmesan. Turn the polenta into an ovenproof bowl, dot with a little butter and place in the oven, covered, to keep warm.

When ready to serve, warm the olive oil gently in a frying pan or skillet, and toss the kangaroo in it quickly. The pan should not be too hot or the kangaroo will discolour and spoil. Turn the warm polenta out onto a serving platter and mound the kangaroo and rocket around it, then shave the remaining Parmesan over the lot with a vegetable peeler. Add a drizzle of balsamic vinegar, if desired.

Serves 4 Recipe: easy to make

Matthew Moran, chef

Pan-fried Chicken Breast
with Moroccan Eggplant and Baby Bok Choy

INGREDIENTS
MOROCCAN EGGPLANT

10 tomatoes, peeled and seeded

2 onions, diced

3 tablespoons olive oil

4 large eggplants (aubergines), diced

2 x 250-g (8-oz) jars mango chutney

4 cups (1 litre/1¾ imp. pints) chicken
stock

2 tablespoons ground cumin

2 tablespoons ground coriander

pinch of saffron threads

juice of 6 lemons

chopped coriander (Chinese parsley)

4 cloves garlic, crushed

4 cornfed chicken breasts, with skin on

2 tablespoons olive oil

4 baby bok choy, steamed

Preheat the oven to 180°C (350°F). To make the Moroccan eggplant, sweat the tomato and onion in the olive oil in a frying pan or skillet for 5 minutes. Add the eggplant, stir and then add the remaining 8 ingredients and cook for 10 minutes.

Pan-fry the chicken breasts in the olive oil in a hot frying pan or skillet, until golden brown. Place in the oven for about 15 minutes, then allow to rest for 10 minutes in a warm place before serving.

To serve, place the steamed baby bok choy on each warm serving plate, add some Moroccan eggplant and place a sliced chicken breast on top.

Serves 4 Recipe: easy to make

Dany Chouet

'I love simplicity above everything and pure flavour. The cooking and the produce have to be perfect. I like my palate to be hit by no more than two flavours—you need something to enhance the main item. It's very hard to do. I prefer simple, elegant, almost stark presentation.'

Dany Chouet was born in the Perigord region of southwest France. She grew up in a family with a

passion for food and, from a young age, she loved to cook the family meals. She studied fine arts in Paris and later worked as a photographer.

When Dany first came to Sydney, she was appalled at the standard of food and, a few months later, opened Upstairs with Monique and Michael Manners to instant success. Two years later, she opened Au Chabrol, which featured a more refined menu and again had packed tables every night. She sold Au Chabrol in 1976, helped the Manners start Glenella, then returned to France. There she met an Australian, Trish Hobbs.

Trish persuaded Dany to return to Australia and, in 1983, they found their dream house in the Blue Mountains and opened Cleopatra as an auberge, a place to stay and eat well. The restaurant grew afterwards. Dany's fine food and Trish's beautifully decorated interiors and garden achieve the charming mood of a colonial family home. Dany's French food is traditional yet innovative, country yet refined, and presented with a unique lightness of

touch. *'My passion is French country cooking. Four hundred years of recipes from peasants and the bourgeoisie can't be wrong. It still exists.'*

The warm atmosphere and friendly service, and the highly acclaimed food make it one of the most desirable out-of-town destinations for food lovers. A fusion of the best of Australia and France.

ABOVE LEFT: Parfait de Foie de Canard et sa Salade (page 68). A very rich parfait with duck livers. Add fresh herb flowers to the salad when you have them.

ABOVE: Poussin aux Raisins (page 121). Garlic and grapes go well together—they inspired this.

ABOVE RIGHT: Oysters and Braised Baby Squid Noodle Salad with Soy, Rocket Oil and Ginger (page 69).

RIGHT: Anise-flavoured Crispy Duck with Kipfler Potatoes, Beetroot and Chervil (page 117).

Dany Chouet and Ralph Potter

Out of Town

Ralph Potter

'I think regional food in Australia should be city, coastal and country food—I want to eat seafood on the coast; when I'm in the country, I'm in the mood for slow-cooked food; and, in the city, I expect multicultural, more diverse food. I think that's an achievable goal. It suits the modern world as you can't turn back the clock. Food has to fit the location and the climate and be sensitive to the location.'

Ralph Potter believes passionately in using top-quality produce for his restaurant, Darleys, at Lilianfels in the Blue Mountains west of Sydney. He is always searching for that extra special quality in  seasonal food. 'Living in the country makes you more aware of the seasons. We have lost the impact of seasonal food now that food travels so widely—game birds, asparagus and mushrooms enjoyed around the area of production are on the whole, a lost aspect of food.'

Ralph started his career in England and then tried to gain further experience in France. Finding many doors closed to a young English chef, he was advised to get himself noticed—so he entered the Robert Carrier Chef of the Year Award and won. Two weeks later, he started at the Les Princes Restaurant in Paris. Ralph went on to work in Geneva, London, Sydney and Alsace. Eventually, he returned to Australia to run Darley's, specialising in modern Australian regional food—wonderful food for which it is well worth travelling.

'I like to make a style of food that suits the materials and environment. The emphasis is on slow-cooked food which is not necessarily heavy. I like to play with different textures and flavours, making my own version. I'm spontaneous and, as I see the weather warming up, I begin to change the menus. I find cooking very enjoyable—you make good food when you're happy.'

Raymond Kersh and Jennice Kersh, chef and restaurateur

Cornfed Chicken Breast
Stuffed with Quandongs on Wild Mushrooms, Warrigal Greens and Native Thyme Broth

INGREDIENTS

4 cornfed chicken breasts

200 g (7 oz) quandongs or peaches

75 g (2½ oz) butter

8 cups warrigal greens or silverbeet
   (Swiss chard), blanched

salt and freshly ground black pepper

4 pieces of pig's caul, about 20 cm
   (8 inch) square

1 tablespoon olive oil

1 small onion, diced

1 clove garlic

100 g (3½ oz) Swiss brown mushrooms,
   sliced

45 g (1½ oz) shiitake mushrooms, sliced

45 g (1½ oz) shijemi mushrooms, sliced

NATIVE THYME BROTH

3¼ cups (825 mL/26 fl oz) chicken stock

½ teaspoon native thyme

1 teaspoon ginger

1 stalk lemon grass, soft part only,
   chopped

2 teaspoons ground coriander

fresh coriander (Chinese parsley) leaves
   to garnish

salt and freshly ground black pepper

Preheat the oven to 200°C (400°F). Butterfly the chicken breast into halves. Sauté the quandongs in a frying pan or skillet in half the butter. When soft, place a quarter of the cooked quandongs in the middle of each chicken breast. Place ½ cup of the warrigal greens on top of each pile of quandongs and season with salt and pepper to taste.

Roll up each chicken breast and then wrap each one in a piece of the pig's caul. Pan-fry the chicken in the olive oil over medium heat until browned, then bake in the oven for 10–12 minutes. Remove pan from the oven and keep warm.

Sauté the onion with the remaining butter, then add the garlic, three types of mushrooms and the remaining warrigal greens.

To make the thyme broth, place the chicken stock, native thyme, ginger, lemon grass and coriander in a large saucepan and bring to the boil. Reduce in volume by half over high heat, then strain through a fine sieve. Season to taste with salt and pepper. Remove the chicken from the pan and slice into 4 rounds. Place the mushroom mixture in the middle of each warmed serving bowl and place the chicken on top. Pour the broth around the outside until it reaches the mushrooms. Garnish with coriander leaves and serve immediately.

Serves 4 Recipe: medium complexity

Vic Cherikoff, native Australian food providore

Barbecued Paperbark Chicken

INGREDIENTS

1 piece of thinned paperbark, dampened

2 tablespoons cooking oil

1 pork loin fillet, trimmed of fat

2 tablespoons Munthari and lemon
myrtle chutney or apple sauce with a
twist of lime

1 red capsicum (sweet pepper), cut into
strips or 1 red chilli, thinly sliced

salt

2 serves steamed rice

¼ teaspoon mountain pepper or freshly
ground black pepper

green salad leaves of choice

½ teaspoon aniseed myrtle

Paperbark torn from the melaleuca tree makes a great wrapping—it imparts a delicate smokiness from the oils that are released when it is heated. Paperbark is also sold in rolls. Using paperbark is the easiest way to smoke and cook meats, especially white meats, which can simply be wrapped in bark and cooked on a barbecue or in a pan. Paperbark is low in tannins and, although indigestible, is harmless when eaten.

Thin out a piece of paperbark about 20 x 38 cm (8 x 15 inches). Choose the side of the paperbark that has the least stringy fibre and brush with a little oil to prevent any bark from sticking to the meat.

Cut the pork fillet lengthwise by cutting back into the fillet, but not all the way through, to cut the loin into a long, thin steak. Open out and spoon in the chutney, then place the capsicum along the length of the slit. Season with salt to taste. Roll up the loin over the filling and cut the whole loin into 2 equal pieces. Place side by side on the oiled paperbark, wrap the bark over lengthwise and then fold the ends over to finish. Tie the parcel with natural fibre string.

Place the paperbark parcel on a hot hotplate over a preheated barbecue and cook until the parcel is smoking. (The parcel can also be cooked in a dry pan on the stove top, but a cast-iron frying pan or skillet must be used as bark damages stainless steel.) Continue cooking until all sides of the parcel are blackened completely. Test for doneness by feel—the meat should feel just firm and spring back when squeezed, then leave to rest for 5 minutes in a warm place.

To serve, remove any remaining string, unfold the paperbark ends and cut these off close to the fillet. Unfold the bark further and fold back, inverting the bark under the fillet. Slice the fillet and transfer the pork and paperbark wrap to each plate. Serve with steamed rice generously seasoned with mountain pepper and a mixed green salad sprinkled with aniseed myrtle.

Serves 2 Recipe: easy to make

Luke Mangan, chef

Salt-crusted Breast of Chicken,
Jerusalem Artichoke Purée and Leek

INGREDIENTS
SALT CRUST

2¾ cups (340 g/11 oz) plain
  (all-purpose) flour

125 g (4 oz) rock salt

1 teaspoon thyme leaves

1 egg

⅔ cup (155 mL/5 fl oz) water

2 skinless chicken breasts (make sure
  you use the best-quality free-range
  chicken you can find, such as Barossa
  Valley)

250 g (8 oz) Jerusalem artichokes,
  peeled

100 g (3½ oz) waxy potatoes, peeled

2 cups (500 mL/16 fl oz) milk

salt and freshly ground black pepper

1 large or 2 medium leeks, sliced
  lengthwise

1 tablespoon butter, plus extra for
  serving

finest quality extra virgin olive oil,
  optional

*Jerusalem artichoke and leeks are my favourite vegetables and these rustic vegetables
are so simple to prepare. The sweetness of the artichokes, the sharpness of the leeks and
the saltiness of the crusted chicken blend together harmoniously.*

To make the salt crust, mix the flour and salt together with the thyme, then add
the egg and water. Knead together to form a ball of dough and let it rest a minute
in the refrigerator while making the artichoke purée.

Sear the chicken on a char grill or in a hot frying pan or skillet until golden
brown on both sides. Set aside to cool.

To make the artichoke purée, roughly chop the artichokes and potato. Cover
with the milk and a little salt, and cook for about 30 minutes, or until soft. Drain
well, purée and place in a saucepan over low heat to evaporate the excess liquid.
Keep warm.

Preheat the oven to 200°C (400°F). Roll out the salt crust to about 2 cm
(¾ inch) thick onto a floured surface. Divide the crust in two and place one
chicken breast in the centre of one half of the crust. Wrap into a pasty shape.
Repeat with the other chicken breast. Place on a greased baking sheet and bake
in the oven for 15 minutes. Remove the sheet from the oven and set aside for
2–3 minutes before breaking open the salt crust.

Meanwhile, place the leeks in boiling, salted water for 30 seconds. Drain and
sauté in a frying pan with the butter until coated.

To serve, slice each chicken breast on an angle into 3 or 4 pieces. Add a knob
of butter to the artichoke purée and season to taste with salt and pepper. Spoon
the purée onto the centre of each serving plate, and place the sliced chicken breast
over each serving. Arrange the leeks around the outside, season and drizzle a little
oil around each plate, if liked.

Serves 2 Recipe: medium complexity

LEFT: Salt-crusted Breast of Chicken, Jerusalem
Artichoke Purée and Leeks. This recipe takes
advantage of an old-fashioned French technique.
The salt crust enhances the flavour of the chicken
breast, giving it an earthiness and also keeping
it moist.

Liam Tomlin, chef

Roast Stuffed Chicken Legs
with Cèpe Cream Sauce

INGREDIENTS

4 chicken legs

salt and freshly ground black pepper

2 teaspoons unsalted butter

225 g (7 oz) button mushrooms, finely chopped

1 large onion, diced

1 clove garlic, finely chopped

100 g (3½ oz) bacon, rind removed and finely diced

2 small chicken breasts, skinned and minced

1 egg

2 teaspoons chopped fresh herbs, such as thyme, parsley and chives

225 g (7 oz) pig's caul, soaked in cold water for 24 hours

2 tablespoons extra virgin olive oil

45 g (1½ oz) button mushrooms or a selection of morels, oyster, cèpes, trompette de la mort, girolles if available, left whole

a little olive oil

CEPE CREAM SAUCE

30 g (1 oz) dried cèpes

2½ tablespoons Madeira

2½ tablespoons port

2 cups (500 mL/16 fl oz) veal stock

1 cup (250 mL/8 fl oz) light (single) cream

salt and freshly ground white pepper

At Banc, we serve the chicken on a garlic pomme purée, but this chicken is also beautiful cold, sliced and served with a salad, some aïoli and some nice crusty bread.

The chicken legs must be boned first—a sharp boning knife will make this easier. Take your time with this as it is important not to cut through the skin. Lay the leg skin side down and cut along the thigh bone, scrape down the bone towards the joint and the thigh meat will come away from the bone easily. Continue until the bone is free of all meat. Keep the point of the knife close to the knuckle joint and cut around it carefully. Force the meat from the drumstick with your knife until you can grip the bone. Pull the bone as you continue to scrape, then pull the bone hard, this will turn the drumstick inside out and make it easy to remove any sinew. Slice across the skin that is holding the bone. Repeat the process with the remaining legs. Turn the legs back so they lie skin-side down, then season with salt and pepper.

To make the stuffing, melt 1 teaspoon of the butter in a frying pan or skillet, and add the mushrooms. Cook until the mushrooms become totally dry. Remove from the heat and allow to cool. Heat the remaining 1 teaspoon butter in another frying pan and cook the onion, garlic and bacon for a few minutes until softened, without colouring. Allow to cool. Place the minced chicken in a mixing bowl with the mushrooms and the onion mixture. Add the egg and herbs, and season to taste with salt and pepper. Combine thoroughly. Fill the boned legs with this stuffing, using enough to reshape the legs to their original form.

Squeeze the pig's caul dry and lay out on your work surface. Place the chicken legs in the centre and wrap the caul around them. Refrigerate for at least 1 hour to set—the legs are then ready to roast. Preheat the oven to 200°C (400°F). Heat a frying pan with the olive oil and seal the legs until they are golden brown all over. Transfer onto a baking sheet and cook in the oven for 20–25 minutes. Test with a skewer—if the juices run clear, the chicken is cooked.

Meanwhile, soak the cèpes in the Madeira and port for 1 hour. Place the steeped cèpes in a saucepan with the soaking liquid and cook until the alcohol becomes a syrupy consistency. Pour over the veal stock and reduce in volume by half. Add the cream and bring the sauce back to the boil, reducing it to a consistency that coats the back of a spoon. Season to taste with salt and white pepper, and pass through a fine sieve, pressing on the cèpes to extract as much of their flavour as possible.

To serve, sauté the button mushrooms in a little olive oil until golden brown and season to taste. Place the chicken legs on a bed of garlic mashed potato or potato gratin, spoon the mushrooms around and then pour the sauce over the chicken.

Serves 4 Recipe: complex

Maggie Beer, food writer and food producer

Boned Chicken
Stuffed with Giblets and Prosciutto

INGREDIENTS

STUFFING

100 g (3½ oz) chicken giblets

100 g (3½ oz) chicken hearts

butter

2 tablespoons freshly chopped herbs,
    preferably rosemary and marjoram

freshly ground black pepper

1 large onion, roughly chopped

2 cups (250 g/8 oz) stale breadcrumbs

extra virgin olive oil

200 g (7 oz) prosciutto, finely sliced

1 teaspoon Dijon mustard

½ cup (125 mL/4 fl oz) verjuice

16 cups (4 litres/6½ imp. pints) jellied
    chicken stock

1.5 kg (3 lb) free-range chicken, boned

salt

Use a Barossa chicken or the best quality free-range chicken you can buy. Verjuice is a gentle acidulant. Its great advantage is adding acid without dominating flavours.

Preheat the oven to 230°C (450°F). To make the stuffing, cook the giblets and hearts in a little butter in a frying pan or skillet with the herbs and a grinding of pepper, then chop them finely and set aside. Sweat the onion in butter over gentle heat in the wiped-out pan, then add to the giblet mixture. Toast the breadcrumbs with a little olive oil in the oven until golden, watching that they don't burn. Add the prosciutto, mustard and breadcrumbs to the giblet mixture.

To make the boned chicken, reduce the verjuice by half over high heat. Pour the reduced verjuice and the stock into a deep saucepan and heat until warm. Flatten out the boned chicken and spread it with the stuffing, then roll up the chicken and wrap in muslin or cheesecloth. Put the stuffed bird into the stock—it is important that at least three-quarters of the bird is immersed. Poach for 20 minutes at a very gentle simmer, then turn the bird over and poach for another 20 minutes. Remove the bird and wrap in foil to rest for 30 minutes. Reduce the poaching liquid over high heat to a sauce. Slice the stuffed chicken and serve with the sauce and a dollop of Salsa Verde (Green Sauce, page 102).

Serves 4 Recipe: medium complexity

Stefano Manfredi, chef

Chicken Palermo Style

INGREDIENTS

DRESSING

juice and zest of 5 lemons

½ cup fresh oregano leaves, chopped

2 cups fresh parsley leaves, chopped

8 cloves garlic, crushed

1 cup (250 mL/8 fl oz) virgin olive oil

salt and freshly ground black pepper

CHICKEN

2 best free-range chickens, cut into legs
    and breasts

salt and freshly ground black pepper

baby rocket (arugula) leaves

16 red radishes

A nice summer dish, fresh and simple—buy a really tender free-range chicken.

To make the dressing, put the lemon zest in a small stainless steel saucepan with some water and bring to the boil. Remove from the heat, strain and refresh. Repeat the process twice more. Squeeze out the excess water and roughly chop the zest. Mix the oregano, parsley and garlic with the olive oil and lemon juice. Do not make this more than an hour or two before using as the lemon will oxidize and go off.

To make the chicken, preheat the oven to 220°C (425°F) and roast the seasoned chicken pieces in a greased baking pan for 15–20 minutes. Cut each leg into thigh and drumstick, and the breasts into two pieces.

Divide the rocket and red radishes among 8 serving plates. In a large bowl, toss the chicken in the dressing. Season with salt and pepper to taste and toss again. Place on top of the rocket and radish, and serve immediately.

Serves 8 Recipe: easy to make

Philippe Mouchel, chef

Rabbit Tagine

INGREDIENTS

1.5 kg (3 lb) rabbit

½ onion

½ carrot

bouquet garni

5 cups (1.25 litres/2 imp. pints) water

salt and freshly ground black pepper

1 cup (250 mL/8 fl oz) olive oil

1 cinnamon stick

1 teaspoon ground cumin

1 teaspoon ground ginger

pinch of saffron threads

1 vanilla bean

250 g (8 oz) glazed apricots, finest
    quality

2 small red chillies

1 cup (155 g/5 oz) small black olives

1 red capsicum (sweet pepper), seeded
    and thickly julienned

2 medium brown onions, sliced

cooked soft polenta to serve

coriander (Chinese parsley) sprigs to
    garnish

I wanted to try something different, so I made this Middle Eastern tagine with rabbit instead of lamb and soft polenta instead of couscous. It is perfumed with cinnamon, cumin, ginger, saffron and vanilla.

To joint the rabbit, separate at the leg joints, then cut the legs in half. Cut the loin into two sections through the backbone and the rib cage into two sections along the backbone. Make a stock with the leftover rabbit bones by adding the onion, carrot, bouquet garni and water to the bones in a large saucepan. Season with salt and pepper, and cook over medium heat for 1½ hours. Remove from the heat, strain and remove any fat from the top using absorbent kitchen paper.

Over high heat, seal the rabbit pieces in some of the olive oil in a deep frying pan or skillet. Season with salt and pepper, and then add the cinnamon, cumin, ginger, saffron and vanilla—one ingredient at a time—making sure the meat absorbs the spices. Add the rabbit stock with the apricot, chillies, olives and capsicum. Add the remaining olive oil and simmer for 30 minutes. Sauté the brown onion in a clean frying pan or skillet for 15 minutes until it is very soft. After the rabbit has simmered for 30 minutes, place the meat in a tagine dish or a heatproof serving dish. Add the sauce and garnish with the onion confit on top. Cover and simmer for another 10 minutes. Serve with the soft polenta, garnished with a few coriander sprigs.

Serves 4 Recipe: medium complexity

RIGHT: 'Rabbit Tagine is a good balance of flavours between the sweetness of the spices and the softness of the polenta and apricot. I always like to keep the bones in the meat to keep it moist—eat this dish with your fingers.'

Marieke Brugman, chef and food teacher

Arroz de Pombas Bravos

Pigeon Rice

INGREDIENTS

SPICE MIX

2 teaspoons ground cumin

2 teaspoons ground coriander

2 teaspoons ground cinnamon

1½ teaspoons ground allspice

1 teaspoon ground cardamom

1 teaspoon ground ginger

1 teaspoon grated nutmeg

2 tablespoons Maldon sea salt

6 x 500-g (1-lb) squab

4 bay leaves

8 cloves garlic

fresh thyme

a few cinnamon sticks

orange peel

spring onion pieces

75 mL (2½ fl oz) olive oil

45 g (1½ oz) butter

scant cup (200 mL/7 fl oz) white wine

3¼ cups (825 mL/26 fl oz) chicken stock

butter

RICE

45 g (1½ oz) butter

¼ cup (60 mL/2 fl oz) olive oil

2 red onions, finely chopped

2 cloves garlic, finely chopped

1 small red chilli, finely chopped

200 g (7 oz) smoked ham or pancetta, diced

2 spicy chorizo, blanched, skinned and diced

500 g (1 lb) Ferron carnaroli or Spanish rice

a few threads of saffron

In Portuguese cuisine, there are many fabulous rice dishes such as duck rice and seafood rice. The grains should be cooked through until creamy but separate, but with more liquid than in a traditional risotto. My favourite poultry is squab from Ian Millburn at Glenloth in the Mallee. He is one of many rural heroes, and was one of the early pioneers developing a range of specialist poultry and diversifying his agricultural base in order to better maintain his land.

To make the spice mix, combine the spices with the salt. Dry the inside of the squab, having removed the heads, feet and wing tips. Rub inside and out with the spices. Place in a non-corrosive dish with the bay leaves and garlic, and leave, covered, in the refrigerator overnight.

The next day, preheat the oven to 180°C (350°F). Wipe off all the spice mixture inside the squab and reserve the garlic and bay leaves. Fill the cavity of each bird with some thyme, a cinnamon stick, orange peel and spring onion. In a heavy-based oven dish, heat the olive oil and butter, and gently brown each squab over medium heat. Add the reserved garlic and bay leaves, and deglaze with the white wine. Place the squab in a single layer in the dish, add the chicken stock and bring to the boil. Place in the oven and cook until the squab are tender, about 40–60 minutes. Remove the dish from the oven and leave the squab to cool. Once cool, peel off the skin and discard. Slice the squab meat into cubes. Cover with some of the liquid to keep moist and seal with plastic wrap. Strain the stock and reserve, removing all fat.

To cook the rice, preheat the oven to 200°–220°C (400°–425°F). Melt the butter with the olive oil and cook the onion, garlic and chilli until aromatic. Add the ham and cook for a further 5 minutes. Add the chorizo and allow to colour. Add the rice and stir to coat, then add the saffron and 4 cups (1 litre/1¾ imp. pints) of the reserved stock and bring to the boil over medium heat. Transfer to a large stainless steel or earthenware pot and cover tightly with foil. Bake in the oven until the rice is tender, about 30 minutes.

Remove the rice from the oven, fork it over and add the squab. Transfer the rice to an ovenproof serving dish if necessary and moisten with a little extra stock, if needed. Dot with butter and reheat, about 10 minutes, until the rice looks dry on top. Serve with a bitter green salad.

Serves 12 Recipe: medium complexity

Ralph Potter, chef

Anise-flavoured Crispy Duck
with Kipfler Potatoes, Beetroot and Chervil

INGREDIENTS

3 cups (750 mL/24 fl oz) duck stock

2 tablespoons star anise

2 tablespoons five-spice powder

1 tablespoon freshly cracked black
peppercorns

4 duck breasts

500 g (1 lb) baby beetroots (red beets)

salt

1 kg (2 lb) kipfler or pink fir apple
potatoes

1 bunch of small-leaf watercress

1 bunch of chervil

1 bunch of spring onions

a little vegetable oil

1 tablespoon Szechuan peppercorns

SOY LEMON DRESSING

⅔ cup (155 mL/5 fl oz) olive oil

1½ tablespoons lemon juice

1½ tablespoons balsamic vinegar

1 tablespoon salt-reduced soy sauce

1 tablespoon sesame oil

½ clove garlic, chopped

freshly ground black pepper

Serve this as a main course in summer at room temperature or hot as a starter in winter. The beetroot salad leaves and potatoes are firm, while the duck is meaty and crispy. Cracked Szechuan pepper gives it a bit of a finish, which makes all the difference to the dish. Serve with a sparkling Shiraz.

Cook the duck the day before. Bring the duck stock to the boil with the star anise, five-spice powder and peppercorns. Allow to simmer for 10 minutes. Add the duck breasts to the stock and simmer for a further 1¼ hours, until the breasts are tender. Remove the breasts from the stock and place in the refrigerator to cool overnight—this makes it easier to cut them into even-shaped pieces.

To make the soy lemon dressing, whisk all the dressing ingredients together and season with plenty of pepper.

Wash the baby beetroot, but do not peel. Bring some salted water to the boil and add the beetroot. When cooked, refresh the beetroot in cold water and rub the skin off. Peel or brush the skin from the potatoes and cook in salted water. When cooked, drain the potatoes and keep warm.

To serve, reheat the beetroot in hot water, drain and cut the warm potatoes and beetroot into 2–3 cm (¾–1 inch) pieces and place in a bowl with some of the soy lemon dressing. Wash and drain the watercress in a salad spinner. Roughly chop the chervil and place on one side. Peel the outside skin away from the spring onions and sauté in a little vegetable oil until soft. Keep in a warm place until needed.

Cut the duck breasts into 1.5-cm (¾-inch) dice. Heat a little vegetable oil in a cast-iron frying pan or skillet, adding the duck when the oil begins to smoke slightly. Sauté the duck until crispy, then remove from the pan and drain on absorbent kitchen paper. Keep warm.

Add the chervil and watercress leaves to the potato and beetroot, and toss together with the soy lemon dressing. Divide the vegetables between 6 serving plates. Add some of the crispy duck pieces to each plate and top each one with 2–3 pieces of warm spring onion. Splash a little extra dressing on each plate, sprinkle with the Szechuan peppercorns and serve immediately.

Serves 6 Recipe: medium complexity

ABOVE: The main dining room at the beautiful Jacques Reymond's Restaurant.

RIGHT: Lamb's Brains with a Papillote of Celeriac and a Warm Salad of Rocket and Baby Spinach (page 101). The fresh, crisp salad and the crunchy texture of the celeriac and hazelnuts lift the soft, rich texture of the brains.

Jacques Reymond

The Dream of My Life

In the early 1980s, Jacques Reymond flew out to Australia from France for a week—just to have a look. Encouraged, he and his wife, Cathy, promptly moved out here and started their first restaurant in Melbourne's Richmond. Now in their third restaurant, they are the undisputed champions of fine dining in Melbourne, with their tables continuing to be fully booked every evening.

Jacques declares it is the dream of his life and indeed it's easy to see why. The exquisite dining room is lavishly decorated in a painterly French style, the perfect setting for his fine creative dishes. He believes he has found the best ingredients, the right country and the right customers.

He is excited and inspired by the high standard of food coming from the small producers, especially in the past eight years (due mainly to encouragement and support from Jacques and his peers). He likes to select the best ingredients and to respect them. He often incorporates Asian influences in his Australian cuisine.

'I live in Australia, I might as well use Australian flavours. If I wanted to be a French cook, I should go back to France. Why copy someone else?'

Jacques grew up in Burgundy, where his parents ran a hotel and restaurant in a small village. He has mostly learnt cooking his own way and has his own unique style.

He thinks he was lucky not to be influenced by anyone. He firmly believes that he has settled in the right place, that Australia gives him the freedom to do what he wants and the customers appreciate it. 'They ask questions, they are

interested in my cooking style and they are very supportive.'

This modest man declared he was just a cook—but what a cook! His dishes are creative and visually appealing; the contrast in flavours is exquisite in its harmonious complexity. A celebration of all the senses.

ABOVE: Gratin of Spiced Strawberries and Quince with a Grand Marnier Sabayon (page 184). Asian flavours enrich the strawberries that peek up from under a bed of a gratinéed, light-as-a-feather sabayon.

Philip Johnson, chef

Salad of Wild Rice, Hazelnut and
Peking Duck

INGREDIENTS
VINAIGRETTE

1 tablespoon Dijon mustard

2½ tablespoons white wine vinegar

⅔ cup (155 mL/5 fl oz) extra virgin
   olive oil

⅔ cup (155 mL/5 fl oz) light olive oil

salt and freshly ground black pepper

1 tablespoon lemon juice

fresh thyme leaves, finely chopped

1 teaspoon sugar

1 cup (155 g/5 oz) wild rice, soaked for
   30 minutes in cold water

1 red onion, diced

1 clove garlic, crushed

few sprigs of fresh thyme

salt and freshly ground black pepper

½ Florence fennel (finocchio) bulb,
   washed and thinly sliced

½ cup (60 g/2 oz) hazelnuts, roasted and
   skinned

2 Jerusalem artichokes, shaved

zest of 1 lemon

1 Granny Smith apple, sliced

1 Chinese-style barbecued duck, cut
   into strips

corn salad (mâche) leaves

red chard or baby silverbeet (Swiss
   chard) leaves

To make the vinaigrette, combine all the ingredients in a screw-top jar, seal and shake well. Taste and adjust seasonings as required. This dressing will keep for weeks in the refrigerator.

To cook the rice, combine the wild rice with the onion, garlic and thyme in a saucepan. Season to taste with salt and pepper, and cover with water. Set over medium heat and bring to the boil. Turn the heat down to simmer, cover the pan securely and cook until the rice is ready, about 30–40 minutes.

Drain the rice, then refresh in cold water and allow to cool. Add the fennel, hazelnuts, artichoke, lemon zest and apple. Moisten with the vinaigrette and mix through well.

In the meantime, warm the duck. Preheat the oven to 180°C (350°F) and place the duck in a single layer on a silicone paper-lined oven tray or baking sheet. Heat the duck until warmed through, about 6–8 minutes.

To serve, arrange the corn salad and red chard leaves on serving plates, placing a pile of rice salad in the centre. Place the warm duck strips on top of the salad and serve.

Serves 6 Recipe: easy to make

Sue Fairlie-Cuninghame, food writer

Barbecued Duck Curry

INGREDIENTS

2 Asian-styled barbecued ducks

3 cups (750 mL/24 fl oz) coconut milk

2 teaspoons best-quality Thai green
curry paste

5 fresh kaffir lime leaves

1–2 tablespoons Thai fish sauce
(nam pla)

2–3 small green chillies, halved and
seeds removed

125 g (4 oz) pea eggplants (aubergines),
optional

This curry can also be made using white chicken or barbecued pork from Asian food stores, or steamed chicken. Steamed sticky rice wrapped in lotus leaf can also be bought and reheated.

Remove the breasts, legs, thighs and all the meaty portions from the duck and chop coarsely. Heat one-third of the cream from the surface of the coconut milk in a wok or heavy frying pan (skillet) over medium heat, stirring constantly. Add the curry paste and continue to stir until fragrant. Tear 4 of the lime leaves and toss into the wok with the remaining coconut milk, fish sauce, chilli and eggplant. Reduce the heat and simmer gently for 15 minutes, or until the eggplant is almost tender. Add the duck meat and simmer for about 5 minutes. Shred the remaining lime leaf very finely and add to the curry, adjusting the flavour with a little more fish sauce if necessary. Simmer for a further 5 minutes, then serve immediately.

To serve, divide the curry between warmed bowls. Serve with a bowl of glutinous rice or boiled basmati rice.

Serves 6 Recipe: easy to make

Dany Chouet, chef

Poussin aux Raisins
Spatchcocks with Green Grapes, Garlic and Parsley

INGREDIENTS

4 spatchcocks (Cornish game hens)

4 sprigs fresh thyme

1 head garlic

salt and freshly ground black pepper

2–3 kg (4–6 lb) seedless green or
red grapes, not too ripe (they should
be acidic)

1 cup (250 mL/8 fl oz) strong
chicken stock

45 g (1½ oz) unsalted butter

juice of 1 lemon

½ bunch of flat-leaf parsley, finely
chopped

Preheat the oven to 220°C (425°F). Clean and dress the spatchcocks. Place the thyme and a half clove of garlic inside each one and season with salt and pepper inside and out. Pluck the grapes from the stems, keeping aside four handfuls of the best-looking ones for garnishing.

Juice the remaining grapes in an electric juicer or food processor. Strain through a fine strainer to remove the skins. It should yield about 1 cup (250 mL/8 fl oz) of grape juice. Pour into a stainless steel saucepan with the chicken stock. Reduce over high heat to about half the volume. Set aside.

Put the spatchcocks on a rack in a baking pan. Roast the spatchcocks in the oven for about 20 minutes, until the skins are crisp and golden. Rest in a warm area, covered. Strain off the roasting juices and remove the fat from the surface with absorbent kitchen paper. Set aside.

Chop 4 cloves of the garlic very finely. Heat the grape sauce, add the chopped garlic and allow to cook for 3–4 minutes. Whisk in the butter and add lemon juice to taste. Add the parsley and reserved roasting juices. Warm the reserved grapes in the sauce for 1 minute, then either cut the spatchcocks in half or leave them whole. Place on warm serving plates and pour the sauce and grapes around.

Serves 4 Recipe: easy to make

Greg Malouf, chef

Marinated and Grilled Quail
with Hummus Bi Tahini and Moorish Spinach Salad

INGREDIENTS

8 x 200-g (7-oz) quail, cut down the
   backbone

MARINADE

1 cup (250 mL/8 fl oz) olive oil

juice and zest of 1 lemon

1 teaspoon chopped fresh thyme leaves

pinch of ground allspice

pinch of sumak (crushed berry available
   from most Middle Eastern delis)

½ teaspoon pomegranate essence

CHICKPEAS

3 cups (500 g/1 lb) chickpeas, soaked
   in plenty of cold water and pinch of
   bicarbonate of soda for 48 hours

juice of 3 large lemons

1 clove garlic, crushed with 1 teaspoon
   sea salt

1 cup (200 g/7 oz) tahini

SPINACH SALAD

2 bunches of spinach, picked over and
   well washed

4 golden shallots, finely sliced

2 teaspoons currants, soaked in
   3 tablespoons sherry

pinch of ground allspice

pinch of ground cinnamon

1½ tablespoons sherry vinegar

2½ tablespoons extra virgin olive oil,
   plus extra to garnish

½ cup (60 g/2 oz) flaked almonds,
   fried in olive oil until golden brown
   and crisp

coriander (Chinese parsley) leaves to
   garnish

Coat the quail in the marinade ingredients and leave for several hours, covered, in the refrigerator, turning once or twice.

Drain the chickpeas, place in a stainless steel saucepan and cover completely with cold water—allow double the volume of water to chickpeas. Bring to the boil, constantly skimming off any white scum on the surface. Gently simmer until the chickpeas are tender, about 40 minutes. Strain and reserve the cooking liquid.

Put the cooked chickpeas in a food processor or blender with ½ cup (125 mL/4 fl oz) of the cooking liquid and the lemon juice, garlic and tahini. Blend until very smooth. If too thick, add more cooking liquid. The hummus should have the consistency of very thick cream.

To make the spinach salad, blanch the spinach in boiling, salted water for 10 seconds. Refresh in cold water and then squeeze out as much moisture as you can. Mix the shallots with the sherried currants. Gently break the spinach leaves apart into a bowl and add the shallot mixture, allspice, cinnamon, sherry vinegar and the 2½ tablespoons extra virgin olive oil. Mix thoroughly, check the seasoning and lastly add the almonds.

To grill the quail, heat a heavy cast-iron frying pan or skillet until smoking hot. Grill the quail, skin-side down, for 3 minutes, turning the flame down to medium in the last minute. Turn the quail over and increase the heat again. Continue cooking for a further 3 minutes. Remove from the frying pan onto absorbent kitchen paper and keep warm.

To serve, spoon the hummus onto the serving plates next to a pile of spinach salad. Cut the quail in half lengthwise and stack 4 halves on top of the hummus. Garnish with the coriander leaves and a little extra virgin olive oil.

Serves 4 Recipe: medium complexity

Chapter 4
Fish and Shellfish

Alan Saunders

Fish and Shellfish

THE OPEN SEAS AROUND AUSTRALIA, the coastal shallows, the mangrove-lined creeks and estuaries, the lakes and inland rivers are all full of life: more than 3600 species of fish and tens of thousands of molluscs, almost all of which were totally neglected until comparatively recently. These days, about 200 of these species of fish and more than 90 species of molluscs and crustacea are exploited commercially. A hundred years ago, however, Philip Muskett couldn't believe how uninterested his compatriots were in the abundance around them.

There were no deep-sea fisheries and such fishing as there was depended on primitive methods and neglected the most modern equipment being used in Europe. Moreover, the fish markets of Sydney and Melbourne were wholly inadequate. How could this be? Muskett wondered. After all, did not Australians come of British stock, 'a stock the most maritime that the world has ever seen?'

Perhaps, but it was left to other people, also of maritime stock, to change things: 'I have an Australian friend who used to catch baby octopus in Double Bay as a small boy, and sell them to "the wogs"—that was us—for two shillings a bucket,' says Stefano Manfredi, who came from Italy with his family as a child, in his book *Fresh From Italy*. So the Anglos may have caught them, but they wouldn't eat them. Now, everybody's eating them and, with a greater variety of fish being eaten, we need more ways of cooking them.

Neil Perry's King Prawn Cake and Scallops with Spicy Prawn Sauce (page 60) is a good indication of where Australians are going with fish and its preparation. The point is not just that it combines European technique and Asian flavours— anybody can do that—but also that it does so with such careful respect to both, being based on a precise observation of what happens when you make a French mousse with coconut cream. Or there's Diane Holuigue, blending French methods and Moroccan ingredients in her Blue-eye Cod on a Bed of Fennel (page 133) and Raymond Capadli's reviving the sadly neglected mediaeval technique of the savoury blancmange in his Confit of Tasmanian Salmon with Blancmange of Cauliflower, Nutmeg, Spinach and Lemon Oil (page 145).

So, an industry which, little more than a century ago, the most astute observer thought primitive and undeveloped, is now capable of providing Australians with a varied and exciting range of fish. We can no longer be accused of neglecting the life around us (indeed, we can sometimes be accused of overfishing, though this is now being properly policed) and, in Sydney—where Philip Muskett threw up his hands in despair over the state of wholesaling and retailing—we have one of the world's finest fish markets. Moreover, while raising sheep and cattle means trying to do as well as possible something that the rest of the world already does, our seafood and freshwater fish and crustacea (with the exception of a few significant imports) are uniquely ours. In many respects, what we get from our rivers and the ocean that surrounds us is the best of Australia.

PREVIOUS PAGE: Janni Kyritsis's Sicilian Stuffed Red Mullet with Parsley Salad and Grilled Lemon. 'Red mullet is a fish that is regarded very highly in Greece, where I was born. Purchasing red mullet is considered similar to buying a lobster—expensive, but very nice to eat. I love its rich flavour and wonderful colour.'

Janni Kyritsis, chef

Sicilian Stuffed Red Mullet
with Parsley Salad and Grilled Lemon

INGREDIENTS

GRILLED LEMONS

2 lemons

salt

olive oil

GREMOLATA BREADCRUMBS

¼ cup finely chopped parsley

grated zest of 1 lemon

1 clove garlic, finely chopped

½ teaspoon ground black pepper

1 cup (60 g/2 oz) fresh breadcrumbs

SICILIAN STUFFING

2 tablespoons pine nuts, toasted and
  finely chopped

3 tablespoons currants

juice of ½ lemon

½ teaspoon salt

pinch of ground black pepper

¼ cup Gremolata Breadcrumbs

6 whole red mullet, or 12 fresh sardine
  fillets cleaned

plain (all-purpose) flour for coating

2 eggs, beaten

olive oil

PARSLEY SALAD

3 tablespoons pitted small black olives

3 cups flat-leaf parsley, very roughly
  chopped

1 red onion, chopped

2 tablespoons small salted capers,
  blanched

4 anchovy fillets, chopped

grated zest of ½ lemon

6 tablespoons virgin olive oil

1 tablespoon lemon juice

*The parsley and olive salad cuts down the richness of the pan-fried mullet, as does
the grilled lemon, which gives acidity and flavour to complete the dish. This
Mediterranean-influenced dish needs a good virgin olive oil. The Sicilian stuffing
with pine nuts is an essential component and is another example of how Australians
combine different cultures in their cooking. Alone, it would have been a Greek dish.
With the stuffing, however, a different dimension is created—one that is celebrated
in Australia.*

To make the grilled lemons, slice the lemons thinly, sprinkle with salt and leave
for 30 minutes. Pat dry and keep covered in oil for 24 hours. When ready to
serve, cook on a char-grill or in a very hot cast-iron frying pan, until the lemon
begins to colour.

To make the gremolata breadcrumbs, mix all the ingredients together and
reserve. To make the Sicilian stuffing, mix all the ingredients together and reserve.

To cook the fish, butterfly the mullet by splitting each fish open so it is flat,
but still joined together. Place a spoonful of the stuffing inside each one. Coat the
fish in the flour, then dip in the egg before coating with the gremolata
breadcrumbs. Heat some olive oil in a frying pan or skillet, and pan-fry the mullet
until golden brown, about 4 minutes on each side. Only turn once.

At the same time, make the parsley salad by mixing all the ingredients
together—this should be done just before serving.

To serve, place the parsley salad in the centre of each plate and top each
serving with a mullet. The grilled lemon is then placed on top of the fish.

Serves 6 Recipe: medium complexity

Kathy Snowball, food writer

Poached Blue-Eye Cod

with Puy Lentils and Warm Tomato and Fennel Dressing

INGREDIENTS

DRESSING

6½ tablespoons olive oil

1 small red onion, finely chopped

6 tablespoons finely chopped fennel

4½ tablespoons Chardonnay vinegar or
fine white wine vinegar

2 vine-ripened tomatoes, seeded and
finely chopped

salt and freshly ground black pepper

1½ cups (300 g/10 oz) Puy lentils

olive oil

155 g (5 oz) smoked speck or smoked
bacon, rind removed and coarsely
chopped

salt and freshly ground black pepper

4 x 200-g (7-oz) blue-eye cod fillets

½ cup firmly packed flat-leaf parsley
leaves

This is a simple, stylish recipe using store cupboard ingredients and a couple of fresh ones. Drink a nice oaky Chardonnay or a light Pinot with it.

To make the warm tomato and fennel dressing, heat 2 tablespoons of the olive oil in a saucepan and cook the onion and fennel over low heat until soft. Stir in the vinegar and bring to the boil. Remove from the heat, stir in the tomato and remaining 4½ tablespoons olive oil and season to taste.

Cook the lentils in boiling, salted water for about 20 minutes, until tender. Drain and rinse under cold water. Heat 1 tablespoon olive oil in a saucepan and cook the speck over medium heat until browned. Add the lentils, season to taste and stir to heat through.

Meanwhile, gently heat 1–2 cups (250–500 mL/8–16 fl oz) olive oil (enough to cover the fish) in a shallow saucepan and poach the cod over very low heat for 2–3 minutes on each side, or until just cooked.

Stir the parsley leaves into the lentil mixture and divide among the serving plates. Top with the fish and drizzle with warm tomato and fennel dressing.

Serves 4 Recipe: easy to make

RIGHT: Poached Blue-Eye Cod with Puy Lentils and Warm Tomato and Fennel Dressing. There are masses of flavours in this dish—the earthy, gorgeous flavour of speck and lentils, and the delicacy of fish poached gently in olive oil. The sharpness of the fine Chardonnay vinegar breaks through the oil.

Mietta O'Donnell, chef and food writer

Roast Baby Snapper

Cantonese Style

INGREDIENTS

6 small snapper, gutted, scaled and head
left on

2 tablespoons peeled and thinly sliced
fresh ginger

4 cloves garlic, sliced

1 tablespoon sesame oil

1½ tablespoons peanut oil

3 tablespoons light soy sauce

zest of 3 mandarins, finely sliced

small bunch of fresh coriander (Chinese
parsley) leaves, stalks removed

Preheat the oven to 180°C (350°F). Make several incisions on both sides of the fish. Stuff with the ginger and garlic. Mix the sesame and peanut oils together and use to brush the fish. Reserve the leftover oil.

Place the fish on an oiled baking sheet and bake in the oven for 15–20 minutes, depending on the size of the fish, until just cooked and the flesh is opaque. Pour over the soy sauce and sprinkle the mandarin zest over the fish. Roast for a further 10 minutes.

Transfer the fish to warmed serving plates and pour the pan juices over. Sprinkle liberally with the coriander. Heat the remaining oil until very hot and spoon over the fish. This will cause it to spit, so take care. Serve at once, accompanied by steamed rice.

Serves 6 Recipe: easy to make

Cheong Liew, chef

Red-Roast Snapper

with Shaved Cuttlefish and Leek Fondue

INGREDIENTS

1 spring onion, finely sliced

1 tablespoon fresh ginger, finely sliced

4 tablespoons peanut oil

1 tablespoon light soy sauce

1 tablespoon dark soy sauce

2 tablespoons rice wine

1 teaspoon sugar

salt and freshly ground black pepper

about 1.25 kg (2½ lb) snapper fillets

SAUCE

2 green chillies

1 tablespoon coriander (Chinese parsley)
  leaves and roots, chopped

2 tablespoons chopped celery greens

2 tablespoons chopped spring onion,
  green part only

1 tablespoon peanut oil

1 teaspoon sesame oil

1 clove garlic, chopped

½ tablespoon chopped ginger

1 tablespoon brown bean paste

1½ tablespoons sugar

½ tablespoon rice wine

2½ tablespoons fish stock

1 tablespoon oyster sauce

½ tablespoon ginger juice

4 x 1-cm (⅜-inch) cubes of chilled
  unsalted butter

LEEK FONDUE

75 g (2½ oz) butter

1 bunch leeks, whites only, finely sliced

3 tablespoons white wine (Noilly Prat
  if possible)

5 tablespoons crème fraîche

salt and freshly ground white pepper

CONTINUED ON NEXT PAGE

This is an intense dish both for the chef to prepare and for the diner to enjoy. The outer skin of the fish is very distinctly caramel in flavour, but inside there is a soft and delicate meat. I call this exciting eating—it combines the oriental method of preparing fish with French provincial earthiness. It can be garnished very briefly with sautéed snow pea shoots.

The fish is very slightly braised by the green sauce, exuding a delicate flavour. The leek fondue goes well with the flavour and texture of the snapper, and the green sauce brings together the separate elements of the dish. The cuttlefish shavings add another dimension.

Combine the spring onion, ginger, 1 tablespoon of the peanut oil, light soy sauce, dark soy sauce, rice wine, sugar and salt and pepper to taste. Marinate the snapper in this mixture for 30 minutes. Remove the fish from the marinade, pat dry and shallow-fry in a frying pan or skillet in the remaining 3 tablespoons peanut oil, skin-side down, until brown and crisp. Turn over, cook for 1 minute, then remove.

To make the sauce, blend in a food processor or pound the chilli, coriander, celery greens and spring onion greens into a paste. In a frying pan, heat the peanut oil and sesame oil, add the garlic, ginger and brown bean paste, then add the sugar and rice wine. Add the chilli paste and sauté gently for 2 minutes. Remove from the heat and strain the mixture through a fine sieve. Push as much of the paste through as possible with the back of a spoon. Return the resulting green jus, or juice, to the heat and add the fish stock, oyster sauce and ginger juice. Reduce in volume by one-third.

To make the leek fondue, in a frying pan, heat a quarter of the butter and then toss in the leeks. Stir for a few minutes, then add the white wine. Add the crème fraîche and reduce until the fondue thickens, then add the remaining butter. Cook slowly for about 20 minutes, until the leek is very tender. Season with salt and pepper to taste.

To make the cuttlefish shavings, cut the cuttlefish into halves lengthwise, then thinly slice from the inside at an angle. Marinate in half the oil and salt to taste. Heat the remaining oil in a frying pan with the ginger and, with a shake of the frying pan, instantly sauté the cuttlefish. (Separate the cuttlefish slices if they stick together.) Season with salt and pepper to taste.

To serve, spread one generous tablespoon of leek fondue onto the centre of each serving plate. Place the red-roast snapper on top of the fondue. Warm the sauce through and add the unsalted butter. Pour the sauce around the leek fondue and place a tablespoon on top of the snapper. Garnish with the cuttlefish shavings.

Serves 4–6 Recipe: complex

CUTTLEFISH SHAVINGS
1 cuttlefish, cleaned and gutted
1 tablespoon peanut oil
salt and freshly ground black pepper
slice of fresh ginger

Tony Bilson, chef

Grilled Fillet of Snapper
with Saffron and Citrus Sauce

INGREDIENTS

20 small spring onions

scant cup (200 mL/7 fl oz) olive oil

pinch of sugar

20 small Florence fennel (finocchio)
  bulbs, steamed

10 globe artichokes, quartered and
  steamed

1 kg (2 lb) button mushrooms

2 cloves garlic, crushed

1 teaspoon coriander seed

pinch of saffron threads

2 tablespoons sliced fresh ginger

salt and freshly ground black pepper

juice of 1 grapefruit

juice of 1 orange

juice of 1 lemon

juice of 2 limes

2 cups (500 mL/16 fl oz) shellfish stock

3 tablespoons butter

200 g (7 oz) trompette de la mort
  mushrooms or black fungus, finely
  sliced

1 tablespoon flat-leaf parsley

GRILLED SNAPPER

2 tablespoons olive oil

10 x 170-g (6-oz) snapper fillets

pinch of sugar

salt and freshly ground black pepper

julienne of orange to garnish

1 tablespoon freshly chopped coriander

The sauce is an unusual combination of fish and shellfish stock reduced with the juice of different citrus fruits.

To make the saffron and citrus sauce, in a large frying pan or skillet over low heat, gently cook the spring onions in the olive oil with the pinch of sugar. Add the fennel, artichoke, button mushrooms and garlic, then add the coriander seed, saffron and ginger. Season with salt and pepper to taste. When soft, deglaze with all the fruit juices. Cook for 7 minutes and then strain through a fine sieve. Reserve the vegetables.

Put the liquid back into a clean frying pan, add the shellfish stock to the sauce and reduce. Whisk 1 tablespoon of the butter into the sauce. Keep warm.

Pan-fry the mushrooms in the remaining 2 tablespoons butter over medium heat in a separate pan. Add the parsley, stir through and then add the reserved vegetables. Keep warm.

To cook the fish, heat the olive oil in a frying pan or skillet over high heat. Cook the snapper for 2 minutes on each side. Season to taste with salt and pepper, and then crisp the skin under a very hot grill or broiler.

To serve, put the fish on warm plates, with the julienne of orange, vegetables and mushrooms around the fish. Dot the sauce around the plate and sprinkle with the coriander.

Serves 10 Recipe: medium complexity

Dany Chouet, chef

Saumon à L'Olive Noire
Tasmanian Salmon, Black Olive Purée and Spring Onions

INGREDIENTS

1 bunch of large spring onions with
    round bulbs
best-quality virgin olive oil
500 g (1 lb) kalamata olives, pitted
freshly ground black pepper
4 x 140-g (4½-oz) salmon fillets, skin on
½ bunch of fresh lemon thyme leaves
juice of 1 lemon
sea salt flakes
thyme flowers to garnish

LEFT: Saumon à L'Olive Noire. 'Strong black olive
purée seasons the fish. Olives go nicely with
salmon—they give the fish a nice strong, olivey
flavour as they cook together. The onions are lightly
cooked and crunchy, and the sauce is a simple
emulsion of virgin olive oil and lemon juice which
balances the salmon and olives.'

RIGHT: Alla Wolf-Tasker's Whole Freshwater Trout
Served on a Warm Salad of Spinach and Puy
Lentils, with Sauce Vierge. 'This is one of my
favourite summer dishes and is excellent with a
fruity Riesling on a sunny day.'

A very simple dish that people love and is easy to make at home.

Preheat the oven to 210°C (410°F). Keep 4 of the spring onions whole, then very finely slice the bulbs only of the remainder. Heat some olive oil in a frying pan or skillet over low heat, then add all the spring onion and half-cook very slowly without colouring. Purée the olives very finely in a food processor with a little pepper and olive oil. Sprinkle pepper on the salmon fillets, then the thyme leaves. Spread 1½ tablespoons of the black olive purée on top of each fillet very carefully (only on top, not on the sides). Place on an oiled baking pan surrounded by the spring onion and cook in the oven for 8–10 minutes. When cooked, place the spring onion on the serving plates and sit the salmon on top. Deglaze the pan with the lemon juice, whisk in some more olive oil, season with salt and pour the sauce on top and around the fish. Garnish with the thyme flowers and serve.
Serves 4   Recipe: easy to make

Alla Wolf-Tasker, chef

Whole Freshwater Trout
Served on a Warm Salad of Spinach and Puy Lentils with Sauce Vierge

We are truly fortunate in frequently having fat, speckled brown trout brought to our kitchen door by enthusiastic local anglers. The local farmed trout are also wonderfully meaty, although possibly not as flavoursome. I prefer fish cooked on the bone, as it retains all its natural moisture and flavour. Cooked this way and served with boiled new potatoes, the trout makes a fabulous luncheon dish or a larger fish could be used as part of a buffet.
CONTINUED OVERLEAF

INGREDIENTS

SAUCE VIERGE

1 large, firm but ripe tomato

¾ cup (185 mL/6 fl oz) good-quality virgin olive oil

juice of 1 lemon

2 tablespoons finely julienned fresh coriander (Chinese parsley)

2 tablespoons finely julienned fresh basil

2 tablespoons finely julienned flat-leaf parsley

8 coriander seeds, crushed

1 clove garlic, finely chopped

salt and freshly ground black pepper

4 cups (1 litre/1¾ imp. pints) vegetable stock

200 g (7 oz) Puy lentils

salt and freshly ground black pepper

4 golden shallots, finely diced

4 x 200–250 g (7–8 oz) brook or farmed freshwater trout

2½ tablespoons quality virgin olive oil

2 tablespoons fresh lemon juice

½ teaspoon balsamic vinegar

4 coriander seeds, crushed

2 handfuls of baby spinach leaves

To make the sauce, peel, seed and finely dice the tomato. Combine the olive oil, tomato, lemon juice, coriander, basil, parsley, coriander seed and garlic in a bowl. Leave at room temperature to infuse. Adjust the seasoning with salt and pepper. When ready to serve, reheat gently to blood temperature.

To make the salad, bring the stock to a boil, add the lentils and cook for 30 minutes, or until tender. Drain and season with salt and pepper. Keep warm.

To bake the fish, preheat the oven to 200°C (400°F). In a frying pan, slowly sauté the golden shallots in a little olive oil until soft and caramelised. Make 3 incisions on each side of each fish, then place them in a shallow roasting pan. In a small bowl, stir together the virgin olive oil, lemon juice, balsamic vinegar, shallots and coriander seed. Brush the fish on both sides with the mixture. Bake for about 12 minutes. Keep warm by 'tenting' the fish with foil while completing the salad.

To serve, warm the lentils either in a steamer or microwave, and transfer to a bowl. Wash and dry the spinach leaves. Add them to the lentils with a little of the warm sauce and toss through until the spinach is just wilted. Make a bed of the lentil and spinach salad on each of the 4 serving plates and carefully lift a whole trout onto each one. Stir the warm sauce and pour a little over each fish. Serve immediately.

Serves 4 Recipe: easy to make

Paul Merrony, chef

Roast Salmon
with Eggplant Purée, Zucchini and Sage

INGREDIENTS

1 eggplant (aubergine)

scant cup (200 mL/7 fl oz) olive oil

salt and freshly ground black pepper

½ tablespoon cumin seed

3 small zucchini (courgettes)

10 sage leaves, stalks discarded

1 small spring onion, white part only, finely chopped

Roasted fish skin, when crispy and scaled, is quite delicious. I have used salmon here, but other fish with skin which crisps well are snapper and blue-eye cod.

Preheat the oven to 240°C (475°F). Cut the eggplant in half lengthwise. Score deep slashes into the eggplant to allow it to cook evenly. Place in a roasting pan, cover the eggplant with 2½ tablespoons of the olive oil, season with salt and pepper, and seal with foil. Bake in the oven for about 30 minutes (the flesh should be soft when cooked). Remove from the oven and allow to cool, but do not turn the oven off.

2½ tablespoons vinaigrette, made with
   olive oil and white wine vinegar
2½ tablespoons reduced veal stock
4 x 155-g (5-oz) escalopes of salmon,
   scaled but with skin left on and small
   bones removed
chervil or chives for garnish
julienne of parsley for garnish

Warm 2½ tablespoons of the olive oil, add the cumin seed and allow to infuse for 15 minutes on the side of the stove. Scoop out the flesh of the eggplant and purée in a blender or food processer, slowly adding the cumin-infused olive oil in a thin stream until it has thoroughly emulsified.

Cut the zucchini into 8-mm (⅜-inch) thick slices. Heat 2½ tablespoons of the olive oil in a heavy-based frying pan or skillet, add the zucchini and brown well on one side only. There should be no need to fry the other side. Remove from the pan and drain on absorbent kitchen paper. Keep hot.

Cut the sage into a fine julienne and mix with the spring onion, vinaigrette and veal stock in a small saucepan. Boil together and keep hot.

To serve, reheat the eggplant purée, either in a saucepan or microwave. Heat a lightly oiled non-stick frying pan to very hot. Place the salmon in the pan, skin-side down, and allow to brown for 1 minute. Put the salmon, still in the pan, into the very hot oven for 2 minutes. Turn the salmon over and cook for a further 2 minutes—the salmon should be pink and moist on the inside. Divide the zucchini (brown side up) among 4 heated plates, placing at regular intervals. Put the eggplant purée in the middle and the salmon on top. Spoon the sauce over the salmon and sprinkle with the chervil and parsley. Serve at once.

Serves 4 Recipe: medium complexity

Diane Holuigue, food writer and teacher

Blue-Eye Cod
on a Bed of Fennel

INGREDIENTS
3 tablespoons butter
1 large or 2 small bulbs of Florence
   fennel (finocchio), very finely sliced
juice of 1 lemon
½ cup (125 mL/4 fl oz) dry white wine
wedge of Moroccan preserved lemon,
   diced, or rind of 1 lemon, in threads
1 tablespoon tiny capers, preferably
   salted ones, rinsed and soaked
freshly chopped dill
salt and freshly ground black pepper
2 tablespoons extra virgin olive oil
6 x 125-g (4-oz) blue-eye cod or ling
   fillets
1 teaspoon oil

This dish is very much a modern Australian dish, painted, as so many dishes in this country are, with the brush of a broad culinary palette. It has overtones of the classic French whiting dish Grenoblaise, incorporates oil and fennel in the Mediterranean tradition and uses the popular Moroccan ingredients of salted preserved lemon and couscous.

To cook the fennel, heat the butter in a frying pan or skillet, and lightly sauté the fennel over medium heat, without colouring. When half-cooked, add the lemon juice, white wine and preserved lemon. Place the lid on the frying pan and sweat the fennel until tender, then remove the lid and reduce any liquid. Add the capers and dill, season with salt and pepper, then spoon through the olive oil.

Cook the fish just before ready to serve. Either put a film of oil onto a non-stick frying pan and fry skin-side down until cooked through, placing a lid on to help steam the fish through, or cook on an oiled cast-iron grill skin-side up.

To serve, make a bed of the fennel on each serving plate. Top with the fish and serve with couscous.

Serves 6 Recipe: easy to make

David Thompson, chef

A Balanced Thai Meal

BELOW LEFT TO RIGHT: Sour Orange Curry of Prawns and Choi Sum, Grilled Fish with Sweet Fish Sauce, steamed Thai jasmine rice, Kai Jiaw Omelette and Salted Beef Ribs Braised in Coconut Cream.

Thais strive to create balance, which is reflected in striking a harmony of flavours and textures within each individual dish and in concert with the accompanying dishes. These recipes are meant to be served together (for four or five people) and almost simultaneously. Serve with steamed Thai jasmine rice—the centre of Thai food culture. A meal is inconceivable without rice. Everything else is merely an accompaniment.

INGREDIENTS
PASTE

5 dried red chillies, deseeded and soaked in warm water for at least 5 minutes

3 tablespoons red shallots, sliced
1 tablespoon gapi or Thai shrimp paste
2 tablespoons steamed fish, any variety, optional
1 teaspoon salt

3-cm (1¼-inch) piece of tamarind paste
2 tablespoons fresh warm water
2 cups (500 mL/16 fl oz) chicken stock or water
2 tablespoons Thai fish sauce (nam pla), plus extra for finishing
1 teaspoon white sugar, optional
1 small bunch Siamese watercress, choy sum or Chinese cabbage, washed and cut into bite-sized pieces
6 large green prawns (shrimp), peeled and deveined, but with tails intact

Geng Som Gung Sy Pak
Sour Orange Curry of Prawns and Choi Sum

This is a boiled-style curry using techniques and readily available ingredients that are easy and convenient—red chillies, either fresh or dried; red shallots; gapi; boiled fish meat and occasionally garlic, lemon grass, galangal and coriander roots. Throughout the markets of Thailand, curry stalls line the narrow alleyways with old women selling prepared food—nahm priks, salads and curries, the most popular of which is sour orange curry. Pot after pot of this curry is on offer—freshwater fish with green vegetables or fermented bamboo, prawns (shrimp) with green papaya or mussels with drumstick beans. So simple to prepare, its antiquity is reflected in its simplicity.

To make the paste, pound the paste ingredients using a mortar and pestle, or blend in a food processor. Rinse the tamarind under running warm water, then soak in fresh warm water until it is soft. Work off the pulp from the seeds and fibre, and then strain. The tamarind water keeps for 3 days in the refrigerator.

Bring the stock to the boil, add the paste and, when it has returned to the boil, season with the 2 tablespoons fish sauce, a little of the tamarind water and sugar, if using. Add the watercress and prawns, and simmer until just cooked. Finish with another tablespoon of tamarind water and a little more fish sauce. Check the seasoning—it should be salty, sour and a little hot. The vegetables add a bitter note.

Pla Yang Nahm Pla Warn
Grilled Fish with Sweet Fish Sauce

This relish is always eaten with grilled fish—traditionally, a catfish, which is a very fatty fish. It is grilled so slowly over a few embers that the fish becomes slightly smoked and any excess fat is rendered, dripping onto the embers and making the smoke even more pungent. The smokiness works deliciously with sweet fish sauce. The sauce can be made in advance, with or without coconut cream. Bitter or sour vegetables and fruit offer a balance to the sweetness of this dish.

INGREDIENTS

1 freshwater fish, such as a Murray River perch, trout or catfish, cleaned

FISH SAUCE

½ cup (90 g/3 oz) palm sugar (jaggery)

3 tablespoons Thai fish sauce (nam pla)
2 tablespoons tamarind water
a little coconut cream
small handful of deep-fried shallots
small handful of deep-fried garlic
a few deep-fried dried red chillies
fresh coriander (Chinese parsley) leaves

RAW VEGETABLES

1 witlof (Belgian endive), washed
fresh ginger, skinned and sliced
white turmeric, if available, sliced
sprigs of Thai basil (ram rau) and mint
sliced cucumber
winged beans, sliced, if available
⅛ cabbage, roughly sliced
fresh coriander (Chinese parsley) sprigs

To make the fish sauce, melt the palm sugar in a small saucepan, add the fish sauce, tamarind water and coconut cream, and simmer for a few minutes. Do not simmer for too long or the sugar will caramelise and, when cooled, become a gluey rock. Skim, strain and cool the sauce. It will taste salty, sweet and slightly sour. Just before serving, mix the sauce with the shallots, garlic, chilli and coriander.

Grill the fish over a barbecue fire as mentioned above or grill for 4 minutes on each side under a hot grill (broiler). The sauce can be served in a bowl with the raw vegetables and the fish on the side; with the sauce masked over the fish and the vegetables by its side; or tossed together like a salad. Garnish with coriander.

Kai Jiaw Omelette

INGREDIENTS

2 eggs
salt and freshly ground white pepper
3 tablespoons oil
3 red shallots, finely sliced
fresh coriander (Chinese parsley) sprigs

Beat the eggs with a pinch of salt. Heat a wok, add the oil and, when hot, pour in the eggs. Cook over medium heat for just a few minutes until it is almost cooked, then slide onto a plate covered with absorbent kitchen paper. Serve sprinkled with the shallots and coriander, and seasoned with pepper.

Neaua Kem Sot
Salted Beef Ribs Braised in Coconut Cream

INGREDIENTS

MARINADE

1 cup (250 mL/8 fl oz) Thai fish sauce
(nam pla) or light soy sauce

1 tablespoon salt

3 tablespoons white sugar

1 tablespoon freshly ground white
pepper

1 cup (250 mL/8 fl oz) coconut cream

3 cups (750 mL/24 fl oz) coconut milk

200 g (7 oz) beef ribs, rinsed

3 stalks lemon grass, soft part only,
finely sliced (use the outer leaves,
roots and stalks for braising)

4 red shallots, sliced

small handful of fresh mint leaves

small handful of fresh coriander
(Chinese parsley) leaves

3–4 small, very hot chillies (scuds),
finely sliced

2 limes, cut into quarters

This is a modern version of salty beef, a favourite condiment of the Thais. The meat should be marinated for at least 3 days—the longer the better, so that the fibres tighten as the meat becomes impregnated with the brine. The meat is then braised in the coconut cream and milk. The fat renders as it simmers and, when the milk evaporates, the meat begins to fry. The sugar from the coconut and marinade begin to caramelise with the salt and the meat becomes salty, succulent and savoury. Beef cooked in this way—or pork, duck or chicken—must be eaten hot and can be served in many forms, as a condiment unadorned, braised and then caramelised, or as a salad with handfuls of fresh herbs, such as mint, coriander and pak chii farang —sometimes known as long-leaf coriander or saw tooth herb—dressed with lime juice and chillies.

Marinate the beef in the marinade ingredients for 3 days.

Put the coconut cream and milk in a saucepan, bring to a simmer and braise the beef with the lemon grass for 3 hours, until most of the liquid has evaporated and the meat has begun to caramelise.

Take the beef carefully out of the saucepan, remove the bones and slice. When serving, sprinkle with the shallots, mint, coriander and chilli, and garnish with the lime quarters.

Serves 4–5 Recipes: easy to make

Greg Malouf, chef

Whiting Fillets Roasted
in Parmesan Kataifi with Syrian Eggplant Relish and Preserved Lemon

INGREDIENTS

EGGPLANT RELISH

2 medium eggplants (aubergines)

extra virgin olive oil

juice of 1 lemon

1 teaspoon chopped fresh thyme

½ teaspoon pomegranate extract
(molasses)

2 egg (Italian plum) tomatoes, diced

1 tablespoon finely chopped parsley

To make the eggplant relish, steam the eggplant until tender. Remove the skin from the pulp and discard. Place the eggplant pulp in a stainless steel bowl and, while still warm, add the olive oil, lemon juice, thyme and pomegranate extract. Let stand for 30 minutes. Add the tomato, parsley, garlic, onion, coriander, sumak, allspice and pepper to taste, mixing gently as you do so.

Preheat the oven to 220°C (425°F). Season the whiting fillets with salt and pepper, and a little of the Parmesan cheese. Unravel the kataifi and cut into 12 x 15 cm (5 x 6 inch) lengths, each one comprising 10–12 threads of kataifi pastry. Brush the pastry with the butter and sprinkle with the remaining Parmesan. Fold the whiting fillets in half, skin-side up. Place a fillet at one end of

1 clove garlic, crushed with ½ teaspoon
  salt
1 red onion, very finely diced
1 tablespoon freshly chopped coriander
  (Chinese parsley)
pinch of sumak
pinch of ground allspice
freshly ground white pepper

12 whiting fillets
sea salt and freshly ground white pepper
1⅓ cups (155 g/5 oz) grated Parmesan
  cheese
1 packet kataifi pastry
200 g (7 oz) unsalted butter, melted
3 egg yolks
1 tablespoon Dijon mustard
juice of 2 lemons
1 preserved lemon, rinsed, rind and pith
  removed, and finely diced
2 cloves garlic, crushed with 1 teaspoon
  sea salt
2 cups (500 mL/16 fl oz) olive oil

the pastry and tightly roll up. Repeat the process with the remaining whiting.

To make the lemon aïoli, whisk the egg yolks with the mustard, lemon juice, preserved lemon and garlic. Add the olive oil, very slowly, until the mayonnaise is emulsified and very thick. Check the seasoning, adding salt and pepper to taste.

To finish the dish, put the whiting fillets on a baking sheet lined with baking parchment. Bake in the oven for 8 minutes or until golden brown.

To serve, arrange the whiting neatly on a plate with a spoonful of eggplant relish on one side and a spoonful of lemon aïoli on the other. Drizzle with a little extra virgin olive oil and serve at once.

Serves 6 Recipe: medium complexity

Tetsuya Wakuda, chef

Roasted Fillet of Barramundi
with Wakame and Truffled Peaches

INGREDIENTS
4 x 155-g (5-oz) small barramundi
  fillets, skin on
2 tablespoons grapeseed oil
2 tablespoons white truffle oil, plus
  2 teaspoons extra
sea salt
½ large witlof (Belgian endive), julienned
1 tomato, peeled, seeded and diced
½ teaspoon fine sherry vinegar
freshly ground white pepper
4 tablespoons dried Japanese wakame
  seaweed, soaked
4 wild peaches in truffle oil, finely sliced
2 tablespoons finely chopped chives

Wild peaches are available from fine food providores and delicatessens, although, for this recipe, you could substitute the peaches with very finely sliced pitted green olives, allowing 2 olives per serve.

Preheat the oven to 180°C (350°F). Trim the barramundi fillets, remove any loose scales and cut each fillet in half crosswise. Lightly coat the barramundi with the grapeseed oil and the 2 tablespoons white truffle oil. Sprinkle with sea salt. Place on a baking sheet and bake in the oven for 10–12 minutes, or until the fish is soft to the touch.

Combine the witlof, tomato, sherry vinegar and extra 2 teaspoons white truffle oil in a bowl. Season with sea salt and white pepper, and mix together gently with a spoon. Squeeze the water from the wakame and divide. To serve, place the wakame in the centre of each serving plate and top with the truffled peaches and barramundi fillets. Spoon the witlof mixture to the side of the barramundi. Garnish with the chopped chives and serve immediately.

Serves 4 Recipe: easy to make

Geoff Lindsay, chef

Yellow Thai Curry of Swordfish
with Green Papaya

INGREDIENTS

YELLOW CURRY PASTE

10 dried red chillies

1 yellow capsicum (sweet pepper), seeds
and stem removed

1 tablespoon ground turmeric

4 golden shallots, peeled and chopped

6 cloves garlic, peeled and chopped

2 stalks lemon grass, white part only,
finely chopped

1 teaspoon shrimp paste

YELLOW CURRY SAUCE

scant cup (200 mL/7 fl oz) coconut
milk

4 tablespoons Yellow Curry Paste

4 cups (1 litre/1¾ imp. pints) chicken
stock

3 tablespoons tamarind water
(page 134)

2 tablespoons palm sugar

juice of 2 limes

COCONUT RICE

1½ cups (250 g /8 oz) jasmine rice

1 cup (250 mL/8 fl oz) water

5 tablespoons coconut milk

1 piece pandan leaf, about 5 cm
(2 inch) long

4 x 185-g (6-oz) swordfish steaks

1 bunch of snake beans

1 green papaya (pawpaw)

8 fresh mint leaves

8 fresh basil leaves

handful of baby spinach leaves

½ cup crispy fried shallots

Thai basil to garnish

This is unashamedly a yellow Thai curry. It is refreshing, a little bit sour, with only a small amount of coconut milk as the swordfish is so rich. Fragrance is added with fresh mint, basil leaves and lime juice.

To make the yellow curry paste, blend all the ingredients together in a food processor to a smooth, even paste. (This quantity makes enough for one curry.)

To make the yellow curry sauce, pour the coconut milk into a heavy-based saucepan and cook over medium heat until it is almost completely reduced. Add the curry paste and fry for 15 minutes, stirring constantly and without colouring the paste. Add the chicken stock, bring to the boil and simmer for 30 minutes. Add the tamarind water, palm sugar and lime juice. Mix well and, when it has reached a thick consistency, remove from the heat and set aside until ready to use.

To make the coconut rice, wash the rice thoroughly in plenty of cold water and drain. Combine all the rice ingredients and place in a saucepan over medium heat. Bring the rice to the boil and simmer for 10 minutes, then cover with a tight-fitting lid. Turn off the heat and allow the rice to steam for a further 10 minutes. It is now ready to serve.

To make the curry, grill the swordfish steaks under a preheated hot grill (broiler) for about 2 minutes on each side. Allow to rest. Blanch the beans and papaya until tender. Heat the yellow curry sauce.

To serve, gently place the swordfish in the sauce, add the papaya and beans, then the mint and basil leaves. Place a slice of papaya on each warm serving plate, then spoon the vegetable mixture on top. Place the swordfish on top of the vegetables and spoon some sauce around each plate. Sprinkle over the crispy fried shallots, garnish with the Thai basil and serve with the coconut rice.

Serves 4 Recipe: medium complexity

RIGHT: Yellow Thai Curry of Swordfish with Green Papaya. 'Green papaya is used as a vegetable by the Thais and I added the snake beans as a bit of a tease for a jungle curry. The textures work well with the meaty white flesh of the fish and the crunchy vegetables—the rice is the comfort zone.'

Jacques Reymond, chef

Broth of Oriental Flavours
with Yellowfin Tuna Tagine and Spaghetti Vegetables

Tagine paste is a spicy blend that intensifies the flavours of the tuna and the broth.

INGREDIENTS

TAGINE PASTE

½ tablespoon cumin seed

1½ cinnamon sticks

½ tablespoon paprika

½ tablespoon ground coriander

½ teaspoon saffron powder

3 large bulbs fresh ginger, julienned and blanched 3 times

2½ tablespoons fresh turmeric, grated, or 1 teaspoon if dried

3 chillies, finely chopped

1 tablespoon vegetable oil

1 bunch of fresh coriander (Chinese parsley) leaves

BROTH

8 cups (2 litres/3¼ imp. pints) reduced chicken stock

6 ripe tomatoes

4 bulbs of fresh ginger

5 lemon grass stalks

8 cloves garlic, crushed

12 golden shallots, finely sliced

3–4 chillies, seeded

2 stalks celery, finely sliced

1 leek, finely sliced

salt

1 bunch of fresh basil

1 bunch of fresh coriander

GARNISH FOR BROTH

red shallots, finely sliced

chilli, julienned

ginger, blanched and julienned

fresh coriander leaves

garlic chives, cut into batons

1 carrot, julienned

ginger, blanched and julienned

1 zucchini (courgette), julienned

½ telegraph cucumber, julienned

1 tablespoon vegetable oil

1 cup bamboo shoots

3 cups pea shoots

morels in season to garnish

6 yellowfin tuna steaks, 2 cm (¾ inch) thick

To make the tagine paste, grind the cumin, cinnamon, paprika, coriander and saffron. Place in a food processor or blender with the ginger, turmeric, chilli and some of the vegetable oil, and blend into a paste. Add a little more oil and then add half the coriander leaves. Blend for a few more seconds before adding the rest of the coriander. Continue to blend into a fine paste. If the paste is too dry, add more oil.

To cook the broth, start from cold and put all the broth ingredients in a large saucepan except for the basil and coriander. Cook over medium heat for 40 minutes. Add the basil and coriander, remove from the heat and infuse for 15 minutes. Strain through fine muslin or cheesecloth.

To serve, heat the broth and the garnishes. Stir-fry the carrot, ginger, zucchini and cucumber in a wok with the vegetable oil. At the last moment, remove the vegetables and add the bamboo shoots and pea shoots to the wok. Toss once or twice, then remove—do not allow to wilt. Place the vegetables in the centre of a large soup bowl and add a few morels if using. Coat the tuna with the tagine paste and grill under a salamander or a hot grill (broiler) for 30 seconds on each side. Place the tuna on top of the vegetables, then pour the broth gently around the tuna and sprinkle the garnishes around the plate. Top the tuna with the bamboo and pea shoots, and serve immediately.

Serves 6 Recipe: medium complexity

Genevieve Harris, chef

Steamed Coconut Pancakes
with Green Curry Sauce

INGREDIENTS

GREEN CURRY SAUCE

1 bunch of fresh coriander (Chinese parsley) leaves, stalks and roots

½ cup fresh mint leaves

1 pandan leaf

1 large green chilli

1 stalk lemon grass

4 cups (1 litre/1¾ imp. pints) coconut milk

1 tablespoon palm sugar (jaggery) syrup

2½ tablespoons fish sauce (nam pla)

1 tablespoon lemon juice

COCONUT PANCAKES

3 eggs

1 tablespoon rice flour

150 mL (5 fl oz) coconut milk

dash of fish sauce

dash of sesame oil

vegetable oil

PANCAKE FILLING

500 g (1 lb) whiting fillets

1 cup coriander (Chinese parsley) leaves

4 fresh kaffir lime leaves, finely sliced

½ cucumber, julienned

2 green spring onions, chopped

½ cup fresh mint leaves, chopped

This dish is perfect for entertaining, as everything can be prepared and assembled ahead of time and takes just minutes to plate up. We are currently using whiting in the pancakes, but it works equally well with any other white-fleshed fish, prawns (shrimp) or yabby (freshwater crayfish) meat. You can also serve the pancake on a salad bed of cucumber, coriander and mint.

To make the green curry sauce, chop the coriander, mint, pandan, chilli and lemon grass. Place in a food processor or blender, and blend to a paste. Put into a stainless steel saucepan with the coconut milk and simmer until the flavours have infused and the sauce has thickened and reduced by about half. Season with the palm sugar syrup, fish sauce and lemon juice. Strain through a fine mesh sieve. Reserve and keep warm.

To make the coconut pancakes, whisk the eggs, rice flour, coconut milk, fish sauce and sesame oil together. Strain through a fine mesh sieve. Heat a teflon crêpe pan or skillet over medium heat. Drizzle a small amount of vegetable oil into the pan, then ladle enough pancake batter in to cover the surface thinly. Cook until the mixture is set and then turn out onto a plate. Continue until all the batter is used—you should have 8 pancakes. Set aside.

To make the pancake filling, clean the whiting fillets and cut them into thin strips. Chop the coriander leaves. Mix all the filling ingredients together, then divide evenly into 8 portions. Place a coconut pancake on a board. Put one portion of the filling on the bottom third of the pancake and roll, folding the edges in like a spring roll. Place the rolled pancakes on baking parchment in a steamer tray. Repeat the process with the remaining pancakes and filling. Steam for 8 minutes and serve with the warm green curry sauce.

Makes 8 pancakes Recipe: medium complexity

Serge Dansereau
Joy of Regional Food

'When I started at Kables, The Regent, in 1983, I began to discover the quality products from different regions of Australia—the lamb from Gippsland, beef from Milawa, the Jervis Bay mussels—and I started moving into cuisine du marche, a more regional type of cooking with more homey food.'

Serge Dansereau was born in Canada and did his training in Quebec. On graduation, he was travelling aide to a district executive chef, helping develop standards in food in small hotels—it was during this time that Serge began to appreciate the value of regional products. He was then in charge of the kitchen in several regional hotels, until moving to Australia and falling in love with the place.

He was at The Regent in Sydney for fifteen years and he says he owes his success, in large part, to the fact that he was given carte blanche in the kitchens and that he has a hands-on approach to his job.

Serge was one of the first chefs to encourage growers to produce quality, rather than quantity, and to develop new products, particularly for salads and cheeses. Kables was the first restaurant to serve a uniquely Australian cheeseboard. Due to his influence on the types of food growers were producing, Serge has made a marked impact on the food in Australian homes and restaurants.

Serge's fine food is distinctively Australian in style. He describes it as 'an intelligent type of cuisine that suits the climate and uses Australian food and products with more sophistication.'

In 1999, Serge moved to the revamped Bathers Pavilion to work in partnership with Victoria Alexander. 'Now more than ever, I feel we have to be more aware of how we treat our unique products. I am trying to understand more about flavour and ingredients. I am taking a more natural approach—using fresh natural juices to make sauces and dressings, cooking more directly with flame. I am feeling more focused on what I do.'

ABOVE: Almond Tart with Amaretto Mascarpone and Poached Figs (page 196). 'One of my favourites. The tart is beautiful when it is freshly made and also reheats very well. This tart has a very, light non-aggressive almond flavour.'

LEFT: Blue Swimmer Crab and Cucumber Salad with Crisp Samosa Pastry (page 156). 'This recipe is influenced by one of my chefs who is half Burmese and half Indian, Terence Rego—he has a knack for blending these two cuisines.'

Janet Jeffs, chef

Summertime Fish and Chips

INGREDIENTS

BEER BATTER

1¾ cups (200 g/7 oz) plain (all-purpose)
 flour

pinch of salt

2 eggs

5 tablespoons good-quality ale

THICK POTATO CHIPS (FRIES)

6 medium Spunta potatoes

2 tablespoons olive oil

sprig of rosemary leaves, chopped

sea salt

GARLIC MAYONNAISE WITH BABY CAPERS

3 egg yolks

juice and grated zest of 1 lemon

1 clove garlic, crushed

2 cups (500 mL/16 fl oz) extra virgin
 olive oil

2 teaspoons salted baby capers, rinsed

12 fillets King George whiting or any
 fine-textured white fish, scaled

plain (all-purpose) flour

3 tablespoons olive oil

A flash of silver in the sea foam and a King George whiting is hauled in with an old rod, the Cooper's Ale is chilled, hot, fat potato chips are cooking, sleek fillets are soon sizzling in olive oil—fond memories of hot days and the food of summer.

To make the beer batter, sift the flour and salt into a mixing bowl and make a well in the centre. Break the eggs into the well and gradually pour in the beer, mixing into the flour. Whisk to a smooth battter.

To make the thick chips, preheat the oven to 200°C (400°F). Peel the potatoes and cut them into very thick chips (fries). Brush a shallow baking pan with some olive oil and spread the potato in an even layer. Brush with the oil and sprinkle with the rosemary and sea salt. Bake in the oven until golden, about 50 minutes. Turn a few times during cooking. Remove the chips from the oven and keep warm.

To make the mayonnaise, whisk the yolks with the lemon juice and zest, and garlic. Slowly drizzle in a little olive oil, drop by drop, whisking continuously until the mixture emulsifies. The oil can be added faster now. Keep whisking until all the oil is incorporated. Mix the capers into the mayonnaise just before serving.

To cook the fish, trim the whiting of all bones, wash and pat dry. Lightly flour and dip the fillets into the beer batter, just before cooking. Heat the olive oil in a large frying pan or skillet over medium-high heat. When very hot (test with a bread cube—when it immediately rises to the surface, the oil is ready), fry the fish fillets in two or three batches, being careful not to overcrowd the pan, and cook until golden brown. Quickly drain on absorbent kitchen paper—the fish must be served immediately for best results.

To serve, place the fish and chips on warm serving plates and spoon the mayonnaise beside the fish. Serve at once.

Serves 6 Recipe: easy to make

André Chouvin, chef

Ocean Trout with Lemon Myrtle

INGREDIENTS

SAUCE

½ carrot, ¾ onion and ½ leek, diced

1 bay leaf

2 teaspoons white vinegar

4 teaspoons white wine

2 cups (500 mL/16 fl oz) water

freshly chopped chervil and chives

1 lemon myrtle leaf

155 g (5 oz) butter

To make the sauce, put the carrot, two-thirds of the onion, leek, bay leaf, vinegar, 2 teaspoons of the white wine and water into a saucepan. Bring to the boil. Turn the heat down and slowly simmer for 30 minutes. Strain the liquid into a container. Put the remaining onion and 2 teaspoons white wine in a frying pan or skillet, and reduce until almost dry. Add one-quarter of the sauce liquid to the frying pan along with the chervil, chives and lemon myrtle leaf. Let it reduce in volume by half for 10 minutes over high heat. Strain through a fine sieve and add the butter. Stir until the sauce amalgamates, about 5 minutes. Keep warm.

To make the pancakes, put the potato, egg and egg yolk, cream and salmon into a bowl and blend with a hand-held blender. Melt some butter in a frying pan

SMOKED SALMON PANCAKE

200 g (7 oz) mashed potato

1 egg, plus 1 yolk

2 teaspoons heavy (double) cream

90 g (3 oz) smoked salmon

butter

4 x 200-g (7-oz) ocean trout

salt and freshly ground black pepper

butter

2 tomatoes, skinned, seeded and diced

2 tablespoons chopped chives

over high heat and skim off any any impurities—this helps to prevent the butter burning. Place spoonfuls of the potato mixture in the pan. Flatten to resemble a little pancake—you should have 8 pancakes in all. Sauté on both sides for about 8 minutes, or until golden brown. Reserve in a warm place.

To cook the fish, fillet and season the fish. In a frying pan, sauté the fish on each side in butter for about 5 minutes, or until pink in the middle. (Once again, skimming any impurities off the top of the melted butter helps prevent burning and tainting the fish with a strong butter flavour.)

To serve, add the tomatoes and chives to the reserved sauce. Put the fish on warm plates and spoon over the sauce. Accompany each serving with 2 smoked salmon pancakes.

Serves 4 Recipe: medium complexity

Raymond Capadli, chef

Confit of Tasmanian Salmon
with Blancmange of Cauliflower, Nutmeg Spinach and Lemon Oil

INGREDIENTS

BLANCMANGE CAULIFLOWER

100 g (3½ oz) potatoes

200 g (7 oz) cauliflower

2 teaspoons unsalted butter

1 clove garlic, crushed

½ cup (60 g/2 oz) ground almonds

zest of ½ lemon

2 cups (500 mL/16 fl oz) Noilly Prat

2 cups (500 mL/16 fl oz) Pernod

1 cup (250 mL/8 fl oz) heavy (double) cream

2 teaspoons gelatine

salt and cayenne

1 x 400-g (13-oz) can goose fat

4 x 185-g (6-oz) salmon supreme

sea salt flakes

thyme flowers

lemon oil

NUTMEG SPINACH

1 bunch fresh of spinach leaves

1 tablespoon unsalted butter

1 clove garlic, crushed

½ teaspoon freshly grated nutmeg

salt and freshly ground black pepper

1 tablespoon lemon juice

I always ask for salmon supreme cut off the bone—it's the best cut for this dish.

The blancmange needs to be made 24 hours in advance. Peel and slice the potatoes and finely slice the cauliflower. Place the butter in a saucepan and add the potato, cauliflower, garlic, ground almonds, lemon zest, Noilly Prat, Pernod and cream. Bring to the boil. Place the gelatine in a little water to dissolve and, once soft, add to the blancmange mixture. Season to taste with salt and cayenne. When the gelatine has dissolved, purée the blancmange mixture in a blender or food processor, then pass through a fine sieve. Refrigerate for 24 hours until set.

To make the confit of salmon, pour the goose fat into the saucepan then bring it to blood temperature. Remove the skin from the salmon. Place the salmon in the goose fat and cover. Remove when it is pink in the middle.

While the salmon is cooking, make the nutmeg spinach. Wash and remove the stalks of the spinach. Melt the butter in a frying pan or skillet, and add the spinach, garlic, nutmeg, salt and pepper to taste, and lemon juice. Cook until the spinach is just wilted.

To serve, drain the salmon and wipe with absorbent kitchen paper. Place a little blancmange on each serving plate. Put the salmon on top and sprinkle with sea salt and thyme flowers. Place the nutmeg spinach on the side and pour the lemon oil decoratively around the plate. Serve at once.

Serves 4 Recipe: complex

Damien Pignolet, chef

A Salad of Mussels
with Saffron Potatoes, Fennel and Basil

INGREDIENTS

2.5 kg (5 lb) mussels, scrubbed

1 small onion, peeled and sliced

bouquet garni of thyme, parsley, bay leaf
and crushed garlic clove

good splash of white wine

250 g (8 oz) waxy potatoes

salt and freshly ground black pepper

1 large or 2 small Florence fennel
(finocchio) bulbs

6–8 sun-dried tomatoes, julienned

6 tablespoons small black olives

1 small bunch of basil leaves, torn

VINAIGRETTE

1 teaspoon saffron threads

1½ tablespoons strained mussel juice
from opening mussels

1 small clove garlic, roughly crushed

½ cup (125 mL/4 fl oz) olive oil

salt and freshly ground black pepper

1½ tablespoons red wine vinegar

RIGHT: A Salad of Mussels with Saffron Potatoes,
Fennel and Basil. The fennel, sun-dried tomatoes
and olives combine beautifully with the inherent
saltiness of the mussels.

This mussel dish is inspired by a visit to Provence in the early 1980s. I had it on the menu at Claude's.

Open the mussels in several batches in a wide shallow saucepan with a tight-fitting lid. Place them in one layer with the onion, bouquet garni and wine, put the lid on and place over high heat. The moment steam begins to escape, lift the lid and remove the mussels as they open. Discard any unopened mussels.

Strain the juices through a muslin cloth and set aside while the mussels are shelled. Examine the inside of each mussel for the beard or tiny crabs, both of which need to be discarded. Retain around 12 mussels in the shells as a decorative garnish. Cover the shelled mussels with the strained juices. Reserve 1½ tablespoons mussel juice for the vinaigrette. Peel the potatoes and cut into 2-cm (¾-inch) dice or slices about 1 cm (½ inch) long if thin potatoes are used. Season with salt and pepper to taste and steam until tender, about 12–14 minutes.

While the potatoes are cooking, make the vinaigrette. Infuse the saffron in the warmed reserved mussel juice. Rub a mixing bowl with the garlic, discard the clove and add the oil and infused saffron. Season with salt and pepper to taste and add the vinegar. Taste for saltiness and acidity.

Transfer the potatoes to a bowl and moisten with two-thirds of the vinaigrette, tossing and coating them well. Taste for salt and adjust seasoning if necessary. If you like, add some of the reserved mussel juice to enrich the steamed potatoes. Trim the top and base of the fennel and shave finely lengthwise.

To serve, toss all the ingredients together, including the fennel, tomato, olives and basil, and distribute between 6 plates, adding 2 mussel shells per serve. Moisten with more vinaigrette and serve.

Serves 6 Recipe: easy to make

Damien Pignolet, chef

Prawn Soufflé Tart

INGREDIENTS

PASTRY

250 g (8 oz) plain (all-purpose) flour

pinch of salt

185 g (6 oz) cold butter

pinch of cayenne

¼ cup (60 mL/2 fl oz) liquid, made up
of 1 egg yolk mixed with cold water

CONTINUED ON PAGE 148

I designed this tart for a soufflé class at Accoutrement, where I did a course on savoury and sweet soufflés. It is important to be exact with your measurements for the pastry and soufflé mixtures.

To make the pastry, sift the flour and salt onto a work surface. Grate the cold butter with a hand grater over the flour. Using a chef's knife or steel spatula, toss the flour and butter together. Combine the cayenne with the liquid using a fork. Sprinkle this over the flour and butter. Smear the ingredients into a dough by using the heel of your hand to push the paste together. Do this quickly and

PRAWN STOCK

1¼ cups (310 mL/10 fl oz) fish stock

salt and freshly ground black pepper

625 g (1¼ lb) prawns (shrimp), peeled
    and deveined (reserve the shells)

2 teaspoons olive oil

2 golden shallots, peeled and sliced

2 teaspoons tomato paste (purée),
    diluted with a little stock

3 tablespoons dry vermouth (Noilly Prat
    if possible)

SOUFFLE MIXTURE

60 g (2 oz) butter

45 g (1½ oz) plain (all-purpose) flour

⅔ cup (155 mL/5 fl oz) milk

⅔ cup (155 mL/5 fl oz) stock, from first
    preparation

2 egg yolks, beaten

5 egg whites

pinch of salt

60 g (2 oz) Gruyère cheese, coarsely
    grated

lightly—it should take two or three actions before a dough emerges. Knead lightly into a disc, wrap in baking parchment and chill for 15 minutes. It should not get too hard.

Dust the bench with flour and roll out the pastry to fit a tart pan with a removable base (26–28 cm/10–11 inch) or one of your choice. Lightly grease the pan and line with the pastry, pushing up the sides at least 1 cm (½ inch) above the edge. Prick the pastry base with a fork and put the shell (pan and all) into a plastic bag and reserve in the freezer.

To make the prawn stock, bring the fish stock to the boil and season well with salt and pepper. Place the prawns in a wide frying pan or skillet in one layer and cover with the boiling fish stock. Leave for 1 minute and then strain the stock into a clean saucepan. Cut the prawns in half and reserve.

Heat the oil in the frying pan. Add the shallots and cook gently for a few minutes. Add the reserved prawn shells, increase the heat and toss until they turn pink. Stir in the tomato paste, then add the dry vermouth and allow to bubble for a few minutes before adding to the fish stock. Bring to the boil, taste and adjust seasoning, and simmer for 20 minutes. Strain through a fine sieve. You will have more stock than you need—this can be frozen until required.

To make the pastry, preheat the oven to 200°C (400°F). Line the tart shell with foil and put some pastry weights or dried beans on the foil and bake blind for 10–15 minutes, reducing the temperature to 180°C (350°F) after the first 5 minutes. Remove the foil and weights, and cook until the pastry is very well cooked and dry. Reduce the temperature as required to dry out the pastry—to about 150°C (300°F) for the last 10 minutes. It may take up to 30 minutes to cook properly.

Meanwhile, to make the soufflé, melt the butter in a saucepan and allow it to cool for a few minutes. Add the flour, stir to a smooth paste and return to a gentle heat for 3 minutes, stirring constantly. Allow the roux to cool. Now bring the milk and stock to the boil. Taste and adjust the seasoning as necessary. Stir the hot liquid onto the roux over low heat to obtain a smooth, thick sauce. Cover with a piece of buttered baking parchment and cook very slowly for 15 minutes. Remove the paper and beat the sauce smooth. Add the beaten yolks, beating thoroughly.

The pastry should be cooked at this point and out of the oven. Set the oven temperature to 180°C (350°F) and pat the reserved prawns dry with absorbent kitchen paper. Beat the egg whites until stiff, adding the salt at the soft-peak stage. Lighten the base sauce with one-quarter of the whites, scatter the prawns and half the cheese over the remaining whites and fold into the base sauce. Spoon this mixture into the tart shell and scatter with the remaining cheese. Bake until risen and coloured, about 15–20 minutes, reducing the oven temperature to 160°C (325°F) after the first 10 minutes of cooking.

Remove the tart from the pan—place it on top of a mould or ramekin so that the outer ring drops down, then slide a spatula between the pastry and the base and lift off the tart. Serve at once.

Serves 6   Recipe: complex

Greg Malouf, chef

Salmon Kibbeh Tartare
with Cracked Wheat and Garlic Cheese

INGREDIENTS

500 g (1 lb) yoghurt

⅓ cup (45 g/1½ oz) fine cracked wheat

1 cup (250mL/8 fl oz) water

625 g (1¼ lb) minced Atlantic salmon

2 purple shallots, finely chopped

small bullet chilli, finely chopped

¼ teaspoon freshly ground white pepper

⅓ teaspoon ground pimento

juice of 1 lemon, plus a little extra

sea salt

1 clove garlic, crushed with ½ teaspoon
   sea salt

½ cup each coriander (Chinese parsley),
   mint, flat-leaf parsley and pickled
   artichoke leaves

⅓ cup red onion, finely sliced

⅔ cup (100 mL/3½ fl oz) extra virgin
   olive oil

sea salt and freshly ground white pepper

1 teaspoon sumak

Place the yoghurt in a double layer of cheesecloth and hang for 24–36 hours.

Chill a stainless steel bowl. In a separate bowl, soak the cracked wheat in the water for 8 minutes, then drain and squeeze. Transfer to the chilled bowl and mix with the salmon, shallot, chilli, white pepper, pimento, lemon juice and sea salt to taste. Form the mixture into 6 discs and refrigerate.

In another bowl, blend the yoghurt cheese with the garlic and form into 6 balls.

To serve, place a salmon disc in the centre of the serving plates. Mix the coriander leaves, mint and flat parsley with the artichoke leaves, onion, a squeeze of lemon juice and a little extra virgin olive oil, and lightly season with salt and pepper. Place the salad on top of the salmon with a ball of yoghurt cheese resting on the salad. Drizzle the remaining extra virgin oil around the salmon and sprinkle with the sumak.

Serves 6 Recipe: easy to make

Stephanie Alexander, chef and food writer

Roasted Yabbies with Thyme Oil

INGREDIENTS

20 yabbies, freshly killed and chilled

freshly ground black pepper

1 tablespoon fresh thyme leaves

½ cup (125 mL/4 fl oz) extra virgin
   olive oil

sea salt

lemon wedges to serve

Yabbies can be served as either a starter or a main course, depending on how many you catch. Encourage fish providores to sell them live. Yabbies may be substituted with freshwater crayfish. Don't forget to sprinkle with sea salt—schnapps goes down well sometimes.

Carefully split each yabby and its shell lengthwise, including the head, using a heavy chef's knife. Remove intestinal thread from each half. Arrange yabby halves, flesh-side up, in a single layer on an oiled baking sheet. Grind a little pepper over each; and scatter with thyme. Paint the flesh with some of the oil. Leave the yabbies at room temperature for up to 1 hour before cooking.

Preheat the oven or griller (broiler) to maximum. Grill or roast the yabbies for 4 minutes until the flesh is just firm. Drizzle with a little more oil before serving with sea salt and a bowl of lemon wedges.

Serves 4–6 Recipe: easy to make

Stephanie Alexander

Cooking from the Heart

'My advice to young chefs and anyone interested in cooking is to follow your own bent—read widely, travel widely in your own country, don't wipe your own cultural background—discover who you are and what your culinary roots are.'

Encouraged by her mother, by thirteen years of age Stephanie was a competent cook. Although she loved cooking, it didn't occcur to her to do it professionally— but eventually her love of cooking involved her in Jamaica House and then her own restaurant, Stephanie's, in Fitzroy.

Melbourne didn't have comfortable grand dining when Stephanie's removed to a classified mansion in Hawthorn in 1980. A new tone and standard for fine dining was set—for years, Stephanie's was regarded as an essential Melbourne experience.

During that period, Stephanie encouraged and trained many fine chefs, including Janni Kyritsis, Geoff Lindsay, Neil Perry and Steven Pullett. She also led the field in education and discovery of new ingredients. She especially supported small specialist suppliers. Her inspirational book, Stephanie's Australia showcased these suppliers and the wealth of superb local food produce.

Stephanie also wrote The Cook's Companion, an encyclopedic work of ingredients and recipes, which became a classic overnight.

Stephanie's closed in 1997, as Stephanie decided to step aside from a hands-on role in a kitchen. She became a partner in Richmond Hill Café and Larder, which includes the first two fully humidified cheese rooms in Australia.

'I am essentially curious and I like to cast a broad net, but I come back to things I really love. I like to feel I'm treating the produce with respect and enjoyment. I am an outspoken champion of the quality and diversity of Australian produce.'

ABOVE: Queen of Nuts Cake on a Simple Rhubarb and Red Fruit Sago Sauce (page 205). A sophisticated Italian cake flavoured with candied citron. It is dry and chewy, and served with a wonderful sweet–tart sauce. Thick cream adds the luscious character.

LEFT: Cheese maturing in the humidified cheese room set up by Will Studd at Richmond Hill Café and Larder. This allows an extra dimension of flavour that is achievable only if the cheese is stored correctly and matured to its peak condition.

FAR LEFT: Roasted Yabbies with Thyme Oil (page 149). 'This dish evokes childhood memories. Why aren't yabbies more loved? It would be nice if another generation of children experienced fresh yabbies, even if they can no longer catch them. Roasted simply over high heat on a barbecue, they have a toasty flavour—eat them with your fingers.'

Cheong Liew, chef

The Four Dances

Soused Snook, Octopus with Aïoli,
Raw Cuttlefish with Black Noodles, Spiced Prawn Sushi

Soused Snook

SNOOK INGREDIENTS

WASABI MAYONNAISE

1 egg yolk

1 teaspoon green wasabi

1 tablespoon rice vinegar

5 tablespoons warm peanut oil

2½ tablespoons sugar syrup

2 medium, very fresh snook fillets, or
any fine, white oily fish

1 tablespoon sea salt

1 tablespoon sugar

2½ tablespoons mirin

5 tablespoons rice vinegar or sherry
vinegar

2½ tablespoons rice wine

6 avocado quarters, cut into 2 slices for
each serving

OCTOPUS INGREDIENTS

2 kg (4 lb) octopus tentacles

¾ cup (185 mL/6 fl oz) olive oil

3 tablespoons black olives, pitted and
crushed

4 cloves garlic, crushed

4 bay leaves

6 stalks fresh parsley

juice of 2 lemons

2 red chillies

AIOLI

6 cloves garlic

1 large red chilli

4 coriander (Chinese parsley) roots

1 egg yolk

5 tablespoons olive oil

1 teaspoon sea salt

juice of ½ lemon

The Four Dances is my most popular dish and one that gave my signature to the menu when I opened the Grange, at the Adelaide Hilton. There are twenty-one elements in the dish and a lot of cooking techniques. It showcases versatility and fresh seafood; four different textures and four techniques create the dance. There are many food cultures in the dish, including Mediterranean, Australian, Japanese, Greek, and Malayan— that is why I call it a dance. This dish serves six but you can make the dishes individually as starters or main courses, and save the four dishes together for a special occasion. Arrange the portions cleanly and harmoniously on large white plates.

To make the wasabi mayonnaise, whisk together the egg yolk, green wasabi and rice vinegar. Pour in the warm peanut oil and whisk until it thickens. Add the sugar syrup, combine and reserve.

Clean and trim the snook fillet, removing any bones and, if possible, the outer skin membrane. Lay the fillet skin-side down and sprinkle the salt and sugar evenly over both fillets. Cover and leave to cure for 2 hours.

Marinate the cured snook with the mirin, rice vinegar and rice wine for a further 1 hour or longer. Slice the fillet at an angle diagonally and serve 3 slices per person. Serve on a bed of 2 slices of avocado with a spoonful of the wasabi mayonnaise.

Octopus with Aïoli

Peel the skin off the octopus, but leave the suckers intact. Pat dry with a clean kitchen cloth. Heat the olive oil in a saucepan until sizzling. Add the olives and fry until smoking. Gather the small ends of the tentacles and gently lower the tentacles into the saucepan to seal the octopus very quickly. Immediately reduce the heat to as low as possible. Add the garlic, bay leaves, parsley, lemon and chilli. Cover the pan and simmer for 35–40 minutes. The octopus should be as soft as lobster flesh.

To make the aïoli, using a mortar and pestle, pound the garlic, chilli and coriander roots into a fine, smooth paste. The quality of the paste depends on the patience of the person pounding.

In a mixing bowl, whisk the egg yolk and garlic paste together with a fork. Slowly add the olive oil, whisking until the mixture emulsifies into a mayonnaise consistency. Add the salt and lemon juice to taste.

To serve, slice the octopus at sucker intervals. Arrange on the serving plate and spoon a little aïoli on top.

Cuttlefish Ingredients

185 g (6 oz) sashimi-quality cuttlefish

300 g (10 oz) squid ink taglierini, cooked and chilled

Asian-style dressing

½ teaspoon sesame oil

½ tablespoon oyster sauce

1 tablespoon balsamic vinegar

2 tablespoons sunflower seed oil

1 tablespoon soy sauce

1 tablespoon mirin

freshly ground black pepper

Prawn sushi ingredients

6 large king prawns (shrimp), shelled and deveined

pinch of salt

2 tablespoons sugar

finely grated zest of 2 limes

3 tablespoons peanut oil

2 tablespoons coconut cream

2½ tablespoons tamarind juice

3 tablespoons light palm sugar (jaggery)

Rempah mixture

2 teaspoons fresh galangal, finely grated

1 teaspoon fresh turmeric, finely grated

6 whole candlenuts, finely grated

1 red chilli, pounded to a paste

6–10 golden shallots, finely chopped

3 cloves garlic, finely chopped

2 teaspoons finely grated fresh ginger

2 teaspoons blanchan (shrimp paste), lightly roasted in foil

Banana leaf sushi

1 cup (200 g/7 oz) glutinous rice, presoaked for 1 hour

1 tablespoon peanut oil

1 teaspoon sea salt

4 tablespoons coconut cream

1 large piece of fresh banana leaf or foil lined with greaseproof paper

Raw Cuttlefish with Black Noodles

Clean the cuttlefish thoroughly and wipe off any ink that has smeared the cuttlefish with a damp cloth. Chill for 30 minutes.

Slice the cuttlefish on the inside of the fish, at a very low angle, and then shave very thinly, to gives it a gentler texture. Gather the flesh together to form a white rose and keep covered in the refrigerator.

In a bowl, mix the Asian-style dressing ingredients together. Pour over the chilled squid ink pasta and toss to combine. Divide the pasta into 6 small portions. Place the cuttlefish on the top of the noodles.

Spiced Prawn Sushi

Cut the prawns in half lengthwise. Lightly sprinkle them with salt, sugar and lime zest. Set aside.

Put all the rempah ingredients into a blender or food processor, and blend to a smooth paste. In a wok, heat the peanut oil over low to medium heat. Add the rempah mixture and coconut cream, and stir-fry slowly and constantly, until half the oil starts to separate from the solid. Add the prawns, tamarind juice and palm sugar, and continue stir-frying until the prawns are cooked, less than a minute.

Banana Leaf Sushi

Steam the rice with a sprinkling of the oil and salt for 15–20 minutes. Mix in the coconut cream with the cooked rice until it is nicely moist. Toast the banana leaf with a hot iron or ridged frying pan or skillet. Trim off the hard stems and hard edges of the leaf. Put the cooked rice on the banana leaf and roll it into a sushi log, about 3–4 cm (1½ inches) in diameter. Wrap the whole rice sushi in foil and char-grill for about 3–4 minutes on each side. Cook for about 15 minutes in a steamer. When unwrapped, the edges of the rice sushi should be slightly brown and toasted with an astonishing fragrance of the smoked banana leaf.

To serve, cut the sushi into 4-cm (1½-inch) logs and spoon the Spiced Prawn Sushi on top.

Serves 6   Recipe: complex

Gary Cooper, chef

Collar of Prickly Ashed Crayfish
in a Shark Fin and Kaffir Lime Leaf Broth

INGREDIENTS

FISH STOCK

300 g (10 oz) trevally bones, or any fine white-fleshed fish bones

1 carrot, roughly chopped

2 brown onions, skin on, roughly chopped

2 stalks celery, roughly chopped

2 bay leaves

1 teaspoon white peppercorns

2 crayfish, no larger than 1 kg (2 lb) each, uncooked

1 tablespoon Szechuan pepper

1 tablespoon salt

3 free-range eggs

⅔ cup (100 mL/3½ fl oz) heavy (double) cream

1 tablespoon butter

salt and freshly ground black pepper

dried shark fin (available at good Asian grocers)

2 kaffir lime leaves (available at good Asian grocers)

1 tablespoon salmon roe

To make the fish stock, wash the fish bones in clean, cold water. Drain the water and repeat to remove any impurities. Place the carrot, onion and celery in a large stockpot, add the fish bones, bay leaves and white peppercorns, and cover the bones with cold water. Bring the water to the boil and simmer for 20 minutes uncovered. Strain and allow to cool.

To prepare the crayfish, remove the head and cut the tail in half. Remove the flesh from the carcass and reserve. To make the prickly ash, roast the Szechuan pepper and salt in a small frying pan or skillet.

To make the scrambled eggs, mix the eggs with the cream and butter, and season to taste with salt and pepper. Put the mixture in a saucepan over low heat and gently cook the eggs, stirring gently until they are creamy and soft. Place in a bowl and keep warm.

To make the shark fin broth, break the shark fin into the fish stock and add a kaffir lime leaf. Gently simmer for 20 minutes until the shark fin is soft.

To serve, while the shark fin broth is simmering, place the crayfish tail meat in the broth—it will take 2 minutes to cook. Divide the crayfish meat among 4 deep, wide bowls—the meat will naturally curl. Top with the warm scrambled eggs and then the salmon roe. Pour the shark fin broth around the crayfish, making sure each serving has some shark fin pieces. Finely slice the remaining kaffir lime leaf and use to garnish each serving. Serve immediately.

Serves 4   Recipe: medium complexity

FAR RIGHT: Collar of Prickly Ashed Crayfish in a Shark Fin and Kaffir Lime Leaf Broth. This is a simple luncheon dish for lovers of crayfish. The shark fin broth is very gelatinous; the crayfish is crunchy, but melt-in-the-mouth; and it is all topped off with soft scrambled eggs and crunchy salmon roe. The dish is called a collar because the crayfish curl up when cut in half.

Serge Dansereau, chef

Blue Swimmer Crab
and Cucumber Salad with Crisp Samosa Pastry

INGREDIENTS

SAMOSA DOUGH

2 cups (250 g/8 oz) plain (all-purpose) flour

⅓ cup (90 mL/3 fl oz) natural (plain) yoghurt

75 g (2½ oz) melted butter, at room temperature

large pinch of salt

2½ tablespoons squid ink

2½ tablespoons saffron reduction (see note)

3 tablespoons olive oil

DRESSING

1 soft poached egg

2½ tablespoons cucumber juice (from the drained cucumber julienne)

2 tablespoons tahini

5 tablespoons vegetable oil

2½ tablespoons white wine vinegar

juice of 1 lime

salt and freshly ground black pepper

SALAD

1 telegraph cucumber, peeled and julienned (reserve juices for dressing)

salt

200 g (7 oz) blue swimmer crab meat, cleaned

1 small red chilli, seeded and julienned

1 punnet young watercress leaves

Blue swimmer crabs are one of the sweetest of seafoods. Buy them really fresh. Sometimes we colour the dough with green spinach or saffron, or any other natural colouring. It adds flavour as well as colour. The pastry is soft and flaky and easy to make. The light dressing is made from vegetable juices.

To make the samosa dough, divide the quantities of flour, yoghurt, butter, salt in two and place in two separate bowls. Place the squid ink in one bowl and the saffron reduction in the other. Mix separately to form two amounts of dough (if too dry, add a little water). Rest each dough, covered, in the refrigerator for 1 hour. Roll each ball of dough out thinly on a floured board and cut either into small circles or triangle shapes. Place on a tray and refrigerate until needed.

To make the dressing, blend the egg, cucumber juice, tahini, vegetable oil, vinegar and lime juice in a food processor or blender. Season to taste with salt and pepper, and reserve.

In a frying pan or skillet, fry the samosa pieces in olive oil over very high heat for 2 minutes until crisp. Drain well on absorbent kitchen paper and reserve.

Drain the cucumber julienne and season with salt. Mix the crab meat with the chilli and some of the dressing to moisten the crab meat.

To serve, set a little crabmeat salad on each plate and top with a samosa pastry and another tablespoon of crabmeat salad. Top with some cucumber and repeat. Moisten the watercress with a touch of vegetable oil and place on top.

Serves 4 Recipe: medium complexity

NOTE: To make saffron reduction, pour ⅔ cup (155 mL/5 fl oz) dry white wine into a small saucepan over medium heat. Add a pinch of saffron threads and reduce in volume by two-thirds. Strain and reserve.

Guillaume Brahimi, chef

Stew of Yabbies,
Clams, Mussels and Scallops with Fresh Tarragon

INGREDIENTS

16 yabbies or freshwater crayfish

12 scallops, Coffin Bay if available

1 kg (2 lb) mussels

500 g (1 lb) clams

2–3 snapper bones

60 g (2 oz) butter

5 carrots, chopped

1 bunch of celery, chopped

12 golden shallots, finely diced

1 kg (2 lb) button mushrooms, chopped

10 vine-ripened tomatoes

3 tablespoons olive oil

salt and freshly cracked black pepper

2 cups (500 mL/16 fl oz) Pernod

1 bunch of spinach

1 bunch of fresh tarragon, stems
   discarded and leaves finely chopped

A sea dish to compliment the food of the sea. It is simple and quick to make. The touch of tarragon at the end really lifts the dish.

Clean the yabbies, scallops, mussels and clams. Reserve. Make the fish stock with the snapper bones by covering them with water and bringing to the boil for 20 minutes. Reserve.

Melt some of the butter in a frying pan or skillet. Add the carrot, celery and half the shallots. Cook until they have softened, then add the mushrooms.

Blanch the tomatoes, remove their skins, deseed and dice the flesh. Place in a clean saucepan with the remaining shallots and cook slowly.

Twenty minutes before serving, heat half the olive oil in a frying pan or skillet. Add the yabbies and mushroom mixture, and season with cracked pepper. After 3 minutes, deglaze with the Pernod. Remove from the heat. Remove the yabby heads from the bodies and discard or save to make a stock.

Strain the fish stock and allow to reduce in a saucepan over high heat for 5 minutes. Reduce the heat and add the confit of tomato, scallops and yabbies. Keep warm. Wilt the spinach in a frying pan with the remaining butter and season to taste with salt and pepper. Heat the remaining olive oil in a frying pan, then add the mussels and clams. Remove from the pan once the shells are open and add to the stew. To serve, place the wilted spinach in the serving bowls with some of the stew on top. Garnish with the tarragon just before serving.

Serves 4 Recipe: medium complexity

Graeme Phillips, chef

Maria Island Clams
on Ginger-pickled Wakame

INGREDIENTS

1 tablespoon peanut oil

4 spring onions, finely sliced

1 red chilli, finely chopped

2 cloves garlic, finely chopped

1 tablespoon finely chopped fresh ginger

45 g (1½ oz) dried wakame, soaked,
   squeezed well and coarsely shredded

5 tablespoons rice wine vinegar

1½ tablespoons black mirin

splash of sesame oil

36 live Maria Island clams or pippies

A combination of two delicious sea flavours—sweet, fleshy clams and wakame seaweed—with a spicy Asian touch. A citrusy young Riesling or Semillon to drink with it would be perfection.

To make the pickle, gently heat the peanut oil in a frying pan or skillet, and sweat the spring onion, chilli, garlic and ginger until perfumed. Add the wakame, vinegar and mirin, toss together and bring to a quick boil for 30 seconds. Remove from the heat and allow to cool. Mix in a splash of sesame oil.

Steam the clams until just opened and the meat is just beginning to come away from the shell, 2–3 minutes. Remove the clams, fill one shell with a pocket of the pickled wakame and replace the clam in the other shell. Serve in the shell.

Serves 6 Recipe: easy to make

Alain Fabrègues, chef

Roasted Marron
from Parkerville with Citrus Sauce

INGREDIENTS

4 x 250-g (8-oz) fresh marron or
  freshwater crayfish
1 lemon
½ grapefruit
1 orange
5 tablespoons vegetable stock
100 g (½ oz) unsalted butter, cold and
  diced, plus extra
salt and freshly ground black pepper
16 stringless green beans, ends trimmed
8 baby carrots
1 tablespoon olive oil
200 g (7 oz) fresh fettuccine
fresh chervil or dill sprigs
fresh chives, finely chopped

When purchasing marron, select only live ones. Marron that die before being cooked have been under stress and the body fluids can make the flesh very soft and mushy, decreasing the yield of meat. It can also be dangerous to eat this shellfish if it is not absolutely fresh.

Immerse the marron in plenty of boiling, salted water, covered, for 90 seconds. Refresh in iced water. Remove the shell and the cord. Crack the claws and remove the flesh, but be very careful not to break it. Preheat the oven to 210°C (410°F).

Wash and clean the marron heads, and carefully shorten them by trimming with sharp kitchen scissors. Reserve for garnishing the dish.

Peel and segment the lemon, grapefruit and orange, and remove all the pips and white pith. Bring the vegetable stock to the boil in a saucepan over high heat and add the citrus segments. Cook for 5 minutes. Place in the food processor or blender, and blend at high speed. Add the 100 g (3½ oz) butter and blend into a smooth sauce. Check the seasoning and adjust with salt and pepper to taste. Set aside in a warm place. Be careful that the sauce does not get too hot—above 55°C (120°F)—otherwise it will separate.

Blanch the beans in boiling, salted water and refresh in iced water. Repeat the process with the carrots.

Season the marron with salt and pepper to taste. Heat an ovenproof frying pan or skillet, add the 1 tablespoon olive oil, and seal the marron tails. Transfer to the oven for 5 minutes. Remove from the oven, add the claws to the pan and allow to rest for 4 minutes.

Cook the fresh fettuccine in plenty of boiling, salted water for about 90 seconds. Drain well. Toss with a dab of butter, a pinch of salt and a little pepper. Heat the beans and baby carrots in 2 tablespoons water and a little fresh butter.

To serve, have 4 hot serving plates ready. Roll one-quarter of the fettuccine onto a long roasting fork, and place the roll in the centre of one of the plates. Repeat the process with the other plates. With a sharp knife, slice each marron tail into 2 pieces lengthwise. Arrange the marron on top of the bed of fettuccine, keeping the shape of the tail. Place the carrots and beans decoratively on either side of the marron. Put one of the reserved heads at the top of each plate, and the claws at the bottom. Emulsify the butter sauce with a hand-held blender and spoon over the tail and fettuccine. Garnish with the chervil and chives. Serve immediately.

Serves 4 Recipe: medium complexity

Chapter 5
Barbecues

Alan Saunders

Barbecues

'Why do people who claim to be sophisticated and knowing in food matters collapse with hysteria at the thought of the backyard barbie, when meats on a stick are regarded as haute cuisine in Balkan, Turkish and Levant cookery?' asked the late Richard Beckett in *Convicted Tastes*, his admirably pugnacious account of food in Australia. It's a good question, and the answer, perhaps, is that the barbie is traditionally the preserve of the male amateur, a category of cook that we don't quite know how to place.

We're all perfectly happy, of course, with male professionals—they're the backbone of the industry, especially when the industry is a very traditional one, as in France—and much romantic ink has been spilt, especially in the prefaces to cook books, on the subject of the female amateur, the mother (amateur only in the technical sense of being unpaid) whose culinary skills and dedication have fed a family and inspired a future professional. The male amateur, however, we still seem to believe is a nuisance—and a show-off, too, which is why he's relegated to the backyard, where he won't do too much harm.

But here, as in so many other areas of cooking, change is already under way. Traditionally, the point about the barbecue, as we all know, is that it gives men a chance to potter purposefully. You put on an apron, perhaps even a chef's toque, and you hover over the burning meat with kitchen pliers in your hands and an intent look on your face. So how will we manage with something like Lucio Galletto's Barbecued Polenta with Mushrooms (right)?

Polenta requires a different sort of attention: you need to hover over the thing for about half an hour, stirring it most of the time. So this is emphatically not a dish for show-offs and what it, along with the rest of the recipes here, reveals is that the barbecue is no longer just a ritual. Sure, it's still a celebration of the outdoors and of Australia's (usually) benign climate, but it's no longer just an excuse for burning the bodies of dead animals. Nowadays, the result has to taste good as well.

Does this mean a loss of spontaneity in the backyard barbecue? Probably, but spontaneity in cooking is not necessarily a good thing if it means that the act of food preparation is just a sort of fit that comes on you from time to time when the weather's good. Cooking should be a part of life's pattern, not a sudden seizure. A dish such as Raymond Capadli's Grilled Whole Barramundi with Lime Pickle Infused with Coriander (page 169) is the way of the future for the barbie—not only because it uses a fine Australian fish, but also because it depends on a condiment (*tracklement* is the technical term) that should have been made months and months in advance.

PREVIOUS PAGE: Damien Pignolet's Grilled Lamb Rump with Red Capsicums, a dish inspired by Provence. Enjoy the complexity of the roasted capsicums, grilled baby garlic and tapenade sauce. The meat is from the rump on the top end of the leg where the hip joint is. It is very tender, but give your butcher some warning of your order so it can be cut for you.

Damien Pignolet, chef

Grilled Lamb Rump
with Red Capsicums

INGREDIENTS

MARINADE

1 clove garlic, roughly crushed

2½ tablespoons walnut oil or olive oil

2–3 sprigs of fresh rosemary, leaves only

1 tablespoon green peppercorns, lightly crushed

1 tablespoon coriander seed

2½ tablespoons olive oil

6 red capsicums (sweet peppers)

6 heads baby garlic

6 rosemary stems

6 x 250-g (8-oz) lamb rumps

125 g (4 oz) tapenade

3 tablespoons virgin olive oil

1 tablespoon balsamic vinegar

salt and freshly ground black pepper

1–2 bunches of rocket (arugula), washed and trimmed

To make the marinade, rub a bowl with the garlic 4–6 hours in advance and discard the clove. Rub the rumps with the walnut oil, place in the garlic-rubbed bowl and scatter the meat with the rosemary, peppercorns and coriander seed. Add the olive oil, cover and refrigerate.

Prepare the barbecue and, before the flames have died down, put on the capsicums. Allow them to blacken quite quickly, then remove to sweat off their skins in a sealed plastic bag. Chargrill the garlic and rosemary stems.

Meanwhile, remove the bulk of the seasoning debris from the lamb and put on the hot grill. Seal the meat quickly close to the fire, then move to a higher position above the flame and cook to your liking. Remove to a warm spot to rest for 10 minutes before carving. While the lamb cooks, the capsicums should be peeled—try to keep them whole. Don't be tempted to rinse them, but you may like to wipe off any little bits of skin with dampened absorbent kitchen paper.

Mix the tapenade and virgin olive oil with the balsamic vinegar, and adjust the seasoning to taste with salt and pepper.

To serve, lay a rustic bouquet of rocket, garlic and rosemary on each plate, along with some capsicum and the carved rump. Moisten each portion with the tapenade sauce and serve.

Serves 6 Recipe: easy to make

Lucio Galletto, restaurateur

Barbecued Polenta with Mushrooms

INGREDIENTS

4 cups (1 litre/1¾ imp. pints) water

sea salt

175 g (5½ oz) polenta flour, medium grain

2 punnets shiitake mushrooms

3 tablespoons olive oil

salt and freshly ground black pepper

Parmigiano-Reggiano cheese, shaved

truffle oil

Bring the water to the boil in a medium saucepan. Add about 1 teaspoon sea salt, lower the heat to a simmer and rain the polenta flour in, stirring with a whisk until completely blended. It will now start to bubble vigorously. Reduce the heat to as low as possible and cook the polenta for about 20–30 minutes, stirring from time to time to prevent it catching on the bottom of the saucepan. The polenta is cooked when it pulls away from the sides of the pan.

Once the polenta is cooked, check the seasoning. Place the polenta on a baking sheet and spread about 2–3 cm (¾ inch–1⅛ inch) thick. Allow to cool and then cut into desired shapes.

Heat the barbecue to medium hot and oil the grill. Brush the polenta and shiitake mushrooms with the olive oil and season with salt and pepper. Place on the barbecue for 3 minutes on each side, brushing again after turning.

To serve, place the polenta on warm plates with the mushrooms on top. Sprinkle the cheese shavings over the top and drizzle with truffle oil.

Serves 4–6 Recipe: easy to make

Alla Wolf-Tasker, chef

Barbecued Lamb Rumps
in Spicy Yoghurt Marinade with Tomato and Chickpea Salad

INGREDIENTS

4 x 185-g (6-oz) lamb rumps, trimmed

SPICY YOGHURT MARINADE

1 teaspoon cardamom pods

1 teaspoon cloves

2 teaspoons black peppercorns

1 teaspoon ground turmeric

1 teaspoon ground cinnamon

3 cloves garlic

½ teaspoon salt

5 small red chillies

1 cup coriander (Chinese parsley) leaves, washed and dried

1¼ cups (310 mL/10 fl oz) plain (natural) yoghurt

2 tablespoons vegetable oil

TOMATO AND CHICKPEA SALAD

250 g (8 oz) chickpeas, soaked overnight

½ onion, chopped

½ carrot, chopped

bay leaf

3 tablespoons good-quality extra virgin olive oil

1 clove garlic, crushed

3 large golden shallots, finely chopped

½ cup coriander (Chinese parsley) leaves, washed and finely chopped

4 medium tomatoes, peeled, seeded and diced

lemon juice

sea salt and freshly ground black pepper

Use strong-flavoured summer lamb for this dish—spring lamb is too delicate for the spicy flavours. I like to marinate it the day before, as well as cook and dress the chickpeas. Flavours are improved and the meat is tender and succulent.

To make the marinade, roast the cardamom pods, cloves and peppercorns in a dry, hot frying pan or skillet. Grind the roasted spices in a spice or coffee grinder, or using a mortar and pestle. Combine all the marinade ingredients in a food processor or blender, adding the yoghurt and oil last. Coat the lamb in the marinade paste, cover and leave in the refrigerator overnight.

To make the tomato and chickpea salad, put the chickpeas in a saucepan, cover with water and place over medium heat. Add the onion, carrot and bay leaf. Cook for at least 1½ hours, or until the chickpeas are tender. Allow to cool in the liquid, then drain.

Heat the olive oil in a frying pan or skillet, add the garlic and shallots, and cook gently until softened. Remove the frying pan from the heat and allow to cool partially, then stir in the coriander and cool completely. Combine with the tomato and adjust the flavour with the lemon juice, salt and pepper. Add to the chickpea mixture and mix through.

To cook the lamb, preheat a covered kettle-style barbecue or the oven to about 220°C (425°F). Place the lamb on the grill or on a baking sheet and cook for about 10 minutes for rare lamb. Remove from the heat and 'tent' with foil, to keep the meat warm, and allow to rest for at least 15 minutes.

To serve, slice the lamb and place on warm serving plates with the tomato and chickpea salad and some good, crusty bread.

Serves 4 Recipe: easy to make

LEFT: Barbecued Lamb Rumps in Spicy Yoghurt Marinade with Tomato and Chickpea Salad. Serve with a good spicy Shiraz, preferably from central Victoria. Barbecued sliced zucchini (courgette) or eggplant (aubergine) drizzled with olive oil would be a perfect accompaniment to this dish.

Raymond Kersh and Jennice Kersh, chef and restaurateur

Barbecue Lamb Loin
and Native Herbs with Illawarra Plum Salsa, Rocket and Macadamia Salad

INGREDIENTS

ILLAWARRA PLUM SALSA

500g (1 lb) Illawarra plums, halved

1 cup (200 mL/7 fl oz) balsamic vinegar

5 tablespoons honey

1 tablespoon fish sauce

1 red chilli, seeded and finely chopped

1 bay leaf

scant cup (200 mL/7 fl oz) red wine

juice and grated zest of 1 orange

juice and grated zest of 1 lemon

½ bunch of basil

1 clove garlic, finely chopped

½ red onion

10 pink peppercorns

1 tablespoon native aniseed

1 tablespoon lemon myrtle

3 tablespoons oil

salt and freshly ground black pepper

4 lamb loin fillets

3 tablespoons macadamia nut oil

1 tablespoon lemon juice

1 bunch of rocket (arugula)

½ cup (60 g/2 oz) macadamia nuts

To make the Illawarra plum salsa, place the plums, vinegar, honey, fish sauce, chilli, bay leaf and red wine in a stainless steel saucepan. Bring to the boil, reduce the heat and simmer for 15 minutes. Remove from the heat and cool. When cool, add the remaining salsa ingredients. This recipe will keep for up to 2 weeks if kept sealed in a jar and refrigerated.

Blend the native aniseed, lemon myrtle, oil and salt and pepper to taste together and rub all over the lamb. Cover and allow the lamb to marinate at room temperature for 2 hours.

Make the dressing by whisking together the macadamia nut oil and lemon juice. Season with salt and pepper to taste. Just before the lamb is ready, select the tenderest rocket leaves and toss lightly with some of the dressing.

To cook the lamb, preheat the barbecue to medium hot. Lightly pat dry the lamb fillets and place on the hot grill. For lamb with a pink centre, cook for 3 minutes, then turn and cook for another 2 minutes on the other side. If you prefer well done, grill for a few minutes more, or to your liking. Remove from the heat and allow to rest for 5 minutes before slicing.

To serve, place some washed and dried rocket leaves on each warm serving plate and top with the sliced lamb. Place some Illawarra plum salsa beside the lamb. Scatter with chopped macadamia nuts over the top and drizzle the leftover dressing over the lamb. Serve immediately.

Serves 4 Recipe: medium complexity

Diane Holuigue, food writer and teacher

Warm Salad of Barbecued Lamb
with Asian Flavours

INGREDIENTS

DRESSING

2 tablespoons plum sauce

2 tablespoons light soy sauce

1 tablespoon mirin or sherry

3 tablespoons light vegetable oil

1 teaspoon sesame oil

1 tablespoon vinegar

few drops of chilli oil, optional

To make the dressing, combine the plum sauce, light soy sauce, mirin, vegetable oil, vinegar and chilli oil (if using) in a jar and set aside. Place the salad greens in a bowl. Cook the green beans in boiling, salted water for a few minutes. Refresh the beans in cold water, then drain and set aside.

Lay the lamb on a plate and coat well with Char Sui sauce, then roll in the Szechuan peppercorns. Cover only superficially—too much becomes gritty. Allow the meat to rest for 30 minutes, then, when ready to cook, grill over a hot, corrugated iron-grill barbecue or fry in a lightly oiled frying pan or skillet. They need about 2½ minutes on the first side and 1½ minutes on the second

baby spinach, tatsoi and rocket
   (arugula), mixed (enough to serve 4)
18 stringless green beans, stalks removed
3 boned eye of loin (backstraps) of
   lamb, well trimmed
4 tablespoons Chinese Char Sui sauce or
   plum sauce
4 tablespoons Szechuan peppercorns,
   crushed finely with a rolling pin
3 tablespoons vegetable oil
12 abalone (oyster) mushrooms
15 snow peas (mange-tout), ends
   trimmed, each cut diagonally into two
3 tablespoons bean sprouts
6 water chestnuts, sliced

(depending on size: the lamb should be charred on the outside and pink in the centre). Transfer to a board to rest for 2–3 minutes, covered with a bowl.

Meanwhile, in a small frying pan, heat the vegetable oil and fry the mushrooms until crisp. Remove from heat and add to the greens. Quickly sauté the snow peas and blanched green beans for 30 seconds, or until warm and brightly coloured. Add the bean sprouts and water chestnuts, toss a moment only, then transfer these, too, to the greens.

Shake the dressing ingredients to blend, then pour over the greens and other ingredients. Mix and make a nest of these on each plate. Slice the lamb slightly on the diagonal and arrange the slices over the nests of green. Serve immediately.

Serves 6 Recipe: easy to make

Matthew Moran, chef

Chargrilled Sirloin
with Mash and Salsa Verde

INGREDIENTS
6 potatoes, peeled
salt
45 g (1½ oz) butter
½ teaspoon freshly ground black pepper
½ cup (125 mL/4 fl oz) light (single)
   cream, hot
4 x 250-g (8-oz) thick sirloin steaks
olive oil
freshly ground black pepper
4 tablespoons demi-glace, heated

SALSA VERDE
½ bunch of flat-leaf parsley
3 eggs, hard-boiled
10 anchovies
4 cloves garlic
2 slices bread, crusts removed, soaked
   in milk and gently squeezed dry
2 tablespoons capers
45 g (1½ oz) Parmesan cheese
5 tablespoons olive oil
juice of 5 lemons
salt and freshly ground black pepper

When buying the beef, choose thick sirloin steaks, grain-fed preferably, and bring to room temperature before cooking. If you choose not to buy the demi-glace, use a brown veal stock reduced to a rich demi-glaze.

To make the mashed potato, put the potato in a saucepan and cover with cold water. Add salt, if desired, and bring to the boil. Cover and simmer for 20–25 minutes, or until tender. Drain and return the potato to the saucepan. Put the saucepan back over low heat and let the saucepan and potato dry for 1 minute. Remove from the heat and sieve or mash the potatoes with a potato masher. Add the butter and pepper. Return to low heat. Stirring vigorously with a wooden spoon, gradually add the hot cream (or as much as necessary), until the mixture is light and fluffy.

While the potatoes are cooking, make the salsa verde. Mix together all the ingredients in a food processor and blend to a paste.

Chargrill the sirloins. Make sure the fire has burnt down to very hot embers or turn on the gas barbecue. Rub olive oil and pepper over the steaks. Place on a grill over the fire and cook for about 8–10 minutes on both sides, for a rare steak. Remove to a warm place and allow to rest for 15 minutes.

To serve, place the steak on warm plates and spoon the hot mashed potato next to it. Pour the heated demi-glace over the steak and top with the salsa verde.

Serves 4 Recipe: easy to make

ABOVE: Sweet Potato Gnocchi with Burnt Butter Sauce (page 65). 'My daughter, Suzanne, is such a splendid cook that we like to plan our meals together. She made the delicious gnocchi so that we didn't have much preparation to do on the day.'

RIGHT: Barbecued Salmon with Wasabi Crushed Potato (page 172) was served with the last of the summer salad leaves. 'This style of meal, enjoyed with my family, is my idea of heaven.'

Margaret Fulton
A Passion for Cooking

'''Now I know the scones are cooked—the tops are brown and golden." They chipped in: "They've got a certain smell." "Yes, isn't it good." Then I tapped them, "We'll remember that sound."

'In my first job at the Gas Company I was asked to give cookery classes for the blind. It taught me to describe and express what I was doing in a clear way that anyone could understand. It was a big turning point in my career. I was doing something useful that I loved. I was discovering the gift of being a teacher.'

Margaret Fulton has been instrumental in teaching generations of people to cook and to appreciate fine food and ingredients. She has written a weekly column in women's magazines for more than thirty-five years and her first cookbook, the Margaret Fulton Cookbook sold more than a million copies.

'My passion for cooking was fuelled, first and foremost, by the sheer joy of eating all the sublime things that came out of my mother's kitchen. A perfectly roasted chicken, a plump young bird, butter roasted with its crisp, golden skin and meltingly tender flesh, was a feast for the eyes and perhaps, best of all, a feast for the soul.'

Margaret extended her knowledge at East Sydney Technical School under the highly skilled Jules Weinberg, whose terms of reference in those days was Escoffier, the great French master chef. While she was learning the techniques and science, she was mixing socially with a French crowd, eating their fine home-cooked food. She was enchanted—she still remembers the first taste of real mayonnaise.

Margaret's continuing success is due also to her ability to simplify the complex and make splendid dishes accessible for all. She has an enviable reputation—cooks know that a Margaret Fulton recipe always works. Among many of her admirers are leading chefs and food writers who learnt from her books. She has encouraged providores and small growers of speciality ingredients. Without a knowledgeable audience, Australia's food revolution could never have taken place. Thank you Margaret.

'I like the skills and tradition of food. I love to know something has been done to absolute perfection.'

LEFT BELOW: From the left, Louise Gibbs, Adrian Smith, Margaret Fulton and Kate, Suzanne and Robert Gibbs enjoying their wonderful lunch.

ABOVE: Globe Artichoke and Bean Spaghetti Salad (page 89) makes a perfect starter for an alfresco lunch. 'I had a case of artichokes, so I decided to make the artichokes with potato and green beans, one of my favourite autumn dishes.'

Neil Perry, chef

Aged Beef
with Grilled Vegetable Salad and Anchovy Butter

INGREDIENTS

ANCHOVY BUTTER

125 g (4 oz) anchovies

250 g (8 oz) unsalted butter

lemon juice

freshly ground black pepper

2 x 625-g (1¼-lb) rump slices, about
   5 cm (2 inches) thick

olive oil

sea salt

GRILLED VEGETABLE SALAD

⅔ cup (100 mL/3½ fl oz) olive oil

6 slices Florence fennel (finocchio)

1 large red onion, peeled and cut into
   1-cm (½-inch) rings

3 cloves garlic, minced

6 large field mushrooms, cut into 1-cm
   (½-inch) slices

5 pink-eye potatoes, cooked for
   20 minutes in boiling, salted water,
   then peeled

4 tablespoons extra virgin olive oil

juice of 2 lemons

sea salt and freshly ground black pepper

We age our beef at Rockpool. Ask your butcher to age a standing rib for you—this would serve about six to eight people. Fillet is more tender, but, for flavour, I prefer rump. At Rockpool, we cut the meat into very large steaks and grill two serves at a time. This allows us to keep it on the grill longer to achieve a really crisp, smoky crust (it is so thick, it will still be melting and rare in the middle). The flavours of the anchovy butter, beef and charred vegetables are meant for each other. Remember to turn the meat only once during cooking.

To make the anchovy butter, purée the anchovies and butter in a food processor or blender until well incorporated. Add the lemon juice and pepper to taste. Roll in foil into a sausage shape and refrigerate. Just before needed, remove from the refrigerator and cut into 6 slices crosswise, allowing the butter to reach room temperature before using.

Make a fire or turn on the gas barbecue. If using a wood fire, wait until the fire has burnt down to very hot embers.

Brush the steaks with olive oil and season well with sea salt. Place on the heated grill. Cook on one side for about 10 minutes, flip and cook for a further 8 minutes on the other side. Transfer to a plate, and allow the meat to rest in a warm place for 15 minutes.

To make the grilled vegetable salad, rub the grill with olive oil and a cloth. Oil the fennel and place on the grill. Cook for 3 minutes. Remove from the grill. Place the onions on the grill with some oil and put the garlic on top. Oil the field mushrooms and place over the heat. Turn after a few minutes and, when they have softened, place in a bowl with the onions, garlic and fennel. Cut the potatoes (they should still be warm) and add to the mix. Add the extra virgin olive oil and lemon juice. Season to taste with sea salt and pepper, and toss through lightly.

To serve, divide the vegetable salad into neat piles between 6 large white plates. Cut the beef into thin slices and place over the salad. Pour the juices from the meat plate over the beef, place a slice of anchovy butter on top of each serving of meat and grind over some pepper. Serve immediately.

Serves 6 Recipe: medium complexity

Raymond Capadli, chef

Grilled Whole Barramundi
with Lime Pickle Infused with Coriander

INGREDIENTS
LIME PICKLE

6 large green limes

3 tablespoons salt

2 tablespoons mustard seed

⅔ cup (155 mL/5 fl oz) olive oil

4 cloves garlic, sliced

3-cm (1¼-inch) piece of ginger, sliced

1 tablespoon ground coriander

1 tablespoon chilli powder

1 tablespoon fennel seed

1 tablespoon cumin seed

1 tablespoon fresh turmeric, if possible,
or 1 teaspoon dried

6 curry leaves

bunch of fresh coriander (Chinese
parsley) stalks, chopped

zest of 3 lemons

1 teaspoon finely chopped ginger

1 teaspoon chopped garlic

⅔ cup (155 mL/5 fl oz) olive oil

2 kg (4 lb) wild barramundi, cleaned

sea salt and freshly ground black pepper

When summer comes, I can't wait to get the barbecue out for one reason—I can use all the chutneys I've prepared over winter—Lime Pickle is one of my favourites.

Barramundi are caught in coastal rivers and estuaries in tropical and subtropical areas of northern Australia. They are excellent eating and are a famed sport fish. The flesh is moist and well textured. Although any large, high-quality fish could be substituted, nothing is as fine as a wild, fresh barramundi.

To make the lime pickle, place the limes in a stainless steel bowl, cover with boiling water and leave to stand for 20 minutes. Drain off the water and cut each lime into 6 pieces and rub with the salt. Put the limes into a glass jar and seal. Leave in the sun or a warm place for 6 days to tenderise.

Place the mustard seed under a hot grill (broiler) to roast until the flavour comes out. Heat the oil, add the mustard seed, garlic, ginger, coriander, chilli powder, fennel seed, cumin seed, turmeric and curry leaves, and cook gently for 2 minutes. Add the limes and any liquid that may have accumulated and cook over low heat, stirring from time to time, for 40–60 minutes or until the limes have cooked and the liquid has thickened. Keeps stored in a sterilised jar for months.

To prepare the fish, put the coriander stalks in a mixing bowl. Add the lemon zest, ginger, garlic and oil, and mix together and allow to infuse for 4 hours.

Brush the infused oil on the barramundi, season with salt and pepper to taste, and wrap foil around the tail end of the fish. Place on the barbecue, basting continually with the marinade. Just before the fish is cooked, take off the foil to cook the tail end. Serve with a potato or rocket salad and the lime pickle.

Serves 4 Recipe: medium complexity

Michael Lambie, chef

Zucchini Chutney for Seafood

INGREDIENTS

3 tablespoons olive oil

4 zucchini (courgettes), diced small

2 onions, diced small

1 clove garlic, finely chopped

3 tablespoons soft brown sugar

1 tablespoon tomato paste

4 tablespoons Worchestershire sauce

225 mL (7 fl oz) white wine vinegar

salt and freshly ground black pepper

5 tablespoons extra virgin olive oil

This is a great, piquant chutney that goes really well with any barbecued fish, scallops or prawns (shrimp).

Heat the olive oil in a saucepan. Add the zucchini, onion and garlic, and cook for 5 minutes. Add the brown sugar, tomato paste, Worcestershire sauce and vinegar, and cook for a further 8 minutes. Season with salt and pepper to taste.

Remove from the heat and add the extra virgin olive oil.

Serves 6–8 Recipe: easy to make

Stephanie Alexander, chef and food writer

Barbecue Vegetables

At Richmond Hill Café and Larder, we serve a platter of these delicious vegetables with several labna balls, the yogurt 'cheese' we sell in the larder.

Select a mixture of vegetables. Some will require a little preliminary preparation.

Capsicums (peppers). Halve, seed, lightly oil and grill over the barbecue until well blackened. Peel and cut into wide strips.

Eggplant (aubergine). Cut into thick slices, lightly salt for 1 hour, rinse, dry well, brush with olive oil and grill over the barbecue until soft.

Mushrooms. Oil the gill-side of opened flat mushrooms, and place under a grill (broiler) until bubbling. Season with sea salt and freshly cracked pepper. Squeeze over the juice of a lemon.

Pumpkin (squash). Cut into thick slices, oil lightly and grill over the barbecue until tender.

Onions. Cut onions into small wedges, oil and roast until tender. When ready to serve the platter, place the soft wedges on the char-grill to reheat and crisp a little.

Zucchini (courgettes). Cut into thick slices, lightly oil and grill over the barbecue until tender.

Cherry tomatoes. Roast in the oven or cook gently in a pan on top of the stove.

Recipe: easy to make

Graeme Phillips, chef

Barbecued Marinated Quail
on Rocket and Parmesan Salad

INGREDIENTS
MARINADE
good handful of fresh thyme
6 garlic cloves
grated zest of 1 lemon
3 tablespoons good balsamic vinegar
scant cup (200 mL/7 fl oz) extra virgin
  olive oil

12 quails, boned
100 g (3½ oz) prosciutto, thinly sliced
1 bunch of rocket (arugula), washed and
  dried
sprigs from 2 bunches of flat-leaf parsley
100 g (3½ oz) Parmesan cheese, shaved
freshly ground black pepper

Simple, quick and light with satisfying, rich flavours—a perfect out-of-doors summer dish. Wash it down with a light Pinot or chilled Chardonnay.

To make the marinade, strip the thyme, pound the garlic to a paste and mix all the marinade ingredients together. Toss and marinate the quail in this for at least 2 hours, but preferably overnight. Cover and keep refrigerated.

Drain the quails, but do not dry, and reserve the marinade. Preheat the flat plate of the barbecue to very hot. Cook the quails, skin-side down, for 1 minute. Turn and cook for a further 2–3 minutes, pressing if necessary to keep the quails flat and so that the juices will caramelise. Crisp the prosciutto on the flat plate of the barbecue. Strain the reserved marinade, firmly pressing the solids, to use as a dressing. Put the rocket and parsley in a mixing bowl, toss in the dressing and then toss the prosciutto through.

To serve, place the salad in the centre of the plates, top with the quail, scatter Parmesan shavings over and season generously with pepper.

Serves 6 Recipe: easy to make

Martin Webb, chef

Barbecued Mussels
with Sweet Chilli Vinegar

INGREDIENTS
SWEET CHILLI VINEGAR

½ cup (125 mL/4 fl oz) white wine
  vinegar

⅓ cup (90 g/3 oz) caster (superfine)
  sugar

2½ tablespoons lime juice

2 tablespoons fish sauce (nam pla)

1 small red chilli, thinly sliced

1 small green chilli, thinly sliced

2 golden shallots

5-cm (2-inch) piece of cucumber, cut
  into small dice

1 tablespoon fresh coriander (Chinese
  parsley) leaves

2 kg (4 lb) mussels

A really easy starter—sweet black-shelled mussels with a spicy sour dipping sauce. This technique for cooking mussels on the barbecue can be used with any shellfish.

To make the sweet chilli vinegar, bring the vinegar and sugar to the boil in a saucepan, stir and remove from the heat. Leave to cool, then add the lime juice, fish sauce, chillies, shallots and cucumber. Stir in the coriander, transfer to a serving bowl and reserve.

Heat the barbecue to medium-hot. Put the mussels on the barbecue and cover loosely with foil (or the lid if you have a kettle-type barbecue). Cook until all the mussels open, about 5–6 minutes—discard any mussels that do not open.

Serve the mussels with the sweet chilli vinegar as a dipping sauce.

Serves 4 Recipe: easy to make

Margaret Fulton, food writer

Barbecued Salmon
with Wasabi Crushed Potato

INGREDIENTS

750g (1½ lb) potatoes, peeled and halved

1 teaspoon salt

1 cup (250 mL/8 fl oz) hot milk, plus
  extra

2 teaspoons wasabi

knob of butter

sea salt and freshly ground black pepper

4 thick Atlantic salmon fillets or cutlets

vegetable oil for grilling

1 teaspoon lime or lemon juice

1 tablespoon light olive oil

deep-fried chervil sprigs, optional

Place the potato in a large saucepan, add the salt and water to cover, and bring to the boil. Cook the potato for 15 minutes, or until tender, then drain and shake over heat until dry. Crush with a masher or push through a mouli or sieve (it is not advisable to mash them in a food processor). Beat in the milk, then add 1 teaspoon of the wasabi to the potato and season to taste with salt and pepper. (To keep hot without spoiling, level the surface of the purée in the pan and cover with 3 tablespoons of hot milk and a good knob of butter, then seal the pan with a tight-fitting lid.)

Rinse the salmon very lightly and pat dry with absorbent kitchen paper. Preheat the barbecue or a ribbed grill pan to medium hot, then brush the rack or pan with vegetable oil. When the oil is hot, but not smoking, brush the salmon fillet lightly with vegetable oil and place on the rack or in the pan. Cook for about 6 minutes, turning once.

Mix the remaining 1 teaspoon wasabi with first the lime juice, and then the oil, until combined.

To serve, spoon the creamed potato onto 4 warm serving plates. Peel away the skin of the salmon steaks and arrange on top. If a char-scored finish is wanted,

172   AUSTRALIAN FOOD

have ready a few metal skewers made red hot over a flame and use to score the top of the fish. Garnish with the chervil sprigs, if using. Drizzle the wasabi mixture around the edge of each plate. Serve with a green vegetable in season.

Serves 4 Recipe: easy to make

Chris Taylor, chef

Chargrilled Tuna Belly
with Oysters and Citrus Soy Dressing

INGREDIENTS

4 x 140-g (4½-oz) tuna belly steaks
2 tablespoons mirin
2 tablespoons light soy sauce
1 tablespoon crushed fresh ginger
1 clove garlic, crushed
2 tablespoons vegetable oil
100 g (3½ oz) bean shoots
1 clove garlic, crushed
1 tablespoon crushed fresh ginger
8 oysters
zest of 1 mandarin, julienned

CITRUS SOY DRESSING

2½ tablespoons dashi stock (dissolve
   ½ teaspoon instant dashi in hot water)
1 tablespoon mirin
1 tablespoon soy sauce
juice of 1 lemon
juice of 1 mandarin

Marinate the tuna in the mirin, light soy sauce, ginger and garlic for 30 seconds. Remove the tuna from the marinade and drain off any excess liquid. Heat a barbecue or an oiled ridged grill pan to very hot. Quickly grill the tuna for 3 minutes on each side—make a criss-cross pattern by rotating the tuna 90 degrees halfway through cooking time on each side. Remove from the heat and keep in a warm place.

To make the citrus soy dressing, heat the dashi stock in a small saucepan. Add the mirin and soy sauce. Remove from the heat and pour in the lemon and mandarin juices, just before serving. Keep warm.

Heat a wok and, when hot, add the vegetable oil. Stir-fry the bean shoots, garlic and ginger very quickly. Arrange on warm plates and slice the tuna into 1-cm (⅜-inch) thick pieces. Place the sliced tuna on top of the bean shoots. Drop the oysters into the hot citrus soy dressing to warm through. Place 2 oysters on each plate, drizzle with the citrus soy dressing and garnish with the mandarin zest. Serve immediately.

Serves 4 Recipe: easy to make

Gary Cooper, chef

Barbecued Piri Piri Prawns

on Daikon Cake with Salad of Pickled Cucumber and Smoked Tea Butter

INGREDIENTS

DAIKON CAKE

1 kg (2 lb) daikon radish

2½ cups (300 g/10 oz) rice flour

1 teaspoon salt

1 teaspoon sugar

PICKLED CUCUMBER

1 Lebanese (continental) cucumber

½ cup (125 g/4 oz) sugar

½ cup (125 ml/4 fl oz) cocoa vinegar or palm vinegar, to cover

SMOKED TEA BUTTER

½ cup (125 mL/4 fl oz) water

2 tablespoons Lapsang Souchong tea

8 tablespoons butter

¼ teaspoon ground ginger

2 tablespoons chopped fresh chives

salt

oil for barbecue

8 fresh, uncooked king tiger prawns (shrimp) or 16 banana prawns (medium size), peeled and deveined, but with heads intact

1 teaspoon sweet paprika

1 teaspoon cayenne

finely sliced spring onion

freshly chopped coriander (Chinese parsley)

The daikon cake is typically Asian—soft and slippery. It softens the chilli prawns. The prawn meat is crunchy and, when eaten with the soft daikon, makes quite a special treat for a barbecue. Piri piri is a South African spice mix of cayenne and sweet Hungarian paprika. Mix it according to taste—1:1 for medium heat, 2:1 for fearless palates. The daikon cake and smoked tea butter can be made a day or two in advance, so there is not so much to do on the day.

To prepare the daikon cake, oil a 20-cm (8-inch) cake pan and line with baking parchment. Grate the daikon fairly coarsely using the shredding device on a food processor. Put in a mixing bowl and add the flour, salt and sugar, and mix together. Fold the mixture into the cake pan and cover with foil. Place the cake pan in a bamboo or metal steamer, and steam over a saucepan of boiling water for 1 hour. Allow to cool.

To prepare the pickled cucumber, slice the cucumbers into a bowl and add the sugar and vinegar. Let stand for 30 minutes.

To make the smoked tea butter, bring the water to the boil. Steep the tea in the water for 20 minutes, then strain through a cloth and squeeze the dark tea out. In a food processor, combine the butter, ginger, chives, salt and tea extract. Once it is mixed, roll out the butter into a sausage and cover with plastic wrap and refrigerate.

Cut the daikon cake into wedges and oil the barbecue. Toss the prawns in the combined paprika and cayenne. Lightly brown the daikon wedges, then quickly cook the prawns (90 seconds on each side).

To serve, place the pickled cucumber in the middle of the serving plates, then the daikon cake. Top with the prawns and finish with slices of the smoked tea butter. Garnish with the spring onion and coriander, and serve.

Serves 4 Recipe: medium complexity

Chapter 6
Fruit and Desserts

Alan Saunders

Fruit and Desserts

Australia has always had something of a sweet tooth. In the old country, sugar was a condiment; in the early days of colonisation, it was a luxury. Sugar, however, soon became an important source of energy. By the 1830s, the bushman's rations—doled out to pastoral employees where shops were few and far between—was 'ten, ten, two and a quarter': ten pounds each of meat and flour, two pounds of sugar and four ounces of tea a week. That's a lot of sugar, the best part of a kilogram, and it's twice what labourers in Britain were consuming at the time. And, yes, it did have an effect on the nation's dental health, but perhaps it also had an effect on the Australian weekend.

Hal Porter, the watcher on the cast-iron balcony, reports that in the early 1920s his mother spent Saturday afternoons baking. A biscuit barrel with nothing in it or a cake tin standing empty around the house was unthinkable, so she got to work on fruit cakes, rock cakes and Banburies, date rolls and ginger nuts. 'These conventional solidities done,' he adds, 'she exercises her talent for ritual fantasy, for the more costly and ephemeral dainties that are to adorn as fleetingly as daylilies the altar of the Sunday tea-table.' So on came the cream puffs and the éclairs and sponge cakes in three tiers topped with icing and glacé cherries, all of them proof to Porter's parents that 'life is being lived on a plane of hard-earned and justifiable abundance.'

To this day, desserts and other sweet things are just about the only part of Australia's British culinary heritage that do not meet with wholesale condemnation from the culinary patriots. Asia—not a great place for desserts (although the Thais and the Indians do them well)—has so far had little effect on what Australians eat at this end of the meal. Our desserts still pay homage to the more northern part of the northern hemisphere, even when (as in the case of Vic Cherikoff's bread and butter pudding, page 192) they use native ingredients. Similarly, Stephanie Alexander's Queen of Nuts Cake on a Simple Rhubarb and Red Fruit Sago Sauce (page 205) pays homage to another northern cuisine, that of the German Lutherans who came to the Barossa Valley, South Australia, in the nineteenth century.

Which is not say that an Asian twist can't be given to these traditional pleasures. Genevieve Harris's Coconut and Apricot Pudding with Coconut Sugar Syrup (page 185) uses Asian ingredients—coconut milk, coconut sugar and a pandan leaf—in that most familiar of northern England comfort foods, the pudding—another example of the way in which compromise and adaptation can liven up every course in a modern Australian meal.

PREVIOUS PAGE: Guillaume Brahimi's Poached Pears with Cinnamon Ice Cream and Vanilla Bean Coulis. A nice, light home-style dessert with beautiful pears, which are at their best in winter. It is a great flavour combination of pear, cinnamon and vanilla.

Guillaume Brahimi, chef

Poached Pears
with Cinnamon Ice Cream and Vanilla Bean Coulis

INGREDIENTS

4 pears, plus 2 extra

1 lemon, halved

1 cup (250 mL/8 fl oz) water

¾ cup (185 g/6 oz) sugar, plus
  1½ tablespoons extra

3 cinnamon sticks

scant cup (200 mL/7 fl oz) milk

scant cup (200 mL/7 fl oz) light (single)
  cream

½ teaspoon ground cinnamon

6 egg yolks

200 ml (6½ oz) double (thick) cream

MILLE-FEUILLE

200 g (6½ oz) unsalted butter, softened

⅓ cup (90 g/3 oz) sugar

1 large egg, beaten

½ teaspoon salt

½ teaspoon vanilla sugar (made by
  inserting a vanilla pod into a jar
  of sugar)

2 cups (250 g/8 oz) plain (all-purpose)
  flour

2 tablespoons ground blanched almonds

icing (confectioners') sugar to garnish

strawberries to garnish

I serve this dish in a stack with mille-feuille pastry, but you can serve it more simply at home without the pastry if preferred.

Peel all of the pears and rub with a cut lemon half to prevent discoloration. Place the water, the ¾ cup (185 g/6 oz) sugar and cinnamon sticks in a saucepan and cook over medium heat until the sugar is dissolved and the liquid is starting to simmer. Place 4 of the pears in the syrup, cover and continue to cook over medium heat. Check on their progress as they poach and remove the pears from the saucepan as soon as they are cooked, about 15 minutes. Keep the syrup warm.

To make the coulis, take the 2 extra pears and cut into pieces. Blend in a food processor until smooth, then slowly add to the syrup while still over the heat.

Boil the milk with the light cream and ground cinnamon. Mix the egg yolks and extra sugar together in a mixing bowl. Pour the milk onto the egg yolks mixture and stir well. Return to the saucepan and heat until the mixture begins to thicken, but do not boil. Pour into a bowl placed on a bed of ice and allow to cool before stirring in the double cream. Freeze in an ice cream maker according to the manufacturer's instructions, or pour into a metal ice cream tray, cover with foil and place in the freezer turned to its coldest setting. When firm, store in the freezer at normal setting.

To make the mille-feuille pastry, preheat the oven to 170°C (340°F). In a large mixing bowl or food processor, combine the butter, sugar, eggs, salt and vanilla sugar. Mix until it is blended.

Sift the flour and gradually add to the butter mixture along with the ground almonds. Be careful not to mix too vigorously or the pastry will toughen. When the dough comes together, divide into two even portions and fold each one into a disc shape. Wrap each piece of dough in plastic wrap and refrigerate for at least an hour, preferably overnight.

Remove one piece of pastry from the refrigerator and roll out until 4 mm (¼ in) thick. Cut into rectangular portions about 7 x 3 cm (3 x 1¼ in). Bake in the oven until golden brown, about 15 minutes.

To serve, lay one piece of mille-feuille on each serving plate. Top with some slices of pear, then add the ice cream. Repeat the process, finishing with a layer mille-feuille pastry on top. Drizzle or pipe the coulis around each plate and sprinkle icing sugar on top. Garnish with quartered strawberries.

Serves 4 Recipe: medium complexity

RIGHT: Passionfruit Tart (page 197). Fine pastry and a beautiful passionfruit curd is as good as you can get. This dish is simplicity with no pretension.

Neil Perry
His Luck

'A dish has to have an integration. It needs a good length of flavour, complexity and interest. You mustn't let your ego get in the way. I keep on refining my food, even my favourite recipes. And beautiful fresh produce is really important—get the freshest, best ingredients and nurture the flavours and texture. When I go overseas, I realise how lucky we are with our wonderful produce.'

Neil Perry is not only creator of Rockpool, one of our top 'modern Australian' restaurants, but he is also a consultant to Qantas, has set up a seafood providore arm with John Susman and owns, with Trish Richardson, the Wockpool, Star Bar and Grill, Rockpool Catering and the Museum of Contemporary Art Cafe. That's quite a feat for a not-quite-forty-something.

Neil believes he has been terribly lucky in his food career. He grew up in a family that cared about food. His father was a butcher and a keen fisherman, who cared enough about authentic food to make up his own spice blends. From a young age, Neil was taught the meaning of freshness and the importance of developing a keen eye for produce.

His luck held up in his choice of jobs and mentors. Neil's first job was in management at Sails Restaurant. He then embarked on a year of learning, working with Damien Pignolet, Stephanie Alexander and Tony Pappas. He cites Steve Manfredi and David Thompson as the greatest influences in his maturation and definition of Rockpool cuisine.

He also believes he's lucky to have been born in the New World and a truly multicultural society. 'It has been easier for me to learn from the many diverse food cultures that made up my cooking style. This involves respecting and blending with sympathy produce from their origins. You will notice that I happily borrow from each culture a myriad of threads that I weave into a dish that I believe is uniquely Australian.'

BELOW: Aged Beef with Grilled Vegetable Salad and Anchovy Butter (page 168). Use the finest well-aged beef—this beef has hung on the bone for four weeks. It is full of flavour and perfect to barbecue with anchovy butter.

FAR BELOW: Thick rump steak achieving a really crisp crust and smoky flavour that only a barbecue in the open air brings out to the full.

Philippe Mouchel, chef

Raspberry Vacherin

INGREDIENTS

MERINGUE

10 egg whites, at room temperature

⅓ cup (90 g/3 oz) caster (superfine)
sugar

⅓ cup (90 g/3 oz) icing (confectioners')
sugar

SORBET

1½ cups (300 g/10 oz) caster (superfine)
sugar

1¼ cups (310 mL/10 fl oz) water

4 cups (1 litre/1¾ imp. pints) raspberry
purée, seeds removed

2 cups seasonal fruit such as
passionfruit, banana, kiwi fruit and
strawberries, cut into small dice

pinch of ground ginger

⅓ cup (100 mL/3½ fl oz) heavy (double)
cream

1 teaspoon icing (confectioners') sugar

pinch of ground cinnamon

mint twigs to garnish

A simple summer dessert, its base is a meringue shell containing fruit salad, which is topped with raspberry sorbet. Whipped cream decorates the sides. The meringue and sorbet can be made days in advance and assembled at the last minute. The photograph on page 187 will make the final assembly easier to follow.

Preheat the oven to 100°C (200°F).

To make the meringue, whip the egg whites with the caster sugar until the whites form soft peaks. Gradually mix in the icing sugar, ensuring the peaks are still soft and not overbeaten. Trace 6-cm (2½-inch) circles on baking parchment 4 cm (1½ inches) apart. Put the egg white mixture in a pastry bag with the star nozzle attached. Pipe the meringue in rounds, adding a final round on top of the outermost edge so that there is a depression in the middle. Bake in the oven for about an hour. Turn off the heat and allow the meringues to cool on a wire rack. Store in airtight containers.

To make the sorbet, put the sugar and water in a large saucepan over medium heat. Dissolve the sugar and bring the liquid to the boil. Allow to cool and reserve a tablespoon for the fruit salad. Mix the remaining syrup with the raspberry purée and blend together in a food processor. Transfer to a sorbetière and follow the manufacturer's instructions or pour the raspberry liquid into flat freezer trays and freeze. When it is just about set, take it from the freezer, cut into blocks and blend in the food processor. Pour back into the trays and return, covered, to the freezer.

To serve, moisten the seasonal fruit with the reserved sugar syrup and add the ground ginger. Whip the cream with the icing sugar and cinnamon. Put the fruit salad in the bottom of the meringues and top with raspberry sorbet. Using a pastry bag fitted with a star nozzle, pipe the sides of the sorbet with the cinnamon cream to meet the vacherin base. Garnish each vacherin with a twig of mint.

Serves 20 Recipe: medium complexity

Janni Kyritsis, chef

Pink Gin and Lemon Granita

INGREDIENTS

SUGAR SYRUP

2 cups (500 g/16 oz) sugar

4 cups (1 litre/1¾ imp. pints) water

PINK GIN GRANITA

½ cup (125 mL/4 fl oz) gin

1 cup (250 mL/8 fl oz) sugar syrup

1 cup (250 mL/8 fl oz) water

2½ tablespoons lime juice

1 teaspoon angostura bitters

LEMON GRANITA

1 cup (250 mL/8 fl oz) sugar syrup

1 cup (250 mL/8 fl oz) water

½ cup (125 mL/4 fl oz) lemon juice

grated zest of ½ lemon

I like finishing lunch with a refreshing granita … and having a pink gin granita is really just an excuse to have another martini!

To make the sugar syrup, dissolve the sugar in water in a heavy-based saucepan over medium heat. Bring to the boil and cook until reduced to about 2 cups (500 mL/16 fl oz) sugar syrup.

To make the pink gin granita, mix all the ingredients together. Pour into a flat freezer tray and put in the freezer. Just before it freezes solid, take it out and stir with a fork to make flakes. Return to the freezer and, when ready to serve, stir once again with a fork. Make the lemon granita in the same way.

To serve, carefully spoon the granitas into tall martini dessert glasses so there is a dramatic division of colour. Accompany with a buttery shortbread biscuit (cookie).

Serves 4 Recipe: easy to make

Leo Schofield, food critic

Pineapple Sorbet

INGREDIENTS

1 large fresh, ripe pineapple

2¾ cups (625 g/1 lb 4 oz) caster (superfine) sugar, or less if preferred or if the pineapple is very sweet

juice of 1 lemon

4 tablespoons white rum, plus extra, chilled, to serve

Here is one of my favourite sorbet recipes.

Skin the pineapple, remove all the eyes, core and cut into small pieces. Purée in a food processor or blender. Pour the fruit into a bowl, add the sugar and stir with a wooden spoon until completely dissolved. Add the lemon juice and the 4 tablespoons rum.

Turn the regulator of the freezer to maximum, pour the sorbet mixture into a sorbetière and allow it to set until firm, but not rock-hard. If you don't have a sorbetière or an ice cream churn, the sorbet can be made in refrigerator ice trays, but should be removed once or twice, stirred and replaced in the freezer. The texture is then close to that of a granita, but is none the worse for that.

Serve in tall glasses and top each with a dash of chilled white rum.

Serves 6 Recipe: easy to make

Alla Wolf-Tasker, chef

Amaretto Parfait

INGREDIENTS

1¼ cups (310 mL/10 fl oz) heavy
(double) cream, plus ⅓ cup
(100 mL/3½ fl oz) extra

½ vanilla bean

4 egg yolks

3 tablespoons caster (superfine) sugar

5–6 tablespoons Amaretto

RIGHT: Amaretto Parfait. 'At Lake House, we pour it into a loaf pan which has layers of praline, apricot purée and Amaretto-soaked sponge in the base. When frozen, the loaf is unmoulded and a slice is served on an apricot coulis with a small apricot strudel.'

This is one of those wonderfully versatile custards which can be served just chilled, perhaps with an accompaniment of poached peaches or apricots, or frozen into a smooth-as-silk parfait. It can be made in advance and left in the freezer. Just serve it as a slice with apricot coulis and a crisp dessert biscuit.

Pour the 1¼ cups (310 mL/10 fl oz) cream into a heavy-based saucepan.

Halve the vanilla bean, scrape the seeds into the cream and heat to boiling point. Cream the egg yolks and sugar together, then pour the hot cream over the top. Return the mixture to the saucepan and heat gently until it coats the back of a spoon.

Chill the mixture. Stir in the Amaretto. Whip the extra cream to soft peaks and fold through the Amaretto mixture until it is smooth and even. Pour into individual glasses or bowls if serving as a custard and chill, or pour it into a loaf pan and freeze overnight. Alternatively, line the loaf pan with Amaretto-soaked sponge before pouring in the parfait. Once frozen, unmould and serve sliced with apricot purée or poached apricots.

Serves 6–8 Recipe: medium complexity

André Chouvin, chef

Gratin of Grapes
in Champagne Sabayon

INGREDIENTS

SABAYON

8 egg yolks

1½ cups (375 g/12 oz) sugar

½ bottle Champagne

¼ cup (60 mL/2 fl oz) heavy (double)
cream

1.5 kg (3 lb) grapes, peeled and seeded

This classic dish works well with many fresh seasonal fruits, especially red berry fruits.

To make the sabayon, whisk the egg yolks and sugar in a heatproof bowl until very pale and thick. Add the Champagne and whisk vigorously. Place the bowl over a bain-marie or a saucepan of simmering water and continue whisking vigorously until the sauce thickens. Remove from the heat and beat until the mixture is cold. Stir in the cream.

To serve, place the seeded grapes in hot shallow bowls, whisk up the sabayon and pour over the grapes. Grill under a hot preheated grill (broiler) until the sabayon begins to colour. Serve immediately.

Serves 6 Recipe: medium complexity

Jacques Reymond, chef

Gratin of Spiced Strawberries
and Quince with a Grand Marnier Sabayon

INGREDIENTS

SPICED BERRIES

300 g (10 oz) raspberries

155 g (5 oz) blackberries

45 g (1½ oz) blueberries

½ cup (125 g/4 oz) sugar, plus 1 cup
   (250 g/8 oz) extra

1 teaspoon black peppercorns

1 vanilla pod

3 star anise

1 cinnamon stick

3 cloves

1 tablespoon kirsch

1 kg (2 lb) fresh strawberries

GRAND MARNIER SABAYON

4 egg yolks

½ cup (125 g/4 oz) sugar

4 tablespoons lightly whipped cream

1½ tablespoons Grand Marnier

500 g (1 lb) poached quinces

fresh mint, finely julienned

The strawberries and quinces are spiced to intensify their flavour and contrast with the light sabayon.

To make the coulis, wash the raspberries, blackberries and blueberries, and purée with the ½ cup (125 g/4 oz) sugar in a food processor. Do not overprocess or it will be too frothy. Only add water if absolutely necessary and then sparingly. Rub the coulis through a fine sieve to remove the seeds. Taste and add more sugar if needed.

To make the caramel, heat the extra sugar in a heavy-based saucepan over gentle heat until the syrup turns a rich golden brown. Remove from the heat and set in a pan of cold water to stop the cooking process.

Roast the peppercorns, vanilla pod, star anise, cinnamon and cloves in a dry frying pan or skillet until the flavours come through, then add to the caramel. Deglaze the caramel with the kirsch and add the berry coulis. Cook over low heat and add the whole strawberries to this coulis and cook until soft. Place the strawberries in a bowl and spoon some of the coulis on top.

To make the sabayon, beat the egg yolks in an electric mixer. Add the sugar with a touch of water and beat until very pale and thick. Put in a heatproof bowl over a saucepan of simmering water and continue to whisk until the sauce thickens and coats the back of a wooden spoon. Remove from the heat and beat until cold. Add the whipped cream and Grand Marnier.

To serve, place the spiced strawberries and quinces in individual soup bowls and sprinkle with the mint. Coat with the sabayon and gratinée (grill) them under a salamander or a hot grill (broiler) until the sabayon begins to colour. Serve immediately.

Serves 10 Recipe: complex

Genevieve Harris, chef

Coconut and Apricot Pudding
with Coconut Sugar Syrup

INGREDIENTS

TOPPING

¾ cup (75 g/2½ oz) desiccated (shredded)
coconut

scant ⅓ cup (75 g/2½ oz) caster
(superfine) sugar

3 egg whites

1 tablespoon melted butter

155 g (5 oz) dried apricots, finely diced

PUDDING

1 cup (200 g/7 oz) caster (superfine)
sugar

4 eggs (55 g/1¾ oz), separated

2 cups (500 mL/16 fl oz) coconut milk

3 cups (375 g/12 oz) self-raising flour,
sifted

1 tablespoon melted butter

75 g (2½ oz) dried apricots, finely diced

COCONUT SUGAR SYRUP

250 g (8 oz) coconut sugar or palm
sugar (jaggery)

1 cup (250 mL/8 fl oz) water

1 pandan leaf, torn and tied

This is an old-fashioned pudding with a slight twist. Adding the coconut milk, pandan and coconut sugar gives the dessert an unusual mix of ingredients. These products are available from most Asian grocery stores. We also use South Australian dried apricots for their intensity of flavour.

To make the topping, mix all the ingredients together in a bowl and set aside.

To make the pudding, preheat the oven to 190°C (375°F). Butter and sugar 8 x 1-cup (250 mL/8 fl oz) pudding moulds, shaking out any excess sugar. Fill each mould one-third full with the topping mixture and set aside.

Cream the sugar and egg yolks together. Add the coconut milk, then fold in the flour and butter. When combined, add the dried apricot. Whisk the egg whites until stiff and gently fold into the mixture. Spoon the pudding mixture into the prepared moulds. Cook in a bain-marie or place in a baking pan filled with simmering water. Cover with foil and bake in the oven for about 40–50 minutes, or until a skewer inserted in the centre comes out clean.

To make the sugar syrup, grate or chop the coconut sugar. Place in a saucepan with the water and pandan leaf. Dissolve the sugar, bring the liquid to the boil and simmer until it is thick and syrupy. Strain through a fine mesh sieve.

To serve, turn the puddings out onto warm serving plates and drizzle with the coconut sugar syrup. They can be served straight from the oven or reheated in a steamer for 10 minutes. Serve immediately.

Serves 8 Recipe: medium complexity

Philippe Mouchel

Sharing the Passion

It has been a long journey from Evreux, the small town in Normandy where Philippe Mouchel grew up in a family that loved eating and drinking, and sharing the passion. His mother and grandmother were good home cooks and his father a chef. Today, Philippe finds himself returning to cuisine conviviale and simple food that people love.

Philippe began his apprenticeship in a one-star Michelin restaurant and consolidated his French techniques working for Paul Bocuse. He left France in 1978 to open the Paul Bocuse Restaurant in Tokyo. He fell in love with Japan—the food and the people really changed him. He had to adapt his food to Japanese expectations—make it lighter, forget about such things as cream and sauces. He even married a Japanese girl.

Ten years later, he was asked to move on to open the Paul Bocuse Restaurant in Melbourne. Japan's loss was Australia's gain.

Another love affair with food began. The new restaurant was a wonderful experience in fine dining, showcasing Bocuse's food style and Philippe's unerring ability to balance the simple and

complex, light and rich dishes. He likes to work with the best produce available, to respect the seasons. He is a stickler for his French techniques, but enjoys using spices and loves to work with the exceptional quality of Australian produce.

Sadly, the restaurant closed, but Philippe emerged a little later with Langton's Restaurant, in partnership with Langton's Fine Wines. This is a more accessible, moderately priced establishment, where the chefs are the stars in their open kitchen, busily cooking at the splendid Le Bonnet stove. Langton's food is still French, but

with an Australian accent, using the best-quality ingredients cooked more simply.

'Its more fun now. I wanted to create a warm atmosphere so everything is on show with nothing to hide. I like to work with the best ingredients as simply as possible to make good food. I try to cook on the bone to keep the flesh moist. I like to enhance the true flavour of food with no masks. I use spices to enhance, not to hide.'

Thank you for sharing the passion.

LEFT CENTRE: Sauté of Calamari Served on a Compôte of Ratatouille (page 57). In this fresh summer dish, the calamari makes a good, chewy contrast with the soft vegetables, and the light sea flavour is infused with basil.

FAR LEFT: The wonderfully theatrical Le Bonnet stove at Langton's Restaurant.

LEFT: Bite into Raspberry Vacherin (page 180) and enjoy the intenseness and acidity of raspberries, well balanced by the crisp meringue and the softness and richness of the cream.

Almond
Bread and Butter Pudding
with Biscotti

INGREDIENTS

1 tablespoon chopped glacé (candied) ginger

1 tablespoon chopped glacé (candied) cedrat (also known as citron)

1½ tablespoons mixed (candied) peel, or 1 tablespoon mixed peel and 1 glacé (candied) orange, chopped

4 tablespoons roughly chopped unblanched almonds

10–15 Italian almond biscotti, depending on size, but try to get the largest

enough butter to spread over biscotti

½ cup (125 g/4 oz) sugar

6 eggs

2 cups (500 mL/16 fl oz) milk

2 cups (500 mL/16 fl oz) heavy (thick) cream

pinch of ground cinnamon

3 tablespoons Amaretto di Saronno (Italian bitter almond liqueur)

icing (confectioners') sugar for dredging

spun sugar for garnish, optional

One of the comfort foods that is seeing new light is the bread and butter pudding. It first took a new twist when chefs began saucing it with fresh raspberry coulis. Here, I have updated it further with some Italian ingredients that make it a veritable splendour—glacé ginger, cedrat (a Mediterranean glacéed fruit the Italians often serve with cheese) and glacé orange. The real difference in technique comes from buttering Italian biscotti instead of bread, and reinforcing this with chopped unblanched almonds and an almond liqueur. The end result is beautiful in its own right, but for those with a flair for the dramatic, and the wherewithal to do it, it can be made downright spectacular for grand dining with spun sugar on top. Biscotti and cedrat or citron are available at better Italian delicatessens.

Preheat the oven to 180°C (350°F). Place the ginger, cedrat and mixed peel in the bottom of a deep 6-cup (1.5-litre/2½-imp. pint) Pyrex or white dish—make sure you use the deeper type, not too shallow. Add about 1 heaped tablespoon of the chopped almond and make a layer of the buttered biscotti in the bottom, not too tightly butted.

To make the custard, place the sugar and eggs in a mixing bowl, whisk together to blend, then whisk in the milk, cream and cinnamon. Pour over the biscotti, then place in the oven for 30 minutes. Lift from the oven and scatter the remaining almonds over the top, drizzle with Amaretto di Saronno and dredge or dust with icing sugar. At the same time, test with a skewer to see if the custard has set. When it has set, the skewer comes out dry and hot, not milky. Return to the oven and cook for a further 5 minutes until the almonds have coloured, or until the custard is fully set. Garnish with spun sugar for a spectacular finish, if liked.

Serves 6 Recipe: medium complexity

Lucio Galletto, restaurateur

Quince, Raisin and Grappa Pudding

INGREDIENTS
½ cup (90 g/3 oz) raisins
½ cup (125 mL/4 fl oz) grappa
4 quinces
45 g (1½ oz) unsalted butter
⅓ cup (90 g/3 oz) sugar
grated zest of 1 lemon
heavy (double) cream to serve

TOPPING
125 g (4 oz) unsalted butter
⅓ cup (90 g/3 oz) sugar
seeds of 1 vanilla bean
3 large eggs, separated
½ cup (60 g/2 oz) plain (all-purpose)
   flour
⅔ cup (155 mL/5 fl oz) milk
4 tablespoons grappa

In a small bowl, combine the raisins and grappa, and allow to soak for about 20 minutes.

Preheat the oven to 180°C (350°F). Peel and core the quinces and cut into 12-mm (½-inch) slices. In a large frying pan or skillet, melt the butter over medium heat and add the quinces and sugar. Cook for about 10 minutes, stirring occasionally. Add the grappa-soaked raisins and lemon zest, stir and remove from the heat. Spread the quince mixture into 4 individual ceramic moulds.

To make the topping, cream the butter, sugar and vanilla seeds in a blender. Add the egg yolks, flour, milk and grappa, and blend until smooth. Transfer to a bowl. In a separate bowl, whisk the egg whites and salt until soft peaks form. Fold the whites into the batter very gradually and place on top of the quince mixture in the moulds.

Bake in the oven for 20–30 minutes, or until firm to touch. Serve at room temperature with the cream.

Serve 4 Recipe: medium complexity

Catherine Adams, pastry chef

Catherine's Strawberry and Ricotta Tart

'Some of the best dishes I know come from the staff dinners. Our wonderful pastry chef, Catherine Adams, decided to make a free-form tart from a few leftover ingredients for breakfast. It tasted so good we thought we would write up the recipe and, as luck would have it, there was a photographer on hand!' JANNI KYRITSIS

Use your favourite shortcrust pastry to line a greased 25-cm (10-inch) tart pan with a loose bottom, or try the pastry on page 192 or 197. Follow the instructions for baking blind as well. The tart also looks great made free-form and cooked on a greased baking sheet.

Preheat the oven to 180°C (350°F). To make the custard, whisk 3 eggs with 2½ tablespoons sugar and a few drops of vanilla essence (extract) for flavouring. Fold in about 300 g (10 oz) ricotta cheese and then pour into the tart shell or spread it on top of the free-form pastry on a greased baking sheet.

Cover the tart with sliced strawberries and sprinkle with sugar. Cook in the lower part of the oven so that the pastry cooks before the topping becomes golden. Bake in the oven for about 20 minutes. Serve warm or cold with icing (confectioners') sugar sprinkled over the top, if liked.

Serves about 10 Recipe: medium complexity

Joan Campbell, food writer

Coconut Cream
with Palm Sugar Syrup

INGREDIENTS

COCONUT CREAM

5 large eggs

½ cup (125 g/4 oz) sugar

1 cup (250 mL/8 fl oz) coconut cream

1 teaspoon vanilla extract (essence)

PALM SUGAR SYRUP

½ cup (90 g/3 oz) soft palm sugar
(jaggery)

½ cup (125 mL/4 fl oz) water

roughie pineapple or cheeks of ripe
mango, peeled, cored and thinly
sliced, optional

This desssert is nice and creamy, with a coconut flavour enhanced by the crunchy texture of sweet pineapple.

Beat all the coconut cream ingredients together until thick. Pour into 4 lightly oiled moulds, leaving room at the top for the mixture to rise. Put the moulds into a steamer basket over simmering water and cover with greaseproof paper or muslin to avoid condensation dripping into the creams. Steam for about 20–25 minutes, or until a clean knife that is inserted into the centre withdraws clean. Remove from the steamer, set aside to cool. Alternatively, the creams can be cooked in a water bath of simmering water in a preheated oven at 170°C (340°F), for 20–25 minutes.

To make the palm sugar syrup, heat the palm sugar and water together until simmering and cook until a light syrup forms. Set aside to cool.

To serve, turn the creams out and drizzle with some of the palm sugar syrup. Serve immediately with the remaining palm sugar syrup and the thinly sliced pineapple or mango.

Serves 4–6 Recipe: easy to make

LEFT: Coconut Cream with Palm Sugar Syrup. A very delicate flavour and typically Asian. Refreshing after a rich Asian meal.

Vic Cherikoff, native Australian food providore

Cootamundra

Bread and Butter Pudding

with Lemon Ironwood and Rum Sauce

INGREDIENTS

375 g (12 oz) day-old Cootamundra
   bush bread (available in Australia at
   Woolworths bakeries) or use plain
   bread and include a mixture of
   20 g (¾ oz) wattle boiled in 1 cup
   (250 mL/8 fl oz) of water
3 cups (750 mL/24 fl oz) heavy
   (double) cream
200 g (7 oz) riberries
¼ cup (60 mL/2 fl oz) brandy
4 eggs, lightly beaten
1¼ cups (300 g/10 oz) sugar
1 cup (250 mL/8 fl oz) milk
30 g (1 oz) butter, melted

LEMON IRONWOOD AND RUM SAUCE
125 g (4 oz) butter
1 egg, beaten
2 cups (500 mL/16 fl oz) lemon
   ironwood syrup or maple syrup and
   ¼ teaspoon lime zest
½ cup (125 ml/4 fl oz) dark rum

I have had great success with this dessert. The beauty of this recipe is that while it is familiar, it is also enriched by flavours from the wattle in the Cootamundra bread—redolent of hazelnut, chocolate and coffee. The highlights are provided by the wild riberries. These fruits have the flavour of tart cinnamon and clove, and add a completely new dimension to the dessert.

Tear the bread into chunks and place in a large bowl. Pour the cream over the bread, mix together and leave until the bread is soft, preferably overnight. Stir occasionally. Combine the riberries and brandy in a small saucepan. Heat to a simmer, cover and set aside.

To make the sauce, melt the butter, stir in the egg and ½ cup (125 mL/4 fl oz) of the lemon ironwood syrup, and simmer until it thickens. Add the remaining 1½ cups (375 mL/12 fl oz) syrup and the rum, and keep warm until ready to serve.

Preheat the oven to 180°C (350°F). Use a portion of the butter to coat a 5-cm (2-inch) deep baking pan—or use individual ramekins if preferred. To make the custard, beat the eggs and sugar until pale, smooth and thick. Scald the milk and whisk into the egg mixture with the butter and brandy-soaked riberries. Fold the custard into the bread until well blended. Pour into the prepared pan and steam over a water-filled baking pan in an oven until browned and almost set, about 45 minutes (less if using ramekins). Serve warm with the lemon ironwood and rum sauce.

Serves 6–8 Recipe: medium complexity

Suzanne Gibbs, food writer

Fresh Fig and Mascarpone Tart

INGREDIENTS
1½ cups (185 g/6 oz) plain (all-purpose)
   flour
⅓ cup (90 g/3 oz) caster (superfine)
   sugar
185 g (6 oz) unsalted butter, melted and
   cooled
a few drops of vanilla essence (extract)
   or seeds scraped from vanilla bean

I also make this lovely fresh mascarpone tart with muscat grapes or blueberries in exactly the same way. The pastry is unusual—it works extremely well with soft fruit tarts such as this. Fresh whipped cream can substitute for the mascarpone, sweetened and flavoured in the same way.

Preheat the oven to 200°C (400°F).

Sift the flour into a bowl and stir in the sugar. Form a well in the centre and add the butter and vanilla. Combine to form a stiff dough. Press the dough out as you would a crumb crust, into a 10 x 34 cm (4 x 13½ inch) flan ring with a loose

1½ cups (375 mL/12 fl oz) mascarpone
honey and vanilla essence (extract), or
   orange blossom water
6–8 fresh figs
sugar for topping, optional

bottom, working up the edges evenly. Prick the base well and bake in the oven for 15–20 minutes, or until golden and cooked. Remove from the oven and leave to cool completely.

Whip the mascarpone and sweeten and flavour to taste with honey and vanilla, until it holds its shape.

When ready to serve, spread the mascarpone cream in the tart case as evenly as possible. Next quarter the fresh figs and arrange cut side up in the tart as tightly as you can. Serve as it is or sprinkle thickly with sugar and place for a minute or so under a preheated very hot griller (broiler). Or, if you have one, use a gas torch to caramelise the figs. Nothing more is needed to decorate the tart. Serve cut into wedges.

Serves 8–10 Recipe: medium complexity

Graeme Phillips, chef

Lemon Tart
with Fresh Berries

INGREDIENTS
1 quantity shortcrust pastry (page 192
   or 197)

TART FILLING
10 whole eggs
1½ cups (375 g/12 oz) caster (superfine)
   sugar
juice and finely grated zest of 10 lemons
1⅓ cups (340 mL/11 fl oz) light
   whipping (double) cream

BERRIES
500 g (1 lb) mixed fresh currants,
   blackberries and blueberries
1 punnet strawberries
½ cup (125 g/4 oz) caster (superfine)
   sugar
⅔ cup (155 mL/5 fl oz) water

1 cup (250 mL/8 fl oz) thick (double)
   cream, King Island or best quality

This tart has a rich and refreshing sweet and sour finish—a botrytised Riesling will make it perfection.

To make the filling, beat the eggs in a bowl with the sugar until smooth. Stir in the lemon zest and juice. Lightly whip the cream and stir into the lemon mixture.

Preheat the oven to 200°C (400°F). Roll out sufficient pastry to line a 20 x 5 cm (8 x 2 inch) deep, loose-bottomed tart pan. Press the pastry into the sides of the pan and trim off any excess. Lightly prick the base and chill for 20 minutes. Line the pastry case with baking parchment and half-fill with dried beans or pastry weights. Bake blind in the oven for about 15 minutes, until the pastry is set. Remove the beans and baking parchment, and pour the filling into the case. Reduce the oven temperature to 170°C (340°F) and bake the tart in the oven for 40 minutes, or until set. Allow to cool completely before serving.

While the tart is cooking, place the berries, sugar and water into a saucepan over medium heat and, just before boiling, remove from the heat. Cool slightly. Gently strain the fruit through a sieve and reserve the fruit. Return the syrup to the saucepan and, over high heat, reduce in volume by two-thirds.

To serve, place wedges of the tart on serving plates with the berries and syrup spooned over and a generous fold of cream alongside.

Serves 8–10 Recipe: medium complexity

Martin Webb, chef

Pavlova with a Passionfruit Curd

INGREDIENTS

4 egg whites

⅔ cup (155 g/5 oz) caster (superfine)
  sugar

1 teaspoon white wine vinegar

1 tablespoon hot water

1¼ cups (300 mL/10 fl oz) double
  (heavy) cream

PASSIONFRUIT CURD

2 eggs, plus 2 extra yolks

5 tablespoons fresh passionfruit pulp

30 g (1 oz) unsalted butter, cut into
  small dice

¼ cup (60 g/2 oz) caster (superfine)
  sugar

*An ideal light summer dessert for people with a busy lifestyle. This pavlova can be
prepared a day or two ahead, leaving only the brief final assembly to be done before
serving. A new look for Australia's favourite dessert.*

Preheat the oven to 150°C (300°F). Oil a large piece of baking parchment on a
baking sheet.

Put the egg whites, sugar, vinegar and hot water in the bowl of a food mixer
and whisk at the highest speed for 5 minutes until soft, white peaks form. Spoon
the mixture into a 20-cm (8-inch) round on the oiled paper—or spoon 4 high
rounds on the paper to make individual pavlovas. Cook in the centre of the oven
for about 1 hour 10 minutes, until crisp. (The individual pavlovas will take less
time, about 1 hour.) Allow to cool on a wire rack.

To make the passionfruit curd, put all the ingredients into a bowl set over a
pan of simmering water and stir constantly until the mixture starts to thicken and
take on the appearance of a thin custard. Continue to cook, still stirring, until it
thickens further, about 10 minutes. Remove from the heat immediately so as not
to overcook. Ladle the curd into a clean jar or container, and leave to cool before
covering and refrigerating.

To serve, whip the cream into soft peaks and place onto the pavlova base
spreading out to the edges with a palette knife. For the individual pavlovas,
place a spoonful of cream on top of each pavlova. Pour the passionfruit curd
over the top.

Serves 4 Recipe: medium complexity

RIGHT: Pavlova with a Passionfruit Curd. The silky
texture of the passionfruit curd breaks through
the crusty exterior of the meringue to the
marshmallow interior. Intense, intriguing and acidic,
the flavour of the passionfruit offsets the sweet
meringue.

Serge Dansereau, chef

Almond Tart
with Amaretto Mascarpone and Poached Figs

INGREDIENTS

FRANGIPANE FILLING

200 g (7 oz) butter, at room temperature

1 cup (200 g/7 oz) caster (superfine)
   sugar

5 eggs

¾ cup (90 g/3 oz) plain (all-purpose)
   flour, sifted

2 cups (200 g/7 oz) ground almonds

SUGAR PASTRY

1 cup (200 g/7 oz) caster (superfine)
   sugar

200 g (7 oz) soft butter, at room
   temperature

2 eggs

3¼ cups (405 g/13 oz) plain
   (all-purpose) flour, sifted

2 drops vanilla essence (extract)

2 tablespoons raspberry jam or conserve

3 tablespoons sliced almonds

2 tablespoons icing (confectioners')
   sugar, optional

AMARETTO MASCARPONE

250 g (8 oz) mascarpone cheese

⅔ cup (100 g/3½ oz) icing
   (confectioners') sugar, sifted

1 teaspoon Amaretto

POACHED FIGS

3 cups (750g/1½ lb) sugar

4 cups (1 litre/1¾ imp. pints) water

12 figs

To make the frangipane filling, begin preparations the day before needed. Beat the butter and caster sugar together, then slowly add the eggs, incorporating them one at a time. Beat well. Mix together the flour and ground almonds. Add to the egg mixture, then beat for a few more minutes. Cover with plastic wrap and allow to rest overnight in the refrigerator before using.

To make the sugar pastry, beat the sugar and butter together, then slowly add the eggs. Add the sifted flour and lastly the vanilla essence. The dough will be very soft to handle. Store in the refrigerator until the next day before using.

To bake the tarts, remove the frangipane mixture from the refrigerator 30 minutes before using. This will allow the butter to soften and pipe more easily. Preheat the oven to 180°C (350°F).

Take the sugar pastry out of the refrigerator and roll out to 3 mm (about ⅛ inch) thick. Using a round cookie cutter, cut shapes in the pastry and press them into small moulds or tart pans. Alternatively, press the pastry into one large pie plate. Cut away the edges.

In the base of the pastry, pipe about 1 teaspoon of raspberrry jam in the middle. Next, using a plain nozzle, pipe the frangipane mixture, until the prepared tart moulds are three-quarters full. Sprinkle with the sliced almonds and bake in the oven for 25 minutes until golden—bake for 45 minutes if making one large tart. Remove the tarts from the pans once cold. Dust with icing sugar, if liked.

To make the Amaretto mascarpone, mix all the ingredients together by hand—do not overmix.

To prepare the poached figs, mix the sugar and water together in a saucepan and bring slowly to the boil. Simmer for several minutes to form a heavy syrup. Clean the figs in cold water and gently place in the simmering syrup using a ladle. Place a circle of baking parchment over the figs. Simmer for 20 minutes, then remove from the heat. Allow to cool.

To serve, set a tart on each serving plate and, using a tablespoon dipped in hot water, scoop out a spoonful of Amaretto mascarpone and place on the tart. Slice the figs in half and place 2 halves on one side of each tart. Drizzle with some syrup from the figs and serve.

Makes individual 12 tarts or 1 large Recipe: complex

Neil Perry, chef

Passionfruit Tart

INGREDIENTS

9 large eggs

1¾ cups (350 g/11 oz) caster (superfine) sugar

1¼ cups (310 mL/10 fl oz) heavy (double) cream (45% butterfat)

1⅓ cups (350 mL/11 fl oz) passionfruit juice, strained

plain (all-purpose) flour for rolling

1 quantity sweet shortcrust pastry

a little egg wash for glazing

icing (confectioners') sugar for serving

SWEET SHORTCRUST PASTRY

2 cups (250 g/8 oz) plain (all-purpose) flour

75 g (2½ oz) unsalted butter, cubed

pinch of sea salt

½ cup (90 g/3 oz) icing (confectioners') sugar, sifted

3 tablespoons milk

2 egg yolks

This tart should be to Australians what lemon tart is to the Poms. If one fruit stands out in my mind as Australian, it would have to be the passionfruit. Its intensity sets it apart from other fruits, and it is an ideal partner for cream and eggs. We have cooked the Roux brothers' luscious lemon tart for many years at Rockpool, and this tart draws its inspiration from that.

To make the passionfruit mix, put it together the day before you wish to bake the tart (resting the custard in the refrigerator helps avoid splitting). Break the eggs into a bowl and whisk. Add the sugar and continue to whisk until well incorporated. While stirring gently, pour in the cream. Add the passionfruit juice and continue to stir until well blended. Cover and refrigerate overnight.

To make the pastry, place the flour, butter, salt and icing sugar in a food processor and process for 20 seconds. Add the milk and egg yolks, and process for a further 30 seconds until a mass forms. Turn out on a lightly floured surface and knead lightly for a few moments. Flatten the dough and form a ball. Wrap in plastic and place in the refrigerator for 1 hour.

Spray a 26-cm (10-inch) tart pan with a light vegetable oil. Lightly flour the work surface and roll out the pastry until it is 2 cm (¾ inch) wider than the tart pan. Roll the pastry over your rolling pin and gently ease into the tart pan, pushing the sides in gently so that the pastry takes the fluting. Rest in the refrigerator for 30 minutes.

Preheat the oven to 180°C (350°F). Remove the tart case from the refrigerator and line with foil. Place uncooked rice or dried beans in the foil and bake blind for 20 minutes. Remove the rice and foil, brush the tart shell with egg wash and cook for a further 10 minutes. Remove from the oven and lower the temperature to 140°C (280°F). Return the tart case to the oven.

With the case sitting in the oven, carefully pour in the passionfruit custard. Fill the tart right to the top, using a cup or a small dariole mould. Bake for 40 minutes. Check—the tart should be halfway set, but still be quite wobbly in the middle. If you take it out too soon, it will not set and run when you cut it; if you leave it in too long, it will set too firmly and lose its elegance. Through experience, you'll find the optimum set for the tart in your oven.

Remove the tart from the oven, balance on a cup and remove the sides of the pan. Place the tart on a wire rack and, with a palette knife, slide the base off the tart pan. This will allow the tart to cool and the pastry to crisp up rather than sweat. Invert the pastry ring back onto the tart to help hold the sides in as it cools and sets. Allow to cool for 1 hour. Carefully cut with a serrated knife and place in the middle of large white plates. Dust with icing sugar and serve.

Serves 8 Recipe: complex

Janni Kyritsis

Dining with Janni and an MG

A bite through a golden, crusty surface reveals a sharp, salty flavour that expands as its lingering fishy taste is savoured. To some, it may be just a deep-fried crumbed anchovy. As part of Janni Kyritsis's cooking repertoire, however, it is a sublime creation—one of the many this highly innovative chef is serving at MG Garage Restaurant. There are little clouds of dried and deep-fried fish skin, a Western Australian sardine fillet on a finger of fried bread, and a warm salad of snails, pig's trotters, pig's ears, purslane and escarole amongst them— and any rainy day blues will definitely lift as you dive into a pink gin and lemon granita.

This highly individualistic food is created by a self-taught chef who arrived in Australia at twenty-three, fresh from working in the Greek merchant navy as an electrician. Janni hardly spoke any English, so his partner, David Bradshaw, gave him a copy of Margaret Fulton's Cookbook, accompanied by the words: 'Learn English through an interest.' David is a brilliant home cook and has been Janni's food influence throughout his career. He is the only person whose opinion Janni takes seriously.

Janni had a sound start to his culinary life, growing up in the north of Greece in a family who were fascinated by food and were good home cooks. Although it was a simple cuisine, it was made with only the freshest of ingredients, many of which they grew themselves.

In Melbourne, Janni persuaded Stephanie Alexander to take him on as a second chef in her first restaurant in Fitzroy. It was very difficult at that time to start without any cooking experience, but Stephanie had the vision to give him a chance. From there, he went to Berowra Waters and soon became chef—and his own style of cooking blossomed. After a few years at Bennelong, Janni, together with business partners Ian Pagent and

visual appeal is secondary. After twenty-two years in professional kitchens, this innovative and sophisticated chef still remains true to his parents' philosophy.

LEFT: Pink Gin and Lemon Granita (page 181). The lemon is an important element of the refreshing qualities of this granita—a buttery shortbread biscuit provides the perfect finish.

BELOW: Spinach and Mushroom Roulade (page 88) is a classic Italian dish—the Italians have been making this dish for hundreds of years. This is the version made in Janni's restaurant.

Greg Duncan, conceived a new concept and opened an MG showroom and stylish restaurant in the one space.

Janni loves the freedom of Australia and thinks he couldn't have worked his way to where he is today in any other country. Although he took his basics from Greece, he is not a Greek-influenced cook—Janni describes himself as a Mediterranean-influenced Australian cook. He still believes in learning the classics first—stocks and sauces, mostly French techniques and cooking methods—and he insists that the ingredients and the flavour are the most important elements. He always tries to cook the best way for the ingredient; the dish's

ABOVE: Some of the staff at MG Garage line up for a talk with Janni while they eat their breakfast.

Raymond Capadli, chef

Anneau of Valrhona Manjari Chocolate
with Seville Orange Coulis and Vanilla Bean Chantilly

INGREDIENTS

ANNEAU

5 teaspoons butter

405 g (13 oz) Valrhona Manjari
  chocolate or similar top-quality
  dark chocolate

4 egg yolks

3 eggs

⅔ cup (150 g/5 oz) sugar

⅔ cup (150 mL/5 fl oz) water

3 cups (750 mL/24 fl oz) heavy (double)
  cream, whipped

SEVILLE ORANGE COULIS

1½ cups (300 g/10 oz) caster (superfine)
  sugar

1 cup (250 mL/8 fl oz) water

125 g (4 oz) rind of Seville oranges,
  julienned

1½ cups (375 mL/12 fl oz) freshly
  squeezed lemon juice

1½ cups (375 mL/12 fl oz) freshly
  squeezed orange juice

1½ cups (375 mL/12 fl oz) freshly
  squeezed grapefruit juice

VANILLA BEAN CHANTILLY

⅔ cup (100 mL/3½ fl oz) heavy (double)
  cream

5 teaspoons caster (superfine) sugar

1 vanilla pod

fresh mint, picked over
vanilla pod, julienned

To make the anneau, butter 4 ramekins and line with baking parchment. Melt the chocolate by placing it in a bowl with another bowl of warm water underneath or melt in the microwave. Whip the egg yolks and the whole eggs to peak consistency.

Meanwhile, bring the sugar and water to the boil and, when the sugar has dissolved, add to the egg mixture. Cool slightly. Fold the chocolate into the egg mixture, then fold in the whipped cream. Pour into the prepared ramekins and leave to set for 8 hours in the refrigerator.

To make the Seville orange coulis, dissolve the sugar in the water over gentle heat, then add the rind. Cook for 45 minutes over low heat. Add the fruit juices and cook until pouring consistency. Pass through a sieve, then allow to cool. Reserve the zest.

To make the vanilla bean chantilly, whip the cream with sugar to peak consistency. Cut the vanilla pod in half, scrape out the seeds and fold them into the cream.

To serve, place some coulis in the middle of each serving plate, turn the anneau out of the ramekins and place one in the centre of each serving of coulis. Using a metal spoon, quenelle or gently scoop the vanilla bean chantilly into an oval on top of each anneau. Garnish with the reserved zest, mint and vanilla julienne, and serve.

Serves 4 Recipe: complex

Tony Bilson, chef

Chocolate Soufflé

A never-fail dish—guaranteed to get a great reception from your guests.

INGREDIENTS

CREME PATISSIERE

1 vanilla bean, split

2 cups (500 mL/16 fl oz) milk

1 cup (250 g/8 oz) white granulated
  sugar

½ cup (60 g/2 oz) plain (all-purpose)
  flour

6 egg yolks

3 tablespoons melted clarified butter
  (made by melting butter until the
  solids settle to the bottom—the clear
  fat is then poured off

3 tablespoons caster (superfine) sugar

1 tablespoon bitter cocoa powder

SOUFFLE MIX

200 g (7 oz) bitter chocolate

1¼ cups (310 mL/10 fl oz) crème
  pâtissière (see above)

1 tablespoon bitter cocoa powder, plus
  extra for dusting

8 egg yolks

MERINGUE

10 egg whites

scant ½ cup (100 g/3½ oz) caster
  (superfine) sugar

icing (confectioners') sugar for dusting

To make the crème pâtissière, place the vanilla bean and the milk in a saucepan and bring to the boil. In a separate bowl, whisk together the sugar, plain flour and egg yolks, and pour the boiling milk into the mixture, whisking all the while. Stir over a low heat until the mixture comes to the boil, simmer for 2 minutes and then press through a strainer to eliminate any lumps. Sprinkle the surface with sugar or melted butter to prevent the formation of a skin. This quantity makes 4 cups (1 litre/1¾ imp. pints).

Preheat the oven 170°C (340°F). To prepare the soufflé moulds, brush the insides of six soufflé moulds (preferably Pilluyvit 6-cm/1½-inch high moulds) generously with the melted butter. Mix together the sugar and cocoa. Tip all the sugar/cocoa mix into the first mould, tip the mould on an angle and turn so that the inside is coated with the mix. Tip the mix not clinging to the mould into the next one and repeat the process until the six moulds are coated. Turn the moulds upside down onto a tray to await filling. This concentrates the butter along the upper lip of the mould and helps achieve an even rise when cooking the soufflés.

To make the soufflés, chop the chocolate into small pieces. Place in a saucepan with the crème pâtissière and warm the mixture over low heat, stirring until the chocolate has melted and is incorporated evenly into the mix. Add the 1 tablespoon cocoa and mix thoroughly. Remove the pan from the heat and incorporate the egg yolks. Cool the mixture and put aside until needed.

To make the meringue, in a separate bowl, beat the egg whites until they are fluffy, then add half the sugar. Beat until soft peaks form, then add the rest of the sugar and whisk a little more. The egg white should be firm, but it should fall off into peaks when lifted with a whisk.

Warm the soufflé mix to lukewarm and then fold one-third of the egg whites into the mixture. Fold this mixture back into the rest of the egg whites.

Fill the moulds with the mixture, mounding it slightly. Take a sharp knife and cut the mixture around on the inside of the moulds (on the outside edge) to a depth of 2 cm (¾ inch) without touching the mould. This will enable the soufflés to rise evenly.

To cook the soufflés, pour 2.5 cm (1 inch) of boiling water into the bottom of a baking pan. Place the filled moulds in the dish and bake in the oven. The soufflés will be cooked in 15–17 minutes. If the oven has uneven heat, it is worthwhile turning the soufflés halfway through cooking so that they rise more evenly. When cooked, dust the soufflés with the extra bitter cocoa powder and icing sugar. Serve with vanilla ice cream, if liked.

Serves 6 Recipe: complex

Geoff Lindsay, chef

Turkish Delight Soufflé
with Rose Petal Ice Cream

INGREDIENTS

ROSE PETAL ICE CREAM

1 cup (250 mL/8 fl oz) milk

1 cup (250 mL/8 fl oz) heavy (double)
  cream

½ cup (125g/4 oz) sugar

1 dark red rose in full bloom, or some
  rose water

6 egg yolks

SOUFFLE

1 cup (250 mL/8 fl oz) milk

½ teaspoon butter

1 tablespoon sugar

⅓ cup (45 g/1½ oz) Dutch cocoa powder

2 tablespoons cornflour (cornstarch)

4 Fry's Turkish Delights

8 egg whites

⅔ cup (155 g/5 oz) caster (superfine)
  sugar

icing (confectioners') sugar for dusting

I tried to make this soufflé really interesting, so I folded Turkish delight into the chocolate soufflé to give it a luxurious feeling and accompanied it with rose petal ice cream. The pink jewels of rose water burst in your mouth.

To make the ice cream, place the milk, cream, sugar and rose petals in a saucepan and place over medium heat to warm. Remove from the heat and allow to infuse for 30 minutes. Beat the egg yolks until light and pour the infused milk over the yolks, stirring well until combined. Pour the mixture back into the saucepan and stir over gentle heat until the mixture coats the back of a spoon. Strain through a fine sieve and cool. Churn in an ice cream machine according to the manufacturer's instructions, or pour into a metal ice cream tray, cover with foil and place in the freezer turned to its coldest setting. When firm, allow to set in the freezer at the normal setting.

To make the soufflé base, place half of the milk in a saucepan over medium heat with the butter and sugar. Allow to heat, but do not boil. Mix the remaining milk with the cocoa and cornflour. Pour the hot milk mixture over the cocoa mixture and stir well. Return to the heat and simmer for 5 minutes, then allow the soufflé base to cool.

To finish the soufflé, cut the Turkish delight into 1-cm (½-inch) cubes. Lightly grease 4 x 1-cup (250 mL/8 fl oz) soufflé dishes and preheat the oven to 200°C (400°F). Place half of the Turkish delight and the soufflé base in a stainless steel bowl and warm over a saucepan of simmering water. Beat the egg whites to soft peaks. Gradually add the sugar and keep beating until all the sugar is incorporated. Gently fold into the hot soufflé base very gradually. Put a few pieces of Turkish delight into the bottom of each prepared soufflé dish. Pour the soufflé mixture into the moulds and sprinkle the remaining Turkish delight over the top. Bake in the oven for 8–10 minutes. Dust lightly with icing sugar. Serve immediately with scoops of the rose petal ice cream.

Serves 4 Recipe: medium complexity

RIGHT: Turkish Delight Soufflé with Rose Petal Ice Cream. A celebratory dessert—there one minute, gone the next. It is all hot air really, scented with the rose petal aroma of the Middle East. A little bit of heaven.

Kelly Leonard, chef

Chocolate Diva
with Cumquat Sauce

INGREDIENTS

½ cup (125 g/4 oz) raw (demerara) sugar

9 eggs

500 g (1 lb) chocolate, melted

200 g (7 oz) crème fraîche

2½ tablespoons kirsch

2½ tablespoons Grand Marnier

1½ tablespoons rum

1 teaspoon ground cinnamon

CUMQUAT SAUCE

500 g (1 lb) cumquats, halved and
    seeded

4 cups (1 litre/1¾ imp. pints) water

2½ cups (500 g/1 lb) caster (superfine)
    sugar

1 cinnamon stick

3 cardamom pods

icing (confectioners') sugar or gold-leaf
    transfer

This fantastic poached chocolate cake is one of our signature dishes—the intense taste of the cumquat sauce offsets the richness of the chocolate cake.

To make the sabayon, preheat the oven to 160°C (325°F). Put the sugar and eggs in a heatproof bowl and stand the bowl in a saucepan of simmering water. Whisk briskly until the sauce becomes thick and the mixture coats the back of a spoon. Fold in the chocolate, then the crème fraîche, kirsch, Grand Marnier, rum and cinnamon. Pour into a 30-cm (12-inch) Teflon cake pan that has been lined on the bottom with baking parchment. Place the cake pan in a shallow dish of simmering water. The water should come halfway up the pan. Bake in the oven for 75 minutes.

Remove from the heat and allow the cake to cool. Once cold, remove from the pan and refrigerate. It is easier to slice after 12 hours.

To make the cumquat sauce, put all the ingredients in a saucepan and bring to the boil. Simmer for 1 hour, then remove from the heat and allow to cool.

To serve, dust the top of the cake with icing sugar or gold-leaf transfer. Place a slice of cake on each plate, with the cumquat sauce beside it.

Serves 12 Recipe: medium complexity

Stephanie Alexander, chef and food writer

Queen of Nuts Cake
on a Simple Rhubarb and Red Fruit Sago Sauce

INGREDIENTS

CAKE

200 g (7 oz) best-quality dark chocolate

1 cup (150 g/5 oz) blanched almonds

⅔ cup (150 g/5 oz) sugar

30 g (1 oz) glacé (candied) citron, cut into tiny dice

5 egg yolks, lightly whisked with a drop of pure vanilla essence (extract)

5 egg whites

1 tablespoon melted butter

1 tablespoon fine, fresh breadcrumbs

SAUCE

375 g (12 oz) rhubarb, chopped into 1-cm (½-inch) slices

grated zest of ½ lemon

¼ cup (60 mL/2 fl oz) water

¾ cup (185 mL/6 fl oz) sweet white wine

1 split vanilla bean

2 tablespoons sago

⅓ cup (90 g/3 oz) sugar

500 g (1 lb) fresh or frozen raspberries

heavy (double) cream to serve, optional

When I was in the Barossa Valley, South Australia, I encountered rote grutze, *made from grape juice, for the first time. It was then I realised the similar turnings my sago recipe featuring raspberries and rhubarb had taken.* Rote grutze, *a traditional Lutheran dessert, means red pudding and there are many versions all involving red fruits and sago. I now wonder if my mother's cherry sago had a similar derivation? Use South Australian almonds in the cake if you can.*

To make the cake, preheat the oven to 160°C (325°F). Grate the chocolate finely and chop the almonds finely or grind separately in a food processor. Mix the chocolate, almonds, sugar and citron lightly, but well. Stir in the egg yolks. Beat the whites until they are satiny and in soft peaks. Gently fold the whites into the chocolate mixture. Line a 22 x 5 cm (9 x 2 inch) round cake pan with the melted butter and breadcrumbs, and pour the cake mixture into it.

Bake for about 35 minutes, until the cake feels firm in the centre—a test skewer will still be moist because of the chocolate. Cool in the pan for 10 minutes and then turn out onto a foil-lined tray. Cool completely. The cake keeps very well in an airtight container.

To make the sauce, place the rhubarb, lemon zest, water, wine and vanilla into a non-aluminium saucepan and bring to simmering point. Add the sago, stir, reduce the heat and place the pan on a simmer mat. Cook gently for 15 minutes, stirring often. Add the sugar, stirring to dissolve. Add fresh or frozen raspberries, and simmer for a few minutes, or just until the berries have thawed if using frozen ones. Stir once or twice.

To serve, spoon the sauce onto the serving plates and place a wedge of cake on top. Serve warm or cold, and add a spoonful of cream on the side, if liked.

Serves 10 Recipe: medium complexity

Gary Cooper, chef

The Bathing Cap

INGREDIENTS

MERINGUE

8 egg whites

2½ cups (500 g/1 lb) caster (superfine)
   sugar

MANGO SORBET

1¼ cups (200 g/7 oz) icing
   (confectioners') sugar

juice of 1 lemon

500 g (1 lb) mango pulp, puréed

2 gelatin leaves, soaked, squeezed and
   gently heated until dissolved

FROMAGE FRAIS

250 g (8 oz) fromage frais (goat's cheese)

3 tablespoons icing (confectioners')
   sugar

juice and zest of 1 lemon

scant cup (200 mL/7 fl oz) water

2 gelatin leaves, soaked, squeezed and
   gently heated until dissolved

ROSE-SCENTED JELLY

2 cups (500 mL/16 fl oz) water

½ cup fresh roses, preferably whole

1 drop of red food colouring

3 tablespoons sugar

2 leaves gelatine, soaked and squeezed

MASCARPONE CREAM

310 g (10 oz) mascarpone

scant cup (225 ml/7 fl oz) heavy
   (double) cream

TO SERVE

pastel pink rose petals for garnish

icing (confectioners') sugar for dusting

I made this first as a tiny condiment to dessert. People loved it so much that I made it into a full-blown dessert and have never been able to take it off the menu. It's a play on pavlova, which Australians love, and looks like Esther Williams' bather's cap. The jellies give it a feeling of the ocean as they wobble and sway. I make it with fresh goat's cheese from the neighbouring Yarra Valley Dairy.

To make the meringue, preheat the oven to 120°C (250°F). Whip the egg whites until soft peaks form. Gradually whisk in the caster sugar, ensuring the peaks are still soft and not overbeaten. Trace 4-cm (1½-inch) circles on baking parchment 2.5 cm (1 inch) apart. Put the egg whites in a pastry bag with the star nozzle attached. Pipe the meringue in rounds to the size of the marked circles. Bake in the oven for about 30 minutes. Turn off the heat and allow to cool in the oven, if liked. Store in airtight containers. This quantity makes 40 meringues—keep the remainder in an airtight container for a rainy day.

To make the mango sorbet, put the icing sugar and lemon juice into a large saucepan over medium heat. Dissolve the sugar and bring to the boil. Allow to cool. Mix the syrup with the mango purée and blend together in a food processor. Stir in the gelatine. Place in a sorbetière and follow the manufacturer's instructions or pour the mango liquid into flat freezer trays and freeze. When the sorbet is just about set, remove from the freezer, cut into blocks and blend in the food processor. Pour back into the trays, cover, and return to the freezer.

To make the fromage frais, pass the fromage frais through a food mill or mash with a potato masher. Gently fold in the remaining ingredients and freeze as for the sorbet above.

To make the rose-scented jelly, boil the water and pour over the roses in a mixing bowl. Infuse the tea for 5 minutes. Strain the roses from the liquid and discard. Add the food colouring, sugar and gelatin leaves to the liquid and stir to dissolve. Leave in a cool place and, when set, refrigerate until serving.

To make the mascarpone cream, whip the mascarpone and cream together until thick.

To serve, use a meringue as a base, then layer with a slice of mango sorbet. Top with another meringue, then a slice of fromage frais, and freeze. Just before serving, place each serving on a plate, cover with the mascarpone cream and dot fresh pastel pink rose petals all around the top and sides. Dust with icing sugar, then place 3 scoops of the rose-scented jelly around each plate.

Serves 20 Recipe: complex

RIGHT: The Bathing Cap. A delicate concoction of layers of meringue, mango sorbet and fromage frais, covered with mascarpone cream and topped with pastel pink rose petals. The jellies are made with an infusion of rose petals. Bliss!

Brief Biographies
of Chefs and Food Writers

Catherine Adams, pastry chef

Catherine Adams *always enjoyed baking at home from a young age. After doing her commercial training in New Zealand, her interest leaned towards pastry. In Australia, she started at MCA and Rockpool as a young pastry chef. Later, Catherine and her partner ran a restaurant near Margaret River in Western Australia. She returned to the Perry group to develop her skills in Asian pastries at Wokpool. Catherine is now happily working as pastry chef at MG Garage Restaurant. Her latest interest is perfecting Mediterranean and Middle Eastern pastries, which is a natural step in her career when she lives with a Turkish chef and works for a Greek one.*

Stephanie Alexander, chef and food writer
(pages 150–151)

Victoria Alexander, restaurateur

Victoria Alexander *rose to the challenge when she saw an old bathers pavilion building in Sydney was for lease, and determined to have it. Its stunningly beautiful location at Balmoral Beach, combined with its casual, but elegant furnishings, more than match the fine quality of the eclectic food. Victoria's background was in photographic styling and fashion, although she always loved fine food and cooking. She hired Genevieve Harris as chef and together they served imaginative food at the forefront of modern Australian cuisine. In 1998, the Bathers Pavilion was closed for major renovation and opened again the following year with highly acclaimed chef Serge Dansereau at the helm. The rest is history.*

Maggie Beer, food writer and producer

Maggie Beer *and her husband, Colin, have been breeding pheasants and growing grapes in the Barossa Valley, South Australia, since 1973. For fifteen years, Maggie ran The Pheasant Farm, a highly acclaimed restaurant based primarily on the local produce. Since closing her restaurant, she has worked on her farm produce, creating her Export Kitchen to supply the export market, as well as the domestic, with Pheasant Farm pâté, verjuice, quince paste, mushroom pâté and an increasing number of regional products. Maggie is an enthusiastic supporter of regional food and the potential of quality niche marketing. She is highly regarded as a food writer, writing the only contemporary book on Australian regional cuisine, Maggie's Farm. Her friend Stephanie Alexander gives this apt description. 'Maggie is well known for her determination to work with what she has around her … There are yabbies and trout in the dam, geese on the lake, olives soaking in brine tubs, corn salad poking through the cold ground outside the kitchen door, and the 100-year-old pear tree was just starting to flower [during one visit].'*

Tony Bilson, chef (pages 78–79)

Guillaume Brahimi, chef

'I love old French recipes and the way they used to cook. I'm always looking for old cooking books and for recipes which I make much lighter for today's tastes and casual approach in Australia. I learnt to cook with my grandfather in Paris. We used to cook for twenty people every Sunday. I love home cooking.'

   Guillaume Brahimi *was an apprentice chef at fourteen and later worked at La Tour D'Argent until he moved to that most celebrated restaurant, Robuchon. Joel Robuchon inspired him—everyone worked really hard for perfection and loved what they were doing. Guillaume came to Sydney for a holiday seven years ago and decided it was time to branch out on his own. He worked for several restaurants until he took up the reins at Quay, formerly Bilson's. He likes to put the pressure on himself to gain perfection in a dish. Fresh ingredients are his inspiration. He tries to find the best produce, and cooks it with the minimum of fuss so the freshness and the original flavours are apparent. 'I believe I'm very lucky—I've got a passion and I can do it for a living.'*

Marieke Brugman, chef and teacher

Nestled in the foothills of the Howqua Valley, Victoria, is a gourmet getaway established by **Marieke Brugman** and her partner Sarah Stegley more than twenty years ago. Later it evolved to include a residential hands-on cooking school—the first in the country. It has deservedly been a tremendous success. Leading Australian chefs periodically demonstrate at the school, including Cheong Liew, Phillip Searle, Tetsuya Wakuda and Janni Kryitsis. Marieke and Sarah have led the way in teaching interested home cooks the secrets of Australia's modern cuisine. They also host gourmet tours in Australia and overseas. 'I cook in two ways. On a daily basis, I cook kitchen food that depends on what is available from my garden, with a variety of rice or good sourdough bread. I never spend more than twenty minutes preparing a meal. When I cook for guests, I cook up to fifteen hours a day. We make everything from breads to stocks, preserves, biscuits and muesli. My food is always evolving—favourites revisited and refined. In our quintessentially Australian environment, we create for our guests meals that are conducive to conviviality, intelligent conversation and uplifted spirits.'

Raymond Capadli, chef

'Cooking today has come from the roots of many cultures. I believe food should always be respected by not confusing the search for the new with producing nightmares for the sake of it. We have come full circle back to simplicity, back to basics which give new depths to marrying food with the right ingredients.' **Raymond Capadli** has cooked in fine hotel restaurants all of his cooking life—from Scotland, Cannes, London, Moscow and Hong Kong to Port Douglas and Melbourne in Australia. Before he became executive chef, he worked under such luminaries as Allan Hill and Anton Mossiman. With his formidable credentials, Raymond built Le Restaurant at the Sofitel in Melbourne into the finest prestige hotel dining room in the city. His innovative cuisine is based on the finest ingredients with intense flavours. It is beautifully crafted and visually stunning. He will be opening Fenix, a more relaxed, bistro-style restaurant in the near future, as well as a cooking school.

'For myself, cooking is pure magic—the smell, results and failures are the passion of being a chef. I always say to my chefs, "There should always be surprises. You should never look at cooking from a crowded city. Look at cooking as if you were standing on a boardwalk looking into a thousand oceans," meaning there should be no end to understanding flavour.'

Joan Campbell, food writer
(page 50)

Robert Castellani, chef

'I am Italian, I live in Australia, my ingredients are Australian—when they are cooked, they speak a few words of Italian.' Trained in contemporary French cooking, **Robert Castellani** also excels in Italian and Mediterranean-style cooking. He was born in Pavia, Italy, and migrated to Australia as a child. His parents were rice farmers and both excellent cooks. He has been head chef at some of Melbourne's most renowned restaurants, including Fanny's, Stephanie's and Florentino, and is currently at Donovan's on St Kilda Beach. Robert is not afraid to serve simple dishes in which the ingredients are well balanced and textured—he believes simplicity is the key to success. He also enjoys creating more complex dishes with harmonious flavours. 'Food should be nutritious and satisfy basic needs; it must be nurturing and cheerful, driven by flavour. If you use the best produce, the best cooking follows.'

Vic Cherikoff, native Australian food providore (pages 14–15)

Dany Chouet, chef
(page 106)

André Chouvin, chef

André Chouvin draws his philosophy from eighteen years cooking experience in three-star Michelin restaurants, working with luminaries such as Paul Bocuse, Marc and Paul Haeberlin, and Michel Lorain. Marc Haeberlin was especially supportive, recognising his talent and persuading André to represent him in Boston, USA, at the Julien restaurant. André and his wife, Tracey, have been steadily building Café de la Gallerie for the past three years as a gastronomic restaurant on the Central Coast of New South Wales. André celebrates the wonderful Australian ingredients available locally that he can enhance with his French craftsmanship. CONTINUED ON PAGE 212

Top: The view of the Yarra Valley from the verandah in early spring where the Hallidays enjoy 'the fairyland of morning mists and fogs; the midday view with the tall buildings of Melbourne; the chequerboard of light and double rainbows after a rain storm; and the incandescent light of late afternoon.'

James and Suzanne Halliday

A loaf of bread, a glass of wine ...

The Yarra Valley's reputation for fine wines and fine food has gathered momentum in the past few years, placing it firmly as one of the outstanding regions in Australia, set in the most stunningly beautiful agricultural landscape.

Victoria's first vineyard was established in the Yarra Valley in 1854, by the pioneering wine-grower

Suzanne, began their vineyard, Coldstream Hills. With their formidable energy and passion, it wasn't long before they were producing outstanding Chardonnay, Pinot Noir, Cabernet/Merlot and Cabernet Sauvignon. Their vineyard is one of the highest profile wineries in the region and was acquired by the giant Southcorp wine company in

herbs, breads, chocolate, pasta, jams and preserves, honey, lavender, nuts, mushrooms, cider, beer and, of course, world-famous wines.

'We are lucky enough to live at once in and above the Yarra Valley, ever offering new vistas. Then there is the change of the seasons in the vineyards carpeting the slopes below our house,

Paul de Castella. His vineyard was soon surrounded by other great wine estates and, by the 1880s, Victoria was the country's major wine-producing state. By the early twentieth century, however, the viticultural districts were going out of production and only a handful survived—economic depression and changing fashion caused table wines to decline in demand. Then, as now, the dynamic of suburban growth threatened to swallow vineyards, orchards and market gardens.

The rebirth of the Yarra Valley vineyards did not begin until the late 1960s. James Halliday, Australia's most widely known and respected wine writer, is also a winemaker and wine judge, and was a partner in a small, high-quality winery, Brokenwood, in the Hunter Valley, until he realised the potential in the Yarra Valley. He and his wife,

1996, although James continues to head the dedicated winemaking team.

The Hallidays, fired with enthusiasm and broad knowledge, have been instrumental in showcasing the quality of the world-class wines and food of the region. Suzanne founded the Yarra Valley Regional Food Group in 1998 to identify small and large specialist food growers in the area and to promote and publicise the primary products of the region.

The group has published a food trail to identify places where visitors can stop to taste and buy seasonal fresh food, catch a trout, bottle local mineral water or enjoy a cheese tasting at the dairy. Among the foods produced are high-quality beef, lamb, poultry and game, salmon and its roe, yabbies, venison, fruit including berries and stone fruit, nashi and olives, all manner of vegetables and

a feast for the senses: the lime green ribbons of spring, the darker green, precisely trimmed rows of summer; the riot of yellow, orange, gold and red of autumn; and finally the strangely compelling architecture of the newly pruned vines in winter. We are indeed part of a lucky country.'

ABOVE LEFT: A few of the splendid local wines.

ABOVE CENTRE: Fine-quality Atlantic salmon roe or caviar, naturally farmed and milked by hand in the Yarra Valley.

ABOVE RIGHT: Wood fungus from the Gourmet Mushroom Farm at Wandin.

FAR LEFT: The fine-quality local apples and pears.

In the evening, they offer à la carte, degustation and prestige menus. The prestige menu includes Australian produce enhanced with foie gras, caviar and black truffles. Terry Durack described André's restaurant in the Good Food Guide as 'a wonderful mix of Oz casual, with big-night-out food.'

Gary Cooper, chef

After cooking professionally for twenty years for high-quality establishments such as Fanny's, Burnham Beeches and Cotswold House, **Gary Cooper** *has realised one of his great dreams. With his wife, Sonia, he is managing the reborn Chateau Yering in the beautiful Yarra Valley, on the site of Victoria's first great wine estate. Food is at the forefront, setting high standards in fine dining and luxury accommodation. Gary's menu showcases the superb local food produce and reflects Gary's penchant for combining unusual ingredients in ingenious ways with exemplary craftsmanship. Gary considers the textures and flavours in a dish first and likes to have a few surprises as well. 'If you stick to the classical way of doing things and then add your own twists, you'll end up with something exciting.' His restaurant, Eleonore's, and Sweetwater Café, also at Chateau Yering, are both a foodies' heaven.*

Serge Dansereau, chef
(pages 142–143)

Peter Doyle, chef

'I like to concentrate on seasonal ingredients and let the food speak for itself. I think visual appeal is important, but I don't put in anything without a reason—it has to taste good.'

The Sydney dining scene has changed dramatically since **Peter Doyle** *was an apprentice learning to cook carpetbag steaks and oysters mornay. As soon as he finished, he went to Europe with his wife, Beverley, and roamed through France, Italy and Spain in a campervan, enthralled with everything that was happening in food. 'It was the beginning of nouvelle cuisine. It was a real buzz. You went to France to eat an oakleaf lettuce because you couldn't get it here. You'd go to Italy to eat mesclun, to taste cheeses. Now we have all that here and it's not such a buzz going to Europe. We have our own particular style of service that's identifiable. Our restaurants look a particular way and the food has changed.' The food Peter cooks now is essentially Australian, utilising classic French techniques. It is strongly influenced by Mediterranean flavours and only a little by Asian cuisines. His restaurant, Cicada, is a friendly, relaxed environment with an elegant dining room and verandah. The service is friendly and the food finely honed with freshness and honesty. 'I like the interplay of classic, harmonious flavours enhancing the main ingredient. Restraint and simplicity are important qualities for a perfectly cooked dish.'*

Alain Fabrègues, chef

While other boys dreamed of train engines and rocket ships, **Alain Fabrègues** *thought only of stoves and white hats. Alain's education in food began early, under the influence of his grandmother, a famous cook of her day. He did his apprenticeship at Le Restaurant du Marché Gate de Brienne in Bordeaux and later furthered his training under Jean Delaveyne, the noted master. He migrated to Western Australia and married Elizabeth and together they opened The Loose Box in 1980. Alain is dedicated to producing the finest cuisine in French brigade style, while celebrating the wonderful fresh produce of Western Australia. All the herbs and most of the vegetables he uses are grown in the large gardens surrounding his luxurious restaurant and cottages. Winner of a staggering number of awards and prizes, Alain has certainly realised his dream of creating the finest cuisine for all his lucky patrons.*

Sue Fairlie-Cuninghame, food writer and regional food promoter
(page 51)

Margaret Fulton, food writer
(pages 166–167)

Lucio Galletto, restaurateur

Lucio Galletto *was brought up in a family of restaurateurs—in fact, he was almost born in a restaurant. He began his cooking life chopping the parsley in his parents' restaurant on the Italian Riviera. Later, to his family's disappointment, he left for Sydney when he fell in love with an Australian girl, Sally, now his wife. Lucio worked a few years at Natalino's then opened his first restaurant in Balmain in 1981, presenting fresh Italian home cooking. This was a bit of a revolution in those days—he was the first to make fresh handmade pasta and large stuffed ravioli. After two years, he bought the*

Hungry Horse in Paddington and, after a few months, employed Eugenio Riva as chef. Together they had a wonderful time changing the menu and discovering new produce. His restaurant, Lucio's, has created wonderfully fine Italian Australian food consistently for nearly twenty years. Riva left to open his own restaurant in 1997 and Lucio is happily working alongside Timothy Fisher. Lucio has been faithful to his philosophy of following the seasons, not the fashion. 'I like to get excited about what I do, as well as keep an eye on tradition. I think it's important to respect it. I think it has been a very exciting time to be in Sydney. When I grew up in Italy, there were special small producers for fresh basil or fish—it wasn't at all like that when I first came to Sydney. Now in Sydney young people are excelling in specialised produce. The fresh ingredients are very exciting. Sydney is a mecca for some of the most inventive chefs in the world. I like being part of the Australian cuisine. And it's possible because the diners are adventurous.'

Suzanne Gibbs, food writer

Suzanne Gibbs *grew up shopping, chopping, listening and watching in the atmosphere of the finest professional cookery. The daughter of best-selling cookery author Margaret Fulton, Suzanne polished her natural talents at the Cordon Bleu School of Cookery in London, graduating with its prestigious diploma. They immediately invited her to be the dessert and pastry chef at the Cordon Bleu Restaurant. She has had a highly successful career back in Australia as a cook, food writer and food stylist. She still enjoys working in the kitchen with Margaret, sharing her passion for the finest ingredients and presenting recipes for home cooks in a clear, easy-to-follow style. Her recipes and brilliant food styling reflect her knowledge of what makes a particular dish appealing to home cooks.*

Suzanne and James Halliday, regional food promoters and wine writer
(pages 210–211)

Genevieve Harris, chef

Genevieve Harris *has cooked in a number of acclaimed restaurants in Australia, including the Bluewater Grill and the Paragon Cafe, as well as working at the Bathers Pavilion as executive chef for four years. She has been praised as a 'perfectionist' and a chef of 'incredible finesse and refinement', with a rare understanding of ingredients and spices. Her food is eclectic, blending Asian and Mediterranean flavours using only the freshest of ingredients. While at the Bathers Pavilion, she was co-author of their highly successful, eponymous cookbook. She is now happily back cooking in her home town of Adelaide, where she is a partner in the well-known restaurant, Nediz Tu.*

Diane Holuigue, food writer and teacher

Diane Holuigue *writes about food with a magical style—she is able to capture the aroma, taste and texture of the dish she is describing and to enthuse the reader. Her clearly set-out instructions make it easy for novices to follow—thoughtful tips and hints make it easier still. She is passionate about communicating her immense knowledge of food, continually being broadened here and in Europe and the USA. Diane has been a leading writer for twenty-six years with both magazines and newspaper columns, and has written more than nine cookbooks. For twenty-eight years, she ran the foremost private cooking school, The French Kitchen, teaching more than 54 000 students. It was characterised by its down-to-earth approach to the demystification of cookery and culinary techniques. Diane was the first to bring international teaching chefs here—Giuliano Bugialli, Ann Willan, Madhur Jaffrey, Roger Vergé and Marcella Hazan, among many. She has made an enormous contribution to the growth of knowledge in the food and wine traditions of Australia.*

Janet Jeffs and Kelly Leonard, chefs

Janet Jeffs *was apprenticed to culinary legend Cheong Liew, at Neddy's in Adelaide. She also had the good fortune to work with Maggie Beer at the Pheasant Farm in South Australia's Barossa Valley. Her first restaurant was Kilikanoon in the beautiful Clare Valley, until she moved to open Juniperberry in Canberra with* **Kelly Leonard**. *Kelly has always been a dessert queen, she assured us. Food and making textiles are her profession and passion. The theatrical elements of dessert making are a feature* of her food-related performances at Juniperberry. The restaurant has a glamorous space which adds drama to the beautifully presented food. It is very well known for its sumptuous desserts, epitomised by Mr Curly, a humorous reference to Michael Leunig's enigmatic cartoon character.

Philip Johnson, chef

'We do as little as possible with the best ingredients available.' **Philip Johnson** understates the fine-flavoured food he presents at e'cco, a bold, bright restaurant with salsa red and eggplant purple walls and plain wooden tables and chairs. New Zealand born, Philip worked in Sydney and Perth before moving to Brisbane, where he opened the highly popular Le Bronx. He has a perfectionist's hands-on attention to detail—'You are only as good as your last meal,' he admits. In 1995, he opened e'cco to packed tables. Philip likes to travel to broaden his outlook and techniques, and regularly writes a column on food. Rick Stein commented: 'e'cco is the sort of restaurant the rest of the world envies ... laid back, totally at ease with itself and the service just slips along nicely ... where the food makes you feel ten years younger. To me, it was just like rock 'n roll, a live show that just makes you go "Yes, that's it" ... That's what it's all about.'

Simon Johnson, food providore
(pages 90–91)

Jennice and Raymond Kersh, restaurateur and chef

'We had to wait for pioneers like Raymond and Jennice to discover what the Aboriginal people had known for a millennia—that the bush offers a bounty which talent can transform into one of the world's most interesting cuisines,' wrote David Dale, journalist. **Jennice and Raymond Kersh** are brother and sister who own and run Edna's Table II in Sydney, specialising in modern Australian cuisine with the delicate flavours of indigenous ingredients. They grew up amongst a melting pot of nationalities in Sydney's colourful docklands. Their childhood revolved around a love of food and hospitality, which made up for the hardship of grinding poverty. Their father was a wonderful cook, and Raymond soon followed in his footsteps. They have spent time living with an Aboriginal settlement in the Kimberley region of Western Australia and travelled widely throughout Australia, extending their knowledge of native food. Raymond combines classic cooking techniques with a preference for native Australian food—lemon myrtle leaves, native aniseed, wild plums, kangaroo, native mint and bush tomatoes.

Janni Kyritsis, chef
(pages 198–199)

Michael Lambie, chef

'The creation of Circa, The Prince has allowed me to establish a place of great food within a great establishment on my own terms. My fundamentals of cooking are top-quality ingredients, simply cooked and not overgarnished, served with a fantastic sauce. I like to stick to the basics.' **Michael Lambie** wanted to cook from an early age. He had a providential start early in his career, working at The Sloane Club in London, Claridges, the Waterside Inn and then under Marco Pierre White. Michael travelled to Australia hoping to establish himself and to be part of the new wave of fine cooking. Following three years at the Stokehouse learning about the Australian palate, he opened Circa, to great acclaim. 'Now there's a much more European style of food developing within Melbourne. Standards have risen, it could be the leader of food in the world, because of the people, the produce and it's a very inviting place.'

Kelly Leonard, chef
(see Janet Jeffs, page 213)

Cheong Liew, chef

Cheong Liew is one of Australia's most influential chefs. He pioneered the fusion of European and Asian cuisines and ingredients—his food has its own unique flavour, texture and visual appeal, with the subtlety of a master. Cheong grew up in Malaysia amidst three food cultures—Chinese, Malayan and Indian. His family was very food orientated—his grandmother did the cooking helped by her daughters. As children, they were encouraged to help and all joined in the fun of making rice in bamboo leaves, grinding rice for rice cakes and cleaning the shark's fin. Cheong came to Australia as a student, but his love of being in the kitchen with his aunties turned him to cooking. He began in a Greek restaurant, The Iliad, where the head chef luckily took a liking to him and encouraged him, plying him with books to read. He enjoyed learning new cooking techniques, but after a while he realised you needed the temperament of a Greek to capture Greek cooking. After that, he learnt and experimented with Indian and French cuisines at Lord Kitcheners, serving Greek and Chinese-style food as well. Barry Ross worked as the dishwasher and, inspired, they decided to open their own restaurant, Neddy's. Cheong went to the market every day and cooked what he felt like. There was no menu—he produced seasonal fresh food and the public responded enthusiastically. Slowly the menu was developed by the patrons. His own

BELOW RIGHT: Simply served with black olives, this white mould sheep's milk cheese is made in the Camembert style, originally created by Richard Thomas.

ABOVE: Damien Pignolet's Prawn Soufflé Tart (page 146). This tart shows the contrast of textures between the pastry, being light and flaky, and the very light and creamy texture of the soufflé. The richness and intensity of flavours is balanced by a touch of cayenne.

style of food evolved and that is how his unique style of fusion came about. He has recently taken his cuisine to the fine dining room, The Grange, at the Adelaide Hilton.

'In my cooking, I'm trying to put together various elements of different cultures into one dish. I can cook a dish the traditional way, but I like to put in an element from somewhere else in the globe to remind many people of their own cuisine. There is a cultural freedom in Australia that accepts this. I wanted to break away from my Chinese traditions, but not their cooking techniques. Fusion has existed for thousands of years as food cultures mix with migration and exchanges of ideas. My upbringing as a Chinese in Malaya made me unafraid of mixing cuisines together.'

Geoff Lindsay, chef

'Dynamic approach, adaptable and flexible, spontaneous, stunning visually, bold combinations of flavours'—there is plenty of praise for **Geoff Lindsay**'s fine-quality food at Stella. Geoff hails from Warrnambool, a small coastal town in Victoria where he began his apprenticeship. Geoff was lucky enough to have food-loving parents who took him travelling and eating around the world from an early age. As soon as he was qualified, he worked for Stephanie Alexander, ending up as head chef for three years. He left to work with Andrew Blake at Blake's Restaurant, with the intention of setting up Stella to showcase his own style of Australian food. Geoff's menu reflects what he likes to eat himself and is broad enough to offer variety.

'I'm still respectful dealing with the individual food cultures. I don't do fusion food, I don't mix cultures on one plate. My approach meanders between the food cultures, it's a thread, but I don't force them together. I make individual dishes true to their culture. Stephanie crystallised my thoughts and made me dig deeper. I like to use local produce—fresh is best. I like being a student of cuisine cultures— understanding what to do with a piece of lemon grass.'

Greg Malouf, chef

Greg Malouf has been classically trained in European cooking, but his greatest inspiration is drawn from his mother's kitchen and the cuisines of Iran, Turkey, Greece and North Africa. His life in hospitality began at Watson's in Melbourne and continued at Two Faces, Mietta's and Stephanie's, as well as overseas in Austria, Hong Kong and Italy. In 1991, Greg created the restaurant at O'Connell's Hotel—a skilful menu of seasonal dishes influenced by the colours and flavours of the Middle East.

'The dishes I remember as a child cooked by my mother and grandmothers are the same dishes made in the Arabic kitchens all over the world; they are the same dishes which have been made for the past 2000 years and they are the same dishes which I interpret in my own kitchen at O'Connell's. This is the essence of Middle Eastern cooking, it's simply rooted deeply in tradition. What I am trying to do in my kitchen is to reinterpret the exotic flavours, aromas and textures of my childhood, combining them with huge ranges of fabulous fresh produce available here in Australia today. So, although my dishes are based on tradition, I try to develop my own modern twists … the possibilities are endless.'

Stefano Manfredi, chef

Stefano Manfredi migrated from Italy as a young boy in the 1960s. He grew up absorbing a traditional food culture using the freshest ingredients from both his mother and grandmother, who were excellent cooks. While working for Jenny Ferguson at You and Me, he decided to open his own restaurant, The Restaurant Manfredi. It is his intuitive response to fine raw ingredients coupled with his Italian traditional skills that make his cooking an important part of the Australian food revolution. In the late 1990s, Stefano and his mother Franca opened the highly successful bel mondo restaurant in The Rocks, close to Sydney's Circular Quay. 'I am Italian. And I am a cook. But I live in Australia and, whenever I can, I seek out and use only the finest and freshest Australian ingredient. My cuisine is informed by the classic Italian approach to food, but relying on the best ingredients in this country, chosen at their peak. We know that the new cannot exist without the traditional, and that tradition is constantly being nourished by the new. This, in itself, was a revolutionary approach—we knew we were on the right track when we had customers telling us they had enjoyed the meal, it was not Italian.'

Luke Mangan, chef

At fifteen years of age, **Luke Mangan** already knew he wanted to be a chef, and embarked on his career with a four-year apprenticeship with Hermann Schneider. He then left for Europe, where he offered to work for Michel Roux for free for a month and ended up working for eighteen. On returning to Australia, Luke wanted to interpret his training in his own style—the CBD was a great success as a direct result of Luke's firm training in the classics and his personal commitment to excellence. Luke enjoys modernising classic food—he likes to work with the freshest seasonal local produce to keep the food simple, letting it speak for itself. He is now in his element in his own restaurant, Salt, working beside his partner, Lucy Allon.

Paul Merrony, chef

'I promote simplicity in my cooking. Ingredients should speak for themselves. Yes, ingredients do talk. All you must do is learn the language.' **Paul Merrony** first trained at Berowra Waters, before broadening his training in London and Paris at one- and three-star Michelin restaurants. After establishing a series of successful and highly regarded restaurants in Sydney, he now owns and cooks his finely crafted food at Merrony's, overlooking Sydney Harbour. He is regarded as one of Australia's finest young chefs. He has a deep commitment to technique and the finest and freshest Australian ingredients. 'Much of the ideology behind the food at Merrony's is French and the majority of techniques used in the kitchen are French. And yet my restaurant is unmistakeably a Sydney restaurant in terms of its lack of rigid formality and, I hope, its elegant and simple food.' His recipes in this volume have been taken from his mouth-watering book, The New French Cooking in Australia.

Michael Moore, chef

Matthew Moran, chef

Philippe Mouchel, chef
(pages 186–187)

Mietta O'Donnell, restaurateur
and food writer

Neil Perry, chef
(see pages 178–179)

Graeme Phillips, chef

Michael Moore returned to Australia in 1998 for the third time to launch the 'new-look' Bennelong at Sydney Opera House, giving it a new energy and excitement for a whole new market—'We need to get a smile on its face.' He has opened up the space to give it a friendlier, yet elegant, casual appeal, with fine food to match. Michael began his career in London, then moved to Sydney to work under Serge Dansereau as chef saucier. He left for London after two years to work at The Ritz Hotel as the youngest Senior Chef de Partie Poissonier. Believing Australia is on the cutting edge of food innovation, Michael returned to Sydney to be part of the great development in Australian fine cuisine. He worked at the Craigend Restaurant, the Hotel Nikko and the Bouillon Eatery. In 1996, he went to London to create Bluebird, a fine eating house and food store gastrodome for Sir Terence Conran. He's back in Oz—we're hoping he stays this time.

Matthew Moran is an innovative chef who has a passionate belief in top-quality fresh produce, changing his menu every six weeks to take advantage of the seasonal produce. His menu is eclectic in nature—from Moroccan spices and Asian flavours to traditional recipes such as home-cooked duck and pea pie. It tastes as good as it looks. Matthew did his apprenticeship at La Belle Helene, then moved on to work at Restaurant Manfredi. He joined forces with Peter Sullivan to open the Paddington Inn Bistro to instant success. After three years, they opened their present lively and contemporary Moran's Restaurant and Café in Sydney's Potts Point.

Mietta O'Donnell developed a love of good food and hospitality from an early age from the Italian side of her family, as well as her Irish and Scottish antecedents. Her mother worked in her grandfather's quality Italian restaurant Mario's, but neither of her parents wanted Mietta to have anything to do with restaurants. Luckily for Melbourne, after a career as a journalist and extensive overseas travel, she succumbed to her love of food and, in 1974, opened Mietta's in North Fitzroy. There she threw out the rule book, creating menus with Chinese, Italian and French dishes, as well as food from other cuisines. Mietta's was one of the first restaurants to offer a multicultural choice of food cuisines. Later she moved to Alfred Place in the city, with its exquisitely restored nineteenth-century dining room, still displaying the 'remarkable and stylish mixture of cuisine, concern and connections that has come to mean Mietta's.' Mietta's closed in 1996 and Mietta picked up her career as a journalist, writing a weekly column and Mietta's Eating and Drinking in Melbourne. We hope she succumbs again.

Graeme Phillips was born into a traditional Anglo-Saxon family where most food was boiled to death. He became inspired by food when living overseas in Argentina, France and Sweden, and these flavours still appear in his cooking today. He taught himself to cook by reading everything he could and was especially inspired by Elizabeth David, Stephanie Alexander and Patrick Juillet at Le Café. He opened Prospect House in Tasmania as a restaurant with accommodation, specialising in wild game, which is in plentiful supply locally. Other regional ingredients were wild salmon, quail, sea urchins, mussels and oysters. The seasons of Tasmania, which are more distinct than the rest of Australia, influence his change of menus. In summer, he prefers fresh, clean flavours and some Asian influences; in winter, he uses the deeper, richer flavours of northern Europe and China. Graeme went on to open a brasserie in Battery Point, Hobart, with a similar menu, but with more casual food and atmosphere. He believes that Australian chefs and their diners are lucky enough to absorb the techniques and flavours of many food cultures subconsciously. 'When I'm cooking, they just pop out—they have become part of my palate armoury. It has been very exciting growing with the food and wine industry in Tasmania these past twenty years.'

Damien Pignolet, chef

BELOW RIGHT: Liam Tomlin's Roast Stuffed Chicken Legs with Cèpe Cream Sauce (page 112). A classic French autumn dish that adds a lot of flavour to a chicken.

BELOW: Victoria Alexander's Warm Tart of Blue Cheese and Caramelised Onions (page 64).

Ralph Potter, chef (page 107)

Jacques Reymond, chef (pages 118–119)

Leo Schofield, food critic

Kathy Snowball, food writer

Damien Pignolet *is a second-generation Australian of French, German and English descent. He began his career in hospitality, but after a while he took a long break and spent time exploring the cuisines of France and Italy. He was fascinated and the experience has influenced his cooking ever since. Damien first realised his great passion to be a restaurateur when he joined Pavilion on the Park. A partnership with master chef Mogens Bay Esbensen ensued, and they opened Butler's Restaurant. The creative ambition to explore his culinary philosophy was realised through his first marriage to Josephine, and their purchase of Claude's French Restaurant.*

From the first, they gained wide recognition with their exquisite food and service. After fourteen years, Damien sold the restuarant to Tim Pak Poy, who continues this fine tradition with his own unique style.

Damien's need for challenge led to a new partnership with Dr Ron White and they conceived a new concept for pub food, resulting in the Bistro Moncur, which draws upon traditional French bistro fare and modern Australian cuisine. Bistro Moncur has flourished and become an institution in Sydney. The team went on to launch the successful Bistro Deux in Rozelle.

'My philosophy of cooking is to be deceptively simple and totally pure.'

Leo Schofield *is currently director of the Sydney Festival and of the Olympic Arts Festival in the Year 2000. In an earlier incarnation, he was, for almost two decades, Sydney's leading restaurant reviewer, writing for the Sydney Morning Herald, the Australian, the Sunday Telegraph, the Bulletin and Vogue. Leo has always been outspoken and fearless in his praise, as well as in his criticism. He has done much to elevate the culinary standards of Australia, encouraging chefs he believed had talent and enthusing and educating his readers to try the new. He is an amateur cook who believes that a commentator need not have the same skills as those on whom he comments. 'It is not expected that a music critic should be able to sing like Pavarotti.' He favours simple food and believes that restaurant food and home cooking are two entirely different skills.*

'Australian Gourmet Traveller has helped to shape the way we eat in Australia. It has introduced a wide variety of cuisines in a stylish and approachable way.' **Kathy Snowball** *started her working life as a merchant banker, but her love of food and wine finally convinced her to switch careers and follow her passion to work with food. After graduating from Prue Leith's School of Food and Wine in London, teaching, catering and editing, she was appointed Food Editor for Gourmet Traveller magazine in 1996. Gourmet, under the guidance of Carolyn Lockhart since 1990, has been instrumental in educating and encouraging home cooks. It has promoted the fine food created by the top and up-and-*

coming chefs. Wonderful fresh seasonal produce has been celebrated with informative text about where to buy it, how to prepare it and how to cook it. Gourmet Traveller gives readers a sense of confidence in the kitchen and in shopping for the finest quality ingredients. Kathy confided, 'The magazine looks gorgeous, but it's totally useful. If a recipe isn't practical, we don't bother with it. I don't believe those that say people don't want to cook any more. If you look at the growth of food magazines and books, a lot of people do cook. We also like to support the small producers and encourage our readers to demand excellence and also to show enthusiasm for fine products, so the message gets back to the producers. After all, they are the ones committing themselves to take big chances marketing their exciting new products.'

John Susman, food providore
(pages 30–31)

Chris Taylor, chef

RIGHT: Luke Mangan's Cauliflower Soup with Truffle Oil and Chives (page 49)

Chris Taylor worked in top hotels in Sydney, Perth and Europe until he opened his own restaurant, Fraser's, in the glorious King's Park in Perth. The location is a large park of natural bushland with views over the Swan River and the heart of Perth. Chris consistently supports the philosophy of using local produce and 'letting the produce speak for itself ... by changing the menu daily, we ensure variety, but there are a few favourites such as freshly shucked Albany

oysters and the silkiest Kervella Goat's cheese that regularly appear.' The seafood dishes account for nearly 70 per cent of the orders, with Western Australian dhu'fish and swordfish equal favourites. Local game is also a speciality. 'The menu has a broad representation of cultures without mixing them up. A Japanese-influenced dish needs to taste Japanese. We try to be uncomplicated. I'm always looking at different techniques and refining what we're doing. And enjoying myself.'

Richard Thomas, cheese maker
(pages 62–63)

David Thompson, chef

'I'm just a Sydney boy. I developed a passion for food from an early age, even though my dear mum was the worst cook in the world. I studied English literature at university—all those things you really need for cooking. I was lucky enough to train at Pavilion on the Park, Butler's with Mogens Bay Esbensen and Bagatelle. I went to Thailand more or less by accident and was seduced by the country, culture, people and especially the cooking. Thai cooking is one of the great cuisines. It has sound techniques and requires Thai ingredients. Thai cooking is a balance between hot, sour, salty and sweet. It is fresh and fragrant with clear flavours.'

It wasn't long before **David Thompson** moved to live there. He learnt the language and studied the food culture. When he returned, he started Darley Street Thai in Newtown, serving a little Thai at first. It was so popular, however, it soon took over. The restaurant was so successful, in 1993, he moved it to Kings Cross into a stunning Iain Halliday-designed dining room. Later, he opened the glamorous Sailors' Thai, with an upstairs noodle bar.

'I'm cooking Thai food, with Thai techniques and philosophy, but not with the same ingredients—it's evolved into our own style with the new and finer seasonal ingredients available here in Australia.'

Liam Tomlin, chef

Although **Liam Tomlin** began his career at the age of fourteen in Ireland, it wasn't until four years later, when he worked for Bruno Enderli in Zurich, that he discovered there was much more to cooking than he had previously known. There and then he set out to be just like Bruno. Inspired, he went on to experience some of the best hotel kitchens in Europe and Australia. He was chef de cuisine at Level 41 and executive chef at Brasserie Cassis, and is now executive chef at the elegant Banc and Wine Banc. Liam believes in keeping the food as simple as possible, concentrating on two or three flavours in a dish. He likes to use top-quality ingredients, in season, for the season. Liam loves working in Australia, where his Irish background isn't the impediment it might perhaps be in other places. He enjoys the feeling that people in Australia aren't afraid to be a bit off-the-track.

Tetsuya Wakuda, chef

Tetsuya Wakuda began his cooking career with high-profile chef Tony Bilson at Kinselas' in Sydney's Taylor Square. He was fascinated by Tony's blend of French classicism and his individual approach. Tetsuya then worked in several restaurants prior to opening Ultimo's Restaurant in 1986. Gradually, he developed his own unique cuisine, based on the Japanese philosophy of natural seasonal flavours, enhanced by classic French technique. He opened his restaurant Tetsuya's in Sydney's Rozelle in 1989, and has had a packed house ever since. Customers continue to return for this truly great food, so individual, so full of flavour, cooked and presented with great precision—truly a master. Tetsuya's offers a set menu, which is finely balanced and changed frequently. It is well worth following Tetsuya's guide for wine by the glass with each course, to experience his flavour selection to the full. When Tetsuya returned from being guest chef for the James Beard Foundation, rumours abounded that he was invited to set up his own restaurant in New York. But he was not interested. 'Being overseas I was introduced as a Japanese-born Australian chef and I thought, ahhh, it felt good. I am an Australian chef. I had to make a choice … I chose Australia … I love what I do here.'

Martin Webb, chef

'I always cook what I want to eat and I like to marry food with the correct partners to cook seasonally and simply. I make the product the hero—I don't do tricks. I use the best products available and let them speak for themselves. Food needs to be democratic and to be accessible—don't make it exclusive.' **Martin Webb** trained as a chef in England and France, and emigrated to Perth in 1982. The relaxed quality of life, proximity to Asia (closer than Sydney), abundant seafood and superb ingredients greatly influenced him. He enjoys cooking good food with a minimum of fuss and likes to fuse different food cultures. Australia lost Martin for a while when he returned to London to work as head chef of Quaglino's. He has, thankfully, returned to Melbourne as food director of Georges' restaurant and food complex. Martin's recipes have been taken from his stunning book, Fusions.

Alla Wolf-Tasker, chef

'I believe you need sound cooking techniques as well as a great deal of creative ability to take our ever widening repetoire of new ingredients and use them in an effective and intelligent manner. I strongly believe in seasonal food and keeping flavours simple. Use the finest ingredients at their peak. A light touch, a bit of romance or whimsy to finish off. I like to make people smile.' **Alla Wolf-Tasker** arrived in Australia as a baby with her Russian parents. They were both excellent cooks—food and hospitality played a major role in family life, as it did with most post-war migrants. When she and her husband opened Lake House restaurant on the shores of beautiful Lake Daylesford, Victoria, they were emulating the wonderful weekend house parties of her parents' dacha or summer house, which had been just up the hill. Lake House soon became a foodie destination and is one of Australia's finest gourmet restaurant/retreats. Menus reflects Alla's passion for seasonal food and, yes, it makes you smile and give thanks for her warm hospitality and sublime food. The dishes Alla shares with us are a simplified example of her style—suitable for the domestic situation or even a chef's day off!

Further Reading

Alexander, Stephanie. *Stephanie's Australia*. Allen & Unwin, Sydney, 1991.

Alexander, Stephanie & Beer, Maggie. *Stephanie and Maggie's Tuscan Cookbook*. Penguin, Melbourne, 1998.

Alexander, Victoria & Genevieve Harris. *The Bathers Pavilion Cookbook*. Ten Speed Press, San Francisco, 1995.

Barker, Anthony. *From A la Carte to Zucchini: An A to Z of Food and Cooking*. Allen & Unwin, Sydney, 1995.

Beckett, Richard. *Convicted Tastes: Food in Australia*. Allen & Unwin, Sydney, 1984.

Beer, Maggie. *Maggie's Farm*. Allen & Unwin, Australia, 1993.

Beer, Maggie. *Maggie's Orchard*. Penguin, Australia, 1997.

Bilson, Tony. *Fine Family Cooking*. Angus & Robertson, Sydney, 1994.

Campbell, Joan. *Bloody Delicious*. Allen & Unwin, Sydney, 1997.

Chang, Kwang-chih (ed.). *Food in Chinese Culture*. Yale University Press, New Haven & London, 1977.

Coe, Sophie D. & Coe, Michael D. *The True History of Chocolate*. Thames & Hudson, London, 1996.

Dansereau, Serge. *Food and Friends*. HarperCollins, Sydney, 1998.

Driver, Christopher. *The British at Table 1940–1980*. Chatto & Windus, London, 1983.

Dunstan, David. *Better Than Pommard!: A History of Wine in Victoria*. Australian Scholarly Publishing & Museum of Victoria, Melbourne, 1994.

Dunstan, Don. *Don Dunstan's Cookbook*. Rigby, Adelaide, 1976.

Dunstan, Don. 'Tradition and renewal in Australian gastronomy', in Anthony Corones, Graham Pont & Barbara Santich (eds), *Food in Festivity: Proceedings of the Fourth Symposium of Australian Gastronomy*. Sydney, 1990

Durack, Terry & Dupleix, Jill. *Sydney Morning Herald Good Food Guide 1999*. Anne O'Donovan, Melbourne, 1998.

Fahey, Warren. *When Mabel Laid the Table: The Folklore of Eating and Drinking in Australia*. State Library of NSW Press, Sydney, 1992.

Forell, Claude. *The Age Good Food Guide 1999*. Anne O'Donovan, Melbourne, 1998.

Fulton, Margaret. *Encyclopedia of Food and Cookery*. Octopus Books, Sydney, 1983.

Fulton, Margaret. *Margaret Fulton's New Cookbook*. Angus & Robertson, Sydney, 1993.

Fulton, Margaret. *A Passionate Cook*. Lansdowne Publishing, Sydney, 1998.

Gibbs, Suzanne. *Sweet Things*. Angus & Robertson, Sydney, 1994.

Hage, Ghassan. 'At home in the entrails of the West: Multiculturalism, "ethnic food" and migrant home-building', in Helen Grace et al., *Home/World: Space, Community and Marginality in Sydney's West*. Pluto Press Australia, Sydney, 1997.

Hobsbawm, Eric & Ranger, Terence (eds). *The Invention of Tradition*. Cambridge University Press, Cambridge, 1983.

Holuigue, Diane. *Classic Cuisine of Provence*. Ten Speed Press, San Francisco, 1993.

Holuigue, Diane. *The French Kitchen: A Comprehensive Guide to French Cooking*. Paul Hamlyn, Australia, 1983.

Kalcik, Susan. 'Ethnic foodways in America: Symbol and the performance of identity', in Linda Keller Brown & Kay Mussell (eds). *Ethnic and Regional Foodways in the United States*. University of Tennessee Press, Knoxville, 1984.

Kapoor, Sybil. *Modern British Food*. Michael Joseph, London, 1995.

Kersh, Jennice & Raymond. *Edna's Table*. Hodder & Stoughton, Sydney, 1998.

Liew, Cheong & Ho, Elizabeth. *My Food*. Allen & Unwin, Sydney, 1995.

Manfredi, Stefano & Newton, John. *Fresh from Italy: Italian Cooking for the Australian Kitchen*. 2nd ed. Hodder Headline, Sydney, 1997.

Mennell, Stephen. *All Manners of Food: Eating and Taste in England and France from the Middle Ages to the Present*. Basil Blackwell, Oxford, 1985.

Merrony, Paul. *The New French Cooking in Australia*. Horan, Wall & Walker, Australia, 1992.

Muskett, Philip E. *The Art of Living in Australia*. Eyre & Spottiswoode, Sydney, 1893; facs. repr., Kangaroo Press, Sydney, 1987.

Newton, John. *Wog Food*. Random House, Australia, 1996.

O'Donnell, Mietta & Knox, Tony. *Mietta & Friends*. Wilkinson Books, Melbourne, 1996.

O'Donnell, Mietta & Knox, Tony. *Mietta's Eating & Drinking in Melbourne, 1999*. Hardie Grant, Melbourne, 1998.

Perry, Neil. *Rockpool*. Reed Books, Australia, 1996.

Pont, Graham. 'Upstart gastronomy: A cuisine without peasants' in Barbara Santich & Michael Symons (eds), *Proceedings of the Third Symposium of Australian Gastronomy*. Adelaide, 1988.

Ripe, Cherry. *Goodbye Culinary Cringe*. Allen & Unwin, Sydney, 1993.

Santich, Barbara. *Looking for Flavour*. Wakefield Press, Adelaide, 1996.

Schofield, Leo. *Leo Schofield's Cookbook*. Methuen, Australia, 1980.

Steingarten, Jeffrey. *The Man Who Ate Everything*. Alfred A. Knopf, New York, 1998.

Symons, Michael. *One Continuous Picnic*. Duck Press, Adelaide, 1982.

Symons, Michael. *The Shared Table: Ideas for Australian Cuisine*. Australian Government Publishing Service, Canberra, 1993.

Trillin, Calvin. 'American fried' (1974), reprinted in *The Tummy Trilogy*. Farrar, Straus & Giroux, New York, 1994.

Walker, Robin & Roberts, Dave. *From Scarcity to Surfeit: A History of Food and Nutrition in New South Wales*. New South Wales University Press, Sydney, 1988.

Webb, Martin & Whittington, Richard. *Fusions*. Ebury Press, London, 1997.

Whittington, Richard & Webb, Martin. *Quaglino's the Cookbook*, Conran Octopus, London, 1995.

Wood, Beverley (ed.). *Tucker in Australia*. Hill of Content, Melbourne, 1977.

Index

Page numbers in italics indicate illustrations

abalone salad 66–68, *66*
Aborigines 17–18
Acland Cake Shop 20
Adams, Catherine 208; recipe 189
Alexander, Stephanie 28, 150; recipes 149, 170, 205
Alexander, Victoria 208; recipe 64
aniseed myrtle *15*, 109
artichoke (globe) and bean spaghetti salad 89, *167*
artichoke (Jerusalem) soup 46
Au Chabrol restaurant 106
Australian cuisine: Asian influence on 11, 29, 32–33, 36–37, 41; concept of 21–23; in colonial times 17–18, 19–20, 27–28; chefs' influence on 40; decorated cakes 23–24; French influence on 40–41; meat and the barbecue 20–21, 24; lack of peasant, agrarian society 27–28; migrant influence 33–35, 37–38; modern, defined 6, 10–11; national dish 21, 23–24, 36; use of native ingredients *14–15*, 17–18, *18–19*, 24, *30–31*

banana leaf sushi 153
Banc restaurant 112, 219
barbecue vegetables 170, *171*
barbecues 20–21, 24, 160; *see also under names of ingredients*
Barbuto, Vince 20
Barossa Valley 25
barramundi: grilled whole, with lime pickle infused with coriander 169; roasted fillet, with wakame and truffle peaches 137
Bathers Pavilion 143, 208
beef: aged, with grilled vegetable salad and anchovy butter 168; braised ox cheek with winter vegetables *98*, 99; chargrilled sirloin with mash and salsa verde 165; neaua kem sot (salted beef ribs braised in coconut cream) 136; slow-cooked cheeks with celeriac and mushrooms *99*, 100; sugar-cured, with pesto beans and olive oil *74*, 75
Beer, Maggie 25, 208; recipes 105, 113

beetroot, roasted, with blood orange, red witlof and asparagus orange oil *71*, 73
beignets, oyster *43*, 45
bel mondo restaurant *38*, *40*, 216
Bilson, Tony 9, *10*, 40, 78; recipes 76, 129, 201
Bistro Moncur *9*
blue-eye cod: on a bed of fennel 133; poached, with Puy lentils and warm tomato and fennel dressing 126, *127*
Bocuse, Paul 186
borlotti beans with parsley and garlic 75, *75*
bouillabaisse fish soup 48
Brahimi, Guillaume 32, 208; recipes 46, 157, 177
British food 11
Brugman, Marieke 209; recipes 92, 94, 116
Bruneteau, Jean-Paul 18
bunya bunya nuts *14*
Burr, Michael 25–26
bush food. *See* native Australian ingredients *and individual names*
bush food restaurants 16, 18–19
Bush Tucker Supply Aust. 14, 18

Café de la Gallerie 209
Cabramatta 32–33
cakes 23–24, *24–25*; queen of nuts *151*, 205; chocolate diva 204
calamari, sauté of 57, *186*
Campbell, Joan 28, 50; recipes 56, 191
Capadli, Raymond 24, 209; recipes 145, 169, 200
Carême, Antonin 23–24
casserole of shellfish, small 56
Castellani, Robert 209; recipes 54, 64, 66
cauliflower soup 49
cheese *28*, 150, *151*; Richard Thomas's impressions and creations 53, 62–63
cheese, blue 62, *63*; tart 64, *218*
cheese, goat's: salad 52; soufflé 70; terrine 54, *55*; with roasted whole garlic and croutons 89
Cherikoff, Vic 14–15, *14*, 18; recipes 109, 192
chicken: barbecued paperbark 109; boned, stuffed with giblets and prosciutto 113; cornfed, breast stuffed with quandongs and wild mushrooms, warrigal greens and native thyme broth 108;

Palermo style 113; pan-fried breast with Moroccan eggplant and baby bok choy 105; poussin aux raisins (spatchcocks with green grapes, garlic and parsley) *106*, 121; roast stuffed legs with cèpe cream sauce 112, *218*; salt-crusted breast, with Jerusalem artichoke purée and leek *110*, 111
Chinese: in Australia 32; cuisine 12, 32, 41; restaurants in country towns 29, 32, 33
Cicada restaurant 212
Circa, The Prince restaurant 214
clams on ginger-pickled wakame 157
Cleopatra restaurant with rooms 106
chocolate: diva with cumquat sauce 204; soufflé *79*, 201
Chouet, Dany 6, 106; recipes 68, 121, 131
Chouvin, André 209–12; recipes 48, 144, 182
chutney, zucchini 169
coconut: and apricot pudding 185; cream with palm sugar syrup *190*, 191; pancakes, steamed, with green curry sauce 141
Cointreau, André 13
Coldstream Hills vineyard *210*, 211
Cook's Companion, The 150
Cooper, Gary 21, 212; recipes 154, 174, 206, *207*
Cordon Bleu cookery school 12–13
corn, feta and pear salad with walnut dressing 81
crab, blue swimmer: and cucumber salad with crisp samosa pastry *142*, 156; salad 82–84, *83*; soup 46, *47*
crayfish (*see also* marron), collar of prickly ashed, in a shark fin and kaffir lime broth 154, *155*
cucumber and yoghurt soup, chilled 45
curry: barbecued duck 50, 121; sour orange, of prawns and choi sum 134; yellow Thai, of swordfish with green papaya 138, *139*
cuttlefish, raw with black noodles 153

Dansereau, Serge 41, 143; recipes 102, 156, 196
Darley's restaurant 107

Davidson's plums *15*
desserts: almond bread and butter pudding with biscotti 188; almond tart with Amaretto mascarpone and poached figs *143*, 196; Amaretto parfait 182, *183*; anneau of Valrhona Manjari chocolate with Seville orange coulis and vanilla bean chantilly 200; the bathing cap 206, *207*; Catherine's strawberry and ricotta tart 189; chocolate diva with cumquat sauce 204; chocolate soufflé *79*, 201; coconut and apricot pudding with coconut syrup 185; coconut cream with palm sugar syrup *190*, 191; Cootamundra bread and butter pudding with lemon ironwood and rum sauce 192; fresh fig and mascarpone tart *167*, 192; gratin of grapes in champagne sabayon 182; gratin of spiced strawberries and quince with a Grand Marnier sabayon *119*, 184; lemon tart with fresh berries 193; passionfruit tart *178*, 197; pavlova with a passionfruit curd 194, *195*; pineapple sorbet 181; pink gin and lemon granita 181, *198*; poached pears with cinnamon ice cream and vanilla bean coulis *175*, 177; queen of nuts cake on a simple rhubarb and red fruit sago sauce *151*, 205; quince, raisin and grappa pudding 189; raspberry vacherin 180, *187*; Turkish delight soufflé with rose petal ice cream 202, *203*
Doyle, Peter 6, 40, 212; recipes 73, 82, 100
duck: anise-flavoured crispy, with kipfler potatoes, beetroot and chervil *107*, 117; barbecued, curry 50, 121; liver parfait salad 68, *106*; Peking, salad with wild rice and hazelnuts 120
Dunstan, Don 24, 36–37

e'cco restaurant 41, 214
Edna's Table II restaurant 16, 214
eggplant: and egg tomato terrine 85; Moroccan 105
Eleonore's restaurant 212
Fabrègues, Alain 212; recipes 77, 85, 158
Fahey, Warren 24

Fairlie-Cuninghame, Sue 51; recipes 93, 121
Fielke, Andrew 19
fig (fresh) and mascarpone tart 192
fish 30, 124; the four dances 152–53; pla yang nahm pla warn (grilled fish with sweet fish sauce) 135; steamed coconut pancakes with green curry sauce 141; summertime fish and chips 144. *See also under fish names; see also* shellfish
Flower Drum restaurant 41
Flying Squid Brothers, The 28, 31
Fraser's restaurant 219
French cuisine 12, 13, 23, 40–41
French restaurants in Sydney 8, 9
frittata: tomato, olive and parsley 84
Fulton, Margaret 6, 167; recipes 89, 172

Galletto, Lucio *41*, 212–13; recipes 161, 189
Gibbs, Suzanne 213; recipes 65, 192
Glenella restaurant 106
gnocchi, sweet potato 65, *166*
Good Food Guide 8, 9
Gourmet magazine 218–19
granita, pink gin and lemon 181, *198*
grapes, gratin of 182
Greek cuisine 22–23

Hage, Ghassan 33, 35, 37–38
Halliday, James and Suzanne *210*, 211
hara kebab 92
Harris, Genevieve 213; recipes 84, 141, 185
Holuigue, Diane 40, 213; recipes 133, 164, 188
home cooking 40

Illawarra plums *14*
'international' restaurants in Sydney 8, 9, 10
Italian cuisine 22
Italian restaurants in Sydney 8, 9

Jamaica House restaurant 150
Jeffs, Janet 213–14; recipe 144
Johnson, Philip 41, 214; recipes 61, 104, 120
Johnson, Simon 37, 90–91; recipe 81
Juniperberry restaurant 213–14

Kables restaurant 143
Kakadu plums *14*
kangaroo: polenta with smoked kangaroo and Parmesan 105
Kersh, Jennice and Raymond 16, 19, 214; recipes 70, 108, 164
Kervella, Gabrielle 28
Kinsela's restaurant 9
Kyritsis, Janni 16, 198–99; recipes 88, 125, 181

Lake House restaurant 220
lamb: barbecue loin and native herbs with Illawarra plum salsa, rocket and macadamia salad 164; barbecued rumps in spicy yoghurt marinade with a tomato and chickpea salad 162, *163*; brains with a papillote of celeriac and a warm salad of rocket and baby spinach 101, *118*; grilled rump with red capsicums *159*, 161; rump with salad of eggplant, salted lemon, chilli and watercress 104; shanks with red capsicum, black olives and tomatoes 95, 97; warm salad of barbecued lamb with Asian flavours 164–65
Lambie, Michael 214; recipes 46, 99, 169
Langton's Restaurant *13*, 186, *186*
Lau, Gilbert *34*
Lebanese cuisine 35, 42
leek risotto 61
Lehmann, Tony 28
lemon aspen fruit *14*, 70
lemon myrtle *15*, 144, 164
Leonard, Kelly 213–14; recipe 204
Liew, Cheong 36, 37, 214–15; recipes 128, 152–53
limes, wild *15*
Lindsay, Geoff 22, 215; recipes 75, 138, 202
Loose Box, The, restaurant 212
Lucio's restaurant 213

macadamia nuts 17, 164
Malouf, Greg 42, 216; recipes 122, 136, 149
Manfredi, Stefano 6, 33–34, 41, 124, 216; recipes 65, 66–68, 75, 113
Mangan, Luke 216; recipes 49, 81, 111
Manners, Michael 106
Margaret Fulton Cookbook, 34–35

marron, roasted, with citrus sauce 158
Matto, Rosa 26–27
Merrony, Paul 40, 216; recipes 54, 97, 132
MG Garage Restaurant 198, *199*
Millburn, Ian 116
mint, native *14*
Moore, Michael 217; recipes 52, 93
Moran, Matthew 217; recipes 48, 105, 165
Mouchel, Philippe 6, *13*, 40, 186–87, *187*; recipes 57, 114, 180
mountain pepper (leaves) *15*
mushroom and spinach roulade 88, 199
mushroom(s), wild: ragoût of, with mille-feuilles of potato 86, *87*; soup with horseradish cream 49
mullet, red: Sicilian stuffed, with parsley salad and grilled lemon *123*, 125
munthari berries *15*
Muskett, Philip 36, 72, 124
mussel(s): barbecued, with sweet chilli vinegar 172; salad 80; salad of, with saffron potatoes, fennel and basil 146, *147*

native Australian ingredients 14–15, 17–18, 18–19. *See also under individual names*
Neddy's restaurant 37
Nediz Tu restaurant 213, 215

O'Connell's restaurant 216
octopus with aïoli 152
O'Donnell, Mietta 41, 217; recipes 45, 52, 126
olives, South Australian 25–27
omelette: kai jiaw 135
One Continuous Picnic 27–28
Orange food festival 27
oyster(s), *30*, *31*; and braised baby squid noodle salad 7, 69; with red onion salsa *58*, 59; velouté of potato and *43*, 45

panzanella 81
papaya, green: salad 93
paperbark 109
parfait de foie de canard et sa salade 68, *106*
parfaits, Amaretto 182, *183*
passionfruit tart *178*, 197

pasta: naked ravioli with ricotta *39*, 64; seared scallops, black orrechiette and mascarpone 66, *67*; saffron corzetti 68
pavlova with a passionfruit curd 194, *195*
pears, poached *175*, 177
pepperberries *15*
Perry, Neil 10, 11, 41, 179; recipes 60, 168, 197
Phillips, Graeme 217; recipes 157, 170, 193
pigeon rice 116
Pignolet, Damien 6, 40, 218; recipes 146–48, 161
polenta 160, barbecued with mushrooms 161; with smoked kangaroo and Parmesan 105
Pont, Graham 24
Porter, Hal 72, 176
potato, mille-feuilles of, with a ragoût of wild mushrooms and fresh truffle 86, *87*
potatoes, new, warm salad of 77
Potter, Ralph 6, 41, 107; recipes 49, 69, 117
prawn(s): barbecued piri piri prawns on daikon cake with salad of pickled cucumber and smoked tea butter 174; king prawn cake and scallops 11, 60; soufflé tart 146–48, *215*; sushi, spiced 153; sour orange curry of prawns and choi sum 134
Punshon, Alistair 18

quail: barbecued marinated, on rocket and Parmesan salad 170; crisp skin 52; marinated and grilled, with hummus bi tahini and Moorish spinach salad 122
quandongs *14*, 108
quince: gratin of spiced strawberries and quince *119*, 184; raisin and grappa pudding 189

rabbit tagine 114, *115*
raspberry, native *14*, *15*
raspberry vacherin 180, *187*
ravioli, naked, with ricotta *39*, 64
Reymond, Jacques 40, *118*, 119; recipes 101, 140, 184
riberries 192
rice: arroz de pombas bravos (pigeon rice) 116
rice, wild: salad of, with hazelnut and Peking duck 120
Richardson, Trish 179

Richmond Hill Café and Larder 150, *151*
Ripe, Cherry 24
risotto, saffron and leek 61
Rockpool restaurant 10, 168, 179
rosella *15*

salads: blue swimmer crab, with avocado, coriander and mint 82–84, *83*; blue swimmer crab and cucumber *142*, 156; duck liver parfait 68, *106*; globe artichoke and bean spaghetti 89, *167*; goat's cheese 52; green papaya 93; grilled baby corn, Yarra Valley Persian feta and fresh pear with walnut dressing 81; Moorish spinach 122; mussel 80; mussels with saffron potatoes, fennel and basil 146, *147*; oyster and braised baby squid noodle, with soy, rocket oil and ginger 7, 69; roasted beetroot, blood orange, red witlof and asparagus orange oil *71*, 73; traditional Australian 72–73; veal shank 65; vine tomato, with bocconcini 93; warm black-lip abalone, shiitake and corzetti *66*, 66–68; warm salad of barbecued lamb with Asian flavours 164; warm salad of new potatoes with a julienne of steamed chicken and freshly smoked salmon, corn salad and herbs 77; wild rice, hazelnut and Peking duck 120
salmon: barbecued, with wasabi crushed potato *166*, 172; confit of, with blancmange of cauliflower, nutmeg spinach and lemon oil 145; kibbeh tartare with cracked wheat and garlic cheese 42, 149; roast, with eggplant purée 42, 132–33; saumon à l'olive noire (Tasmanian salmon, black olive purée and spring onions) *130*, 131
salsa, red onion 58, *59*
Santich, Barbara 24
scallops: Coffin Bay *30*, 31; with saffron and leek risotto 61; seared, with black orrechiette and mascarpone *66, 67*

Schofield, Leo 218; recipes 56, 80, 181
Searle, Phillip 27
Shaul, Oliver 32
Sheila's Bar Barbie (London) 35–36
shellfish: small casserole of 56; stew of yabbies, clams, mussels and scallops with fresh tarragon 157. *See also under individual names; see also fish*
snapper: grilled fillet with saffron and citrus sauce *10*, 129; red-roast, with shaved cuttlefish and leek fondue 128; roast baby, Cantonese style 126
snook, soused 152
Snowball, Kathy 218–19; recipe 126
Sokolov, Raymond 17
sorbet, pineapple 181
soufflé, chocolate *79*, 201; lemon aspen and goat's cheese 70; prawn soufflé tart 146–48, *215*; Turkish delight 202, *203*
soups: artichoke 46; blue swimmer crab, with black mussels and aïoli 46, *47*; bouillabaisse 48; broth of Oriental flavours with yellowfin tuna tagine and spaghetti vegetables 140; cauliflower, with truffle oil and chives 49; cucumber and yoghurt 45; poor man's 54, *55*; roast tomato and basil 48; velouté of potato and oyster with oyster beignets *43*, 45; wild mushroom, with horseradish cream 49
spinach: cakes 92; and mushroom roulade 88, *199*
squab: arroz de pombas bravos (pigeon rice) 116
squid: deep-fried rings *51*, 56; and oyster noodle salad 7, 69
starters (*see also salads and soups*): crisp skin quail 52; deep-fried squid rings *51*, 56; double-baked lemon aspen and goat's cheese soufflé 70; goat's cheese salad 52; goat's cheese terrine 54, *55*; king prawn cake and scallops with spicy prawn sauce *11*, 60; naked ravioli with ricotta 64; oyster and braised baby squid noodle salad with

soy, rocket oil and ginger 7, 69; rock oysters with red onion salsa 58, 59; saffron and leek risotto with scallops and vodka 61; sauté of calamari served on a compote of ratatouille 57, *186*; seared scallops, black orrechiette and mascarpone 66, *67*; small casserole of shellfish 56; squid ink tagliatelle with things Mediterranean 59; sugar-cured beef with Miss Jane's pesto beans and black olive oil *74*, 75; sweet potato gnocchi with burnt butter sauce 65, *166*; tomato, olive and parsley frittatas 84; warm tart of blue cheese and caramelised onions 64
Stegley, Sarah 209
Stella restaurant 215
Stephanie's Australia 28, 150
Stephanie's restaurant 150
Steingarten, Jeffrey 41
stew, seafood 157
stockpot 44
strawberries: gratin of strawberries and quince *119*, 184; strawberry and ricotta tart 189
Studd, Will *28*, 63
Susman, John 13, 28, 31
sushi, spiced prawn 153; banana leaf 153
sweet potato gnocchi 65, *166*
Sweetwater Café 191, 212
swordfish: yellow Thai curry, with green papaya 138, *139*
Symons, Michael 27–28

tagine, rabbit 114, *115*
tagliatelle, squid ink 59
tarte tatin, tomato 94
tarts: almond *143*, 196; fresh fig and mascarpone 192; lemon, with fresh berries 193; passionfruit *178*, 197; prawn soufflé 146–48, *215*; strawberry and ricotta 189; blue cheese and caramelised onions 64, *218*
Taylor, Chris 219; recipe 173
terrine, goat's cheese 54, *55*; of eggplants and Roma tomatoes on a tapenade sauce 85
Tetsuya's restaurant 220
Thai cuisine 41, 219; balanced Thai meal 134–36

Thomas, Richard 6, 28, 53, 62–63, *215*; recipes 59, 89
Thompson, David 33, 41, 219; recipes 134–36
thyme, native 108
tomato(es): and basil soup 48; braised in Pernod with snails and periwinkles 76, *78*; and eggplant terrine 85; salad with bocconcini 93; tarte tatin 94
Tomlin, Liam 8, 40, 219–20; recipes 45, 86, 112
trout, freshwater: whole, served on a warm salad of spinach and Puy lentils with sauce vierge 131–32, *131*
trout, ocean: with lemon myrtle 144
Tucker in Australia 37
tuna: chargrilled tuna belly with oysters and citrus soy dressing 173; yellowfin tuna tagine 140

Upstairs restaurant 106

veal shank: boiled, with green sauce 102, *103*; salad 65
vegetables, barbecue 170, 171. *See also individual names of vegetables*
Vietnamese restaurants 32–33
vinegars 72

Wakuda, Tetsuya 9, 220; recipe 137
Walker, John and Mary 28
warrigal greens *14*, 108
Webb, Martin 25, 220; recipes 59, 172, 194
White, Marco Pierre 40
whiting: fillets roasted in Parmesan kataifi with Syrian eggplant relish and preserved lemon 136; in steamed coconut pancakes 141; summertime fish and chips 144
wild foods. *See* native Australian ingredients *and under individual names*
Wockpool restaurant 44, 179
Wolf-Tasker, Alla 220; recipes 131, 163, 182
Wood, Beverley 37

yabbies, roasted with thyme oil 149, *150*

zucchini chutney 169